V|D
M|A

LUTHERAN QUARTERLY BOOKS

Lutheran Quarterly Books will advance the same aims as *Lutheran Quarterly* itself, aims repeated by Theodore G. Tappert when he was editor fifty years ago and renewed by Oliver K. Olson when he revived the publication in 1987. The original four aims continue to grace the front matter and to guide the contents of every issue, and can now also indicate the goals of *Lutheran Quarterly Books:* "to provide a forum (1) for the discussion of Christian faith and life on the basis of the Lutheran confession; (2) for the application of the principles of the Lutheran church to the changing problems of religion and society; (3) for the fostering of world Lutheranism; and (4) for the promotion of understanding between Lutherans and other Christians."

For further information, see www.lutheranquarterly.com.

The symbol and motto of *Lutheran Quarterly,* VDMA for *Verbum Domini Manet in Aeternum* (1 Peter 1:25), was adopted as a motto by Luther's sovereign, Frederick the Wise, and his successors. The original "Protestant" princes walking out of the imperial Diet of Speyer in 1529, unruly peasants following Thomas Müntzer, and from 1531 to 1547 the coins, medals, flags, and guns of the Smalcaldic League all bore the most famous Reformation slogan, the first Evangelical confession: The Word of the Lord remains forever.

For the complete list of *Lutheran Quarterly Books*, please see the final pages of this work.

TEACHING REFORMATION

TEACHING REFORMATION

Essays in Honor of Timothy J. Wengert

Edited by
Luka Ilić *and* Martin J. Lohrmann

FORTRESS PRESS
MINNEAPOLIS

TEACHING REFORMATION
Essays in Honor of Timothy J. Wengert

Cover image: © iStock 2020; Midnight blue coloured wall by desifoto © iStock 2020; Luther rose monochrome calligraphic illustration by PeterHermesFurian
Cover design: Alisha Lofgren

Print ISBN: 978-1-5064-6766-5
eBook ISBN: 978-1-5064-6767-2

Contents

Part 2: Reading and Interpreting Texts in the Reformation

Part 3: Forming the Faith

Contributors

Ulrich Bubenheimer studied Protestant theology at the Universities of Tübingen and Göttingen, as well as paleography and history of law. He worked as an assistant to Professor Heiko A. Oberman at Tübingen and completed his doctor of theology degree at Tübingen University in 1971 with a thesis on the Wittenberg reformer Andreas Bodenstein von Karlstadt. Dr. Bubenheimer has served as professor of Protestant theology and religious education at the Universities of Education at Reutlingen and Heidelberg. His main topics of research are late-medieval and Reformation history, sixteenth-century paleography, and the history of libraries in the sixteenth century. He has published works on Luther, Karlstadt, Müntzer, Melanchthon, and Reformation libraries and manuscripts.

Amy Nelson Burnett is Paula and D. B. Varner University professor of history at the University of Nebraska–Lincoln, where she teaches early modern European history. Her research focuses on the dissemination of the Reformation in southern Germany and Switzerland through print, preaching, and educational reform. She is the author of *Debating the Sacraments: Print and Authority in the Early Reformation* and *Karlstadt and the Origins of the Eucharistic Controversy: A Study in the Circulation of Ideas* and co-editor of *A Companion to the Swiss Reformation.*

Derek Cooper is associate dean of the faculty and associate professor of Global Christianity at Reformed Episcopal Seminary in Blue Bell, Pennsylvania. He is also managing director of Thomas Institute, an educational travel company offering learning experiences in the lands of the Bible. Dr. Cooper is the author of a dozen books, including *Basics of Latin*, *Introduction to World Christian History*, *Exploring Church History*, and *Twenty Questions That Shaped World Christian History.*

Theodor Dieter is senior research professor at the Institute for Ecumenical Research in Strasbourg, France, after having served as research professor there since 1994 and as its director from 1998 to 2018. He studied Protestant theology and philosophy at the Universities of Heidelberg and Tübingen. He did his doctorate in theology at the Faculty of Protestant Theology in Tübingen in 1991 and qualified as a professor at the same university in 1998. He served as consultant for the international Lutheran / Roman Catholic dialogue for twenty-five years as well as for the Lutheran/Mennonite dialogue and the Lutheran / Mennonite / Roman Catholic trialogue. In 2017, he was awarded honorary doctorates from the Catholic Theological Faculty of the University of Erfurt, Germany (the faculty where Luther studied theology), and the Catholic University of Leuven, Belgium (the faculty that was among the first to condemn Luther's theology). In the same year, he received the prestigious Ratzinger Prize from Pope Francis.

Irene Dingel has been director of the Leibniz-Institute of European History (IEG) in Mainz since 2005 and professor for church history and history of dogma at the Johannes Gutenberg-University in Mainz since 1998. She studied Protestant theology and romance studies in Heidelberg (University of Heidelberg) and Paris (Sorbonne University and Faculté libre de Théologie Protestante). She was a lecturer on German language and culture at the École Normale Supérieure (ENS), Fontenay-aux-Roses/Paris, and simultaneously, Élève à titre étranger. In 1986, she earned her doctorate (DPhil) at the University of Heidelberg. She was awarded her Habilitation at the University of Heidelberg in 1993 and was professor for historical theology at the Goethe University Frankfurt (1994) before taking her current positions.

Mary Jane Haemig is professor emerita of church history at Luther Seminary in St. Paul, Minnesota. She taught there from 1999 to 2018 and at Pacific Lutheran University from 1994 to 1999. She is the editor of volume 4, *Pastoral Writings*, of *The Annotated Luther* and an associate editor of the *Dictionary of Luther and the Lutheran Traditions*. The author of numerous scholarly articles, she focuses on the Lutheran Reformation of the sixteenth century as well as topics in American Lutheran history. She received her ThD from Harvard University (1996) and her JD from Harvard Law School (1981).

Scott Hendrix graduated from Duke University and the Lutheran Theological Southern Seminary before earning his doctorate while studying Reformation history and theology with Heiko A. Oberman at Tübingen. He then taught church history at three Lutheran seminaries before retiring from teaching at

Princeton Theological Seminary in 2007. From 2008 to 2012, he was the chair of the International Luther Congress. His latest book, *Martin Luther: Visionary Reformer*, was published in 2015 by Yale University Press.

Erik H. Herrmann is associate professor of historical theology and the director of the Center for Reformation Research at Concordia Seminary in St. Louis, Missouri, having received his PhD from the same institution in Renaissance and Reformation studies. His areas of research include the history of biblical interpretation, the history of medieval and Reformation / early modern Europe, and twentieth-century interpretations of Martin Luther and his theology. Some of his recent publications can be found in *The Oxford Handbook of Martin Luther's Theology*, *The Oxford Encyclopedia of Martin Luther*, *The Annotated Luther*, and *Lutherjahrbuch*.

Luka Ilić, PhD, is pastor on the roster of the Evangelical-Lutheran Church in Württemberg, currently serving in Balzheim, and former research associate at the Leibniz Institute of European History in Mainz. His work focuses on the Protestant Reformation in continental Europe, especially on its lesser-known impact on the southern and eastern peripheries. He is the author of *Theologian of Sin and Grace: The Process of Radicalization in the Theology of Matthias Flacius Illyricus* and co-editor of *Matthias Flacius Illyricus: Biographical Contexts, Theological Impact, Historical Reception*.

Robert Kolb is professor emeritus of systematic theology at Concordia Seminary in St. Louis, Missouri. With Timothy Wengert, he is co-editor of *The Book of Concord* (Fortress, 2000). He is also the author of several monographs on Luther and on Luther and Melanchthon's impact on their students.

Gordon Lathrop is Charles A. Schieren Professor of Liturgy Emeritus at the United Lutheran Seminary in Pennsylvania. He is the author of several volumes, including *Holy Things: A Liturgical Theology*, *Saving Images: The Presence of the Bible in Christian Liturgy*, and, with Timothy Wengert, *Christian Assembly: Marks of the Church in a Pluralistic Age*. He has been president of both Societas Liturgica and the North American Academy of Liturgy.

VOLKER LEPPIN is Horace Tracy Pitkin Professor of Historical Theology at Yale Divinity School. Before that, he served as professor of church history and director of the Institute for Medieval and Reformation Times at Tübingen University. After studying in Marburg, Jerusalem, and Heidelberg, he earned his doctoral degree and Habilitation in Heidelberg. He is a member of the Heidelberg Academy of Sciences. The main topics of his research are late-medieval and Reformation piety and theology. He has written major biographies on William of Ockham, Martin Luther, and Francis of Assisi, as well as a history of medieval Christianity, a history of Christian mysticism, and several textbooks on the Reformation.

MARTIN J. LOHRMANN is associate professor of Lutheran Confessions and Heritage at Wartburg Theological Seminary in Dubuque, Iowa. He is the author of *Stories from Global Lutheranism: A Historical Timeline* and *Book of Harmony: Spirit and Service in the Lutheran Confessions*. He is also co-editor with Derek Cooper of *1–2 Samuel, 1–2 Kings, 1–2 Chronicles* in the Reformation Commentary on Scripture series.

MICKEY L. MATTOX is professor of historical theology at Marquette University, where he directs the graduate program in Luther Studies in a Catholic Context. He received his PhD from Duke University. His books include *Defender of the Most Holy Matriarchs*, *Changing Churches*, and *Johannes Oecolampadius*. He serves as associate editor for *Pro Ecclesia* and for *Reformation & Renaissance Review*, and in 2017, he was associate editor for the *Oxford Encyclopedia of Martin Luther*. He is also a contributor and Catholic co-editor for *Luther at Leipzig: Martin Luther, the Leipzig Debate, and the Sixteenth-Century Reformations*.

RICHARD A. MULLER is P. J. Zondervan Professor of Historical Theology and emeritus and senior fellow of the Junius Institute for Digital Reformation Research at Calvin Theological Seminary. He earned his PhD at Duke University. He is the author of *Dictionary of Latin and Greek Theological Terms*, *The Unaccommodated Calvin*, *Post-Reformation Reformed Dogmatics* (four volumes), *Calvin and the Reformed Tradition*, *Divine Will and Human Choice*, and *Grace and Freedom: William Perkins and the Early Modern Reformed Understanding of Free Choice and Divine Grace*.

Stefan Rhein has been the director of the Luther Memorials Foundation in Saxony-Anhalt since 1998. The foundation manages several Reformation history museums: Luther's and Melanchthon's houses in Wittenberg, Luther's birthplace and the house where he died in Eisleben, and Luther's parents' home in Mansfeld. He is trained as a classical philologist and wrote his dissertation on Melanchthon's Greek poetry. His scholarly contributions focus on leading figures of the Wittenberg Reformation: Philip Melanchthon, Martin Luther, Paul Eber, and Johannes Stigel. His most recent publications are *The Beginning of the Reformation: Wittenberg in 1517* and, together with Gottfried Naumann and Matthias Dall'Asta, volume 6 of *Melanchthon deutsch, Sonntagsvorlesungen und Anekdoten.*

Paul Rorem is Benjamin B. Warfield Professor of Medieval Church History at Princeton Theological Seminary. He is also the editor of *Lutheran Quarterly, New Series*, a role he continues to hold after retiring from teaching in June 2021. His publications include *St. Augustine, His Confessions, and His Influence.*

Kirsi Stjerna, a native of Finland, is professor of Lutheran history and theology at the Pacific Lutheran Theological Seminary of California Lutheran University. She is also a member of the core doctoral faculty at Graduate Theological Union in Berkeley, California, and a docent for Helsinki University. Her books include *Lutheran Theology: A Grammar of Faith* and *No Greater Jewel: Thinking about Baptism with Luther.* With Brooks Schramm, she coedited *Encounters with Luther* and *Martin Luther, the Bible, and the Jewish People.* She served as co-general editor with Timothy Wengert and Hans Hillerbrand of *The Annotated Luther*, volumes 1–6, and was the volume editor of—as well as a contributor to—volume 2, *Word and Faith.*

Mark D. Tranvik is professor of Reformation history and theology at Luther Seminary in St. Paul, Minnesota. An ordained Evangelical Lutheran Church in America pastor, he was previously a professor of religion for twenty-five years at Augsburg University in Minneapolis, Minnesota. Tranvik edited and translated Martin Luther's *The Freedom of a Christian* and is the author of *Martin Luther and the Called Life.*

Hans Wiersma is associate professor of religion at Augsburg University, Minneapolis, Minnesota. His published scholarship includes the second edition of James Kittelson's *Luther the Reformer*, as well as *Crazy Book: A Not So Stuffy Dictionary of Biblical Terms*, many catechetical resources, and a variety of Reformation reference work entries and Luther-oriented journal articles.

Abbreviations

BC	*The Book of Concord: The Confessions of the Evangelical Lutheran Church*. Edited by. Robert Kolb and Timothy J. Wengert. Minneapolis: Fortress, 2000.
BSELK	*Die Bekenntnisschriften der Evangelisch-Lutherischen Kirche: Vollständige Neuedition*. Edited by Irene Dingel. Göttingen: Vandenhoeck & Ruprecht, 2014.
CO	*Corpus Reformatorum: Ioannis Calvini opera quae supersunt omnia [Calvini Opera]*. Edited by Guilielmus Baum, Eduardus Cunitz, and Eduardus Reuss. Brunswick and Berlin, 1863–1900.
CR	*Corpus Reformatorum: Philippi Melanthonis opera quae supersunt omnia*. Eds. Karl Bretschneider and Heinrich Bindseil. 28 vols. Halle/Braunschweig: A. Schwetschke & Sons, 1834–1860.
LW	*Luther's Works*. American edition. 55+ vols. Philadelphia: Fortress; St. Louis: Concordia, 1955–.
MBW, MBWR, and MBWT	*Melanchthon's Briefwechsel* [MBW], with *Regesten* [MBWR] and *Texte* [MBWT]. Edited by Heinz Scheible et al. Stuttgart: Frommann-Holzboog, 1978–.
TAL	*The Annotated Luther*. Edited by Hans Hillerbrand et al. 6 vols. Minneapolis: Fortress, 2015–2017.
WA	*Luthers Werke: Kritische Gesamtausgabe [Schriften]*. 65 vols. Weimar: H. Böhlau, 1883–1993.
WA Br	*Luthers Werke: Kritische Gesamtausgabe: Briefwechsel*. 18 vols. Weimar: H. Böhlau, 1930–1985.
WA DB	*Luthers Werke: Kritische Gesamtausgabe: Bibel*. 12 vols. Weimar: H. Böhlau, 1906–1961.
WA TR	*Luthers Werke: Kritische Gesamtausgabe: Tischreden*. 6 vols. Weimar: H. Böhlau, 1912–1921.

ABBREVIATIONS

Preface

Luka Ilić and Martin J. Lohrmann

The idea for this volume was born at Dr. Wengert's sixtieth birthday party in his home in Riverton, New Jersey, in 2010. As we celebrated this important milestone in his life, we looked back at some of his achievements in a circle of family, friends, colleagues, and doctoral students, which included both of us at the time. In the years following, career choices, transatlantic and out-of-state moves, as well as our growing families occupied our minds and time. However, as the next major milestone of seventy years was approaching, we did not want to let pass the opportunity of honoring our preceptor with a collection of essays.

As a Doktorvater, Professor Wengert had high standards, but as time went on, our relationship slowly changed. One marker of this transition took place when he organized a session sponsored by the Society for Reformation Research and invited us to present papers with him at the Sixteenth Century Society & Conference, held in Minneapolis that year. In our PhD seminars, we sometimes felt transported to sixteenth-century Wittenberg, where the subjects of our research—especially Melanchthon, Bugenhagen, and Flacius—were having theological conversations with one another. One semester, the three of us read *Loci communes* in Latin with Dr. Wengert. We worked so hard on our Latin, but we were no match for his knowledge of the text, which it seemed he could almost recite by heart. Surely, we were not the only ones he impacted in such profound ways. Therefore, with this volume, we say a big thank-you to our mentor, colleague, and friend.

When we contacted scholars about the possibility of a Festschrift in honor of Timothy Wengert's seventieth birthday, the response was immediate and energetic. This testifies to the great impact of Dr. Wengert's career as a teacher, pastor, colleague, and scholar. Even more, it testifies to the positive relationships he has cultivated over the years in a variety of settings.

Contributors to this volume have worked with Dr. Wengert in many ways. Several were fellow doctoral students of the late David Steinmetz at Duke University or of Dr. Steinmetz's teacher, Heiko A. Oberman, who influenced generations of Reformation historians. Others have been involved in international Reformation research and ecumenical dialogues, participating in conferences and publishing projects together, while still others have been teaching colleagues in the fields of Lutheran theology and North American Lutheranism. Many scholars who work with the journal *Lutheran Quarterly, New Series* appear here. Among them is Paul Rorem, who wrote the introduction to Dr. Wengert's career (and who surreptitiously provided the bibliography featured at the end of this book), as well as Robert Kolb, with whom Dr. Wengert edited the monumental English-language edition of the *Book of Concord* that was published in the year 2000. Three of the authors completed doctoral dissertations under Dr. Wengert's supervision at the Lutheran Theological Seminary at Philadelphia, the school where Wengert taught for nearly thirty years with dear scholars and colleagues like Gordon Lathrop, whose essay on ecumenism concludes this book.

Indeed, the authors collected here represent only a small fraction of those who have had mutually enriching relationships with Dr. Wengert over the years. Some people we asked to write essays were not able to do so due to other commitments. We also had to limit the number of contributors because we could only publish one volume. While this book focuses on the relatively narrow topic of Reformation history and theology, Dr. Wengert has also served as a pastor in the Evangelical Lutheran Church in America, a participant in international and ecumenical Christian dialogues, and a scholar of global Lutheranism and Christianity around the world. A Festschrift for Timothy Wengert could have just as easily followed those paths, adding even more voices of those who share a common interest in great scholarship within diverse and rich global Christian traditions. As the editors of this volume, we are aware of the limits that have come with focusing on Reformation history and know that many other ways to honor Dr. Wengert's far-ranging career could have been chosen.

Even with such built-in limitations, this Festschrift makes its own rich contribution to Reformation history. It stands as something of a time capsule to future readers, as it gathers essays by many outstanding scholars of our day. We asked participants to send pieces that would relate to the primary areas of Dr. Wengert's research and writing: the development of Reformation theology (including the contributions of Philip Melanchthon), the history of biblical interpretation, and the importance of catechesis, both past and present.

Part 1 of this volume, therefore, begins with essays on the early Reformation by Theodor Dieter and Irene Dingel. It then examines important collegial relationships of the Reformation. Studying the first generation of reformers, Scott Hendrix writes on the relationship between Melanchthon and Urbanus Rhegius, while Amy Nelson Burnett examines the Eucharist debates between Melanchthon and Oecolampadius. Moving into the following decades, Robert Kolb explores the career of Wittenberg student Joachim Mörlin, and Hans Wiersma tells a story of conflict between the next generation of reformers in the city of Bremen.

Much of the Reformation can be described as a "word event" that revolved around new readings of Scripture and other classical texts. This focus on texts and their interpretation is the subject of part 2, which begins with Volker Leppin questioning the authorship of a series of Wittenberg-based lectures on Judges that has been long attributed to Luther. The section continues with Erik H. Herrmann's study of the importance of grammar for early Reformation theology, and then moves to two pieces of Reformation biblical interpretation: Richard A. Muller examines Calvin's use of Acts 2:23 and 4:28 with respect to the doctrine of predestination, and Derek Cooper looks at Reformation-era responses to the deceased prophet Samuel's appearance to King Saul in First Samuel 28. In two essays that each demonstrate the Wittenberg reformers' great familiarity with biblical, classical, and medieval literary traditions, Ulrich Bubenheimer shows how Melanchthon and Luther tackled challenges of biblical chronology, and Stefan Rhein explores the ways in which Melanchthon used stories from history for effective teaching.

Attention to the ways that Christian faith gets shared—the process of catechesis—forms the basis for part 3. On topics directly related to Luther's *Small Catechism*, Mickey L. Mattox provides a study of Luther and the Sabbath, while Mark D. Tranvik examines the doctrine of baptism in Luther and other sixteenth-century catechists. In a paper that resonates with Dr. Wengert's research on North American Lutheranism, Mary Jane Haemig discusses the importance of Luther's catechism in the ministry of Henry Melchior Mühlenberg in colonial Pennsylvania. Moving on to more contemporary evaluations of catechesis and the application of faith in daily life, Martin J. Lohrmann makes the case that "faith and love" can provide a useful bifocal lens through which to understand the *Small Catechism*, Kirsi Stjerna applies core Reformation convictions to the contemporary challenges of racial injustice and a global pandemic, and Gordon Lathrop connects a visit to La Sagrada Família in Barcelona with the enduring ecumenical values of the Lutheran Reformation.

One other way the Festschrift echoes Dr. Wengert's life is that it stands with one foot in the United States and one in Germany. This also represents the life of our laureate, who spends considerable time in Germany almost every year, researching at the Herzog August Bibliothek in Wolfenbüttel, visiting friends in Tübingen and Reutlingen, leading a "Luther Tour" or giving lectures. Dr. Wengert is fluent in German and loves spending time in the country from which many of his ancestors came. We are grateful that today's communication technology has made it possible not only to recruit and stay in seamless contact with a significant number of contributors from Europe but also to conduct the editing process transcontinentally, with one of the editors being based in Iowa and the other in southern Germany.

In summary, this book presents a rich study of Reformation sources and themes that both honor the career of Timothy Wengert and will benefit readers on a number of levels. These essays introduce key figures and aspects of the Lutheran Reformation, they provide excellent examples of contemporary scholarship, and they share new content that will inform any interested reader. Many of the essays have interdisciplinary resonance beyond what we initially planned: Dingel and Stjerna both write on the theme of Christian freedom, Kolb's and Wiersma's respective pieces feature overlapping characters like Tilemann Heshusius and Albert Hardenberg, and Rhein and Cooper both talk about how people in the sixteenth century viewed ghost stories and the devil. In many cases, readers might feel like they have stepped into a graduate class or research seminar on a piece of Reformation history that is entirely new to them; we hope they enjoy splashing around in the deep end of the pool.

We are deeply thankful for the energy and support of the authors whose works are gathered here. We also appreciate the contributions of so many others who have been dear colleagues to Dr. Wengert over the years and whose scholarship has similarly enriched students, local communities, the academy, and the church at large. We are sorry that we could not include all voices. But with a single voice, we together say thank you and *Herzlichen Dank* to the Rev. Dr. Timothy J. Wengert for so much faithful preaching, teaching, and living. In the words Melanchthon adopted as his motto and that have often been heard in Dr. Wengert's churches and classrooms, "What then shall we say? If God is for us, who can be against us?" (Rom 8:31).

Soli deo gloria!

Season after Pentecost, 2020

Introduction

Timothy J. Wengert's Scholarship for the Church

Paul Rorem

Tim Wengert was and is a parish pastor first, and it shows. His ministry of word and sacrament at Cross Lutheran Church in Roberts, Wisconsin, has informed his scholarly career not only in seminary teaching but also in research, writing, and editing. Working with him for twenty-five years now in editing *Lutheran Quarterly* and Lutheran Quarterly Books, I have seen up close that Wengert's scholarship is for the church. Whatever his academic accolades, such as honorary doctorates or the Bretten Melanchthon Prize or plenary addresses at the International Luther Congress meetings, his vocational focus has always been on parish ministry, on the local congregation—namely, preaching and the means of grace.

Of course, his teaching career has obviously been about ministry. Not only did he spend a quarter century at the Lutheran Theological Seminary in Philadelphia, but he is now, in "retirement," at Princeton Theological Seminary. But even for a seminary professor, Wengert has always been especially active in church life, from worldwide ecumenical dialogues and churchwide task forces within the Evangelical Lutheran Church in America (ELCA) to synodical committees and local congregations.

Through the Lutheran World Federation and the ELCA, Wengert has given major time and service to dialogue with Mennonites, Methodists, and Roman Catholics, as well as work with the World Council of Churches (including its Faith and Order Commission) and the National Council of Churches. For the ELCA, he served on the major task force on sexuality and has often spoken at synod assemblies and regional pastoral conferences. For his home New Jersey Synod, he has been a frequent lecturer, a faithful member of its candidacy committee, and a regular supply or interim pastor. Roy Riley, now retired New Jersey Synod bishop, testifies, "Seminary professors who have a passion for parish ministry are a particular treasure. They enable the translation of powerful theology and faithful church teaching into the lives of the people of God. Tim Wengert is a stellar example of such teaching."[1] To the present day, Tim still conducts adult education classes regularly and loves the interim pastorates where he can preach every Sunday. Wengert has also contributed to ecclesial relationships on the inter-Lutheran level through frequent speaking invitations to schools of the Lutheran Church–Missouri Synod and especially the coedited and widely used *Book of Concord* with his frequent collaborator Robert Kolb.

As for other publications, even his scholarly titles on Luther, Melanchthon, or Osiander have stressed topics central to the life of the church. Many of his shorter essays have been explicitly for lay readers and/or busy pastors. Just glancing at his extensive bibliography in this Festschrift, what stands out is the frequency of terms pertaining to the local church: Scripture and Bible, worship and liturgy, church and ministry, confessions and catechisms, law and gospel, word and sacrament, parish and pastor, prayer and preaching, the Lord's Supper and baptism. Just within the Lutheran Quarterly Book series, we see the same pattern in *A Formula for Parish Practice: Using the Formula of Concord in Congregations* and two 2020 volumes: *A Minister's Prayer Book* and *The Augsburg Confession: Renewing Lutheran Faith and Practice.*

It is no accident that such an emphasis tracks Martin Luther's own focus on local church life, as in the tomes Wengert has edited, like *Harvesting Martin Luther's Reflections on Theology, Ethics, and the Church* or *The Pastoral Luther: Essays in Luther's Practical Theology*, or many others in his bibliography, such as *The Annotated Luther.* That pastorate in Roberts, Wisconsin, still echoes through decades of teaching and scholarship, which is all for the church and its message—namely, as countless seminarians have heard him say, "Preach the damn gospel!"

1 Personal email, March 27, 2020.

Part 1

Luther, Melanchthon, and Reformation Colleagues

MARTIN LUTHER'S *TRACTATUS DE INDULGENTIIS*

A COMMENTARY ON AN UNKNOWN TEXT

Theodor Dieter

It may seem strange to call Martin Luther's *Tractatus de indulgentiis*[1] "an unknown text," since in 1967, Jared Wicks not only translated it into English but also offered an in-depth commentary on it.[2] Nevertheless, Wicks himself speaks of it as "the forgotten document in Luther's action" of October 31, 1517,[3] and it seems that this has not considerably changed since then.[4] Thus it may be helpful to present once more an interpretation of this text, pointing to several further aspects that Wicks did not highlight.

In the first volume of the Weimar edition of Luther's works, the text of the *Tractatus* was published as a sermon delivered on July 27, 1516,[5] but it does not fit into the series of sermons on the First Commandment there.[6] In the correspondence of Archbishop Albrecht of Mainz and the Mainz University Faculty

1 WA Br 12:5–10, nr. 4212a. The text is regarded as a letter; thus it suffices mentioning the lines of a quote, in brackets, after identifying the quote in Jared Wicks's translation (see the following footnote).

2 Jared Wicks, "Luther's Treatise on Indulgences, 1517," *Theological Studies* 28 (1967): 481–518; now in Jared Wicks, *Luther's Reform: Studies on Conversion and the Church* (Mainz: Philipp von Zabern, 1992; repr. Eugene, OR: Wipf and Stock, 2019), 87–116. In what follows, all English quotes from Luther's text are taken from Wicks's translation, published in *Luther's Reform*.

3 Wicks, 87.

4 The text was not included in the first volume of TAL.

5 WA 1:65.7–69.8.

6 Wicks, *Luther's Reform*, 88.

of Theology, a copy of the text has been found. In a letter to his diocesan officials, Albrecht spoke of the documents he had received as "the treatise and conclusion about the holy *negotium indulgentiarum* [indulgence business or affair] and about our subcommissioners [Tetzel], written by an audacious monk in Wittenberg."[7] The "treatise" that Albrecht mentions is our *Tractatus*, and the "conclusion" is the *Ninety-Five Theses*. In the same letter, Albrecht speaks again of "the treatise, conclusions, and other writings" and "articles, position, and treatise."[8] So he mentions the *Tractatus* three times in his letter. Thus there is strong evidence that on October 31, 1517, Luther sent not only a letter together with the *Ninety-Five Theses* to the archbishop but also the *Tractatus*.[9] Wicks assumes that the *Tractatus* was written "in early autumn of 1517."[10] The text was published again in an improved version in volume 12 of Luther's *Briefwechsel* (Correspondence).[11]

The *Tractatus* is quite different in form and tone from the *Ninety-Five Theses*. Analytically, and without polemics, Luther discusses the problem step by step. As Wicks describes, "Luther sought clarity on the nature of indulgences and their function in Christian living, and he went about his task with remarkable objectivity."[12]

1. Two Graces, Indulgences, and Luther's Understanding of Punishments

It comes as a surprise that Luther begins his treatise by saying, "Indulgences are the very merit of Christ and of his saints and so should be treated with all reverence."[13] This is different from what Luther declares in the *Ninety-Five Theses*,[14] but he immediately adds in the *Tractatus* that the indulgences have become "a

7 Wicks, 90, translated from *Dokumente zur Causa Lutheri (1517–1521)*, ed. Peter Fabisch and Erwin Iserloh (Münster: Aschendorff, 1988), pt. 1, 305.

8 Wicks, 90.

9 See for the discovery of the treatise in Wicks, 88–97.

10 Wicks, 93. See also 93n27: "Thus the period March-October 1517 seems most probable." Differences in content from the *Ninety-Five Theses* indicate a relatively early date in 1517.

11 Wicks, 93n1.

12 Wicks, 93.

13 Wicks, 97.

14 See theses 56–66 (TAL 1:41–42).

shocking exercise of greed." He complains that "you hear no one instructing people about what indulgences are, about how much they grant, or what purpose they serve."[15] In his treatise, Luther attempts to answer these questions, but he does it in a tentative way, partly acknowledging his ignorance.

From the outset, Luther uses the distinction between two graces to address the problem. This may be seen as the second surprise of the *Tractatus*. In the context of indulgence theologies and practices, the word *grace* was very often used with different meanings. Luther identifies one type of grace "as remission of penance and imposed satisfaction"[16] or as "a release from the temporal punishment imposed by a confessor." He calls this grace of remission "extrinsic." Later, Luther would no longer call this remission of penalties "grace." But here he distinguishes this extrinsic grace from an intrinsic one that he calls "infused grace"[17] or "the grace which makes a person righteous or more righteous."[18] Luther's main theological interest is in the inner condition of human beings and in how "infused grace" transforms them, while due to his topic, he first discusses punishments and their remission. In doing so, he offers a new understanding of punishments.

A third surprise might be that Luther speaks of purgatory as something to be taken for granted. He talks about a "temporal punishment imposed by a confessor, which one must undergo either on earth or in purgatory, if it still remains [at death]."[19] Insofar as penalties are imposed by a priest, indulgences are able to take them away, even if a person has to suffer them in purgatory! "The pope can, of course, release a soul from purgatory with regard to the penance he has himself imposed or could impose. The wording of the papal bull indicates this: 'so far as the keys of holy mother Church extends' and 'mercifully release from imposed penances.'"[20] This is quite remarkable, especially in light of theses 8 to 13 of the *Ninety-Five Theses*,[21] which argue that canonical penalties

15 Wicks, *Luther's Reform*, 97.

16 Wicks, 97.

17 Wicks, 100.

18 Wicks, 97.

19 Wicks, 100.

20 Wicks, 100. The first line Luther quotes here stems from the "Instructio summaria" of Archbishop Albrecht of Mainz (see *Dokumente zur Causa Lutheri*, pt. 1, 280). The source for the second quote has not been identified.

21 TAL 1:36.

are imposed only on people living on earth and should not be changed into the penalty of purgatory. In any case, this remission of penalties only relates to punishments imposed by a priest.

Here we face a problem that seems to have been overlooked by most Luther scholars. In our *Tractatus* as well as in the *Ninety-Five Theses*, Luther addresses those punishments imposed by the church rather than by God.[22] In thesis 5, he states, "The pope neither desires nor is able to remit any penalties except those imposed by his own discretion or that of the canons."[23] But the much more serious problem for medieval Christians was the punishments that were understood as being demanded by divine justice—punishments that one had finally to endure in purgatory and from which one hoped to get indulgence. Penalties imposed by a confessor allow for suffering the penalties on earth that are demanded by divine justice, although the latter requirements might go far beyond what the priests imposed. The final point of reference concerning satisfaction is the punishments called for by divine justice. It is highly astonishing that Luther does not address this point, because it is of central importance for understanding indulgences. A basic principle in the medieval understanding of penance was that "God does not forgive any sin unpunished," a principle stemming from Augustine that was developed throughout medieval times.[24] Already Tetzel, in his first reaction to the *Ninety-Five Theses*, appeals to this principle: "This satisfaction (*since God does not suffer any offence without penalty*) happens by punishment or by an equivalent that is accepted by God."[25]

It seems that it was Luther's opponents who challenged him to address the question of punishment due to divine justice in his *Explanations*, and he was reluctant to do that. In the fifth explanation, Luther identifies different kinds of penalties, raising the question of which punishment could be remitted

22 See thesis 5 (TAL 1:35).

23 TAL 1:35.

24 See Arnold Angenendt, "Deus, qui nullum peccatum impune dimittit. Ein 'Grundsatz' mittelalterlicher Bußgeschichte," in *Und dennoch ist von Gott zu reden*, ed. Matthias Lutz-Bachmann (Freiburg: Herder, 1994), 142–56. See also Theodor Dieter, "Martin Luther's Ninety-Five Theses—Reconstructing a Disputation Which Never Took Place," in *Luther@500 and Beyond: Martin Luther's Theology Past, Present and Future*, ed. Stephen Hultgren, Stephen Pietsch and Jeffrey Silcock (Adelaide: ATF, 2019), 9–17.

25 *Dokumente zur Causa Lutheri*, pt. 1, 322 (italics added).

by the pope. The sixth kind of punishment "is that which they say divine justice requires in order that it may be satisfied."[26] The phrase *they say* indicates that Luther takes up an idea of others while distancing himself from it. He is not quite clear what this kind of punishment should be. For him, it is one of two things: either the third kind of punishment that he mentions and calls "that voluntary and evangelical punishment which is to put into effect by spiritual penance in accordance with 1 Cor. 11[:31]: 'If we were to judge ourselves surely we should not be judged by the Lord'"[27] or the fifth kind of punishment, "the canonical punishment, which is instituted by the church."[28] But he makes his own objection that it must be different from these two kinds if it is meant to be the sixth kind of punishment. Luther considers that it is an intensification of those two kinds, but finally, he states: "I am absolutely convinced that there is no such punishment. First, because by no authority of Scripture, of teachers, or of the accepted interpretation of the canons can it be taught that there is such punishment."[29] As indicated, there was a long history of this understanding; it is very difficult to explain why Luther does not seem to have been aware of this. Even if he completely disagreed with it, one would expect him to address it as a serious error. Nevertheless, in his *Explanations* he continues to consider whether this might be associated with the fourth kind of punishment he mentions: namely, that God punishes the sins of his people with the rod according to Psalm 89:30–33.[30] But this would not create a new type of punishment; it would only emphasize the third or the fourth ones. In *A Sermon on Indulgence and Grace*, Luther declares, "No one can defend the position with any passage from Scripture that God's righteousness desires or demands any punishment or satisfaction from sinners except for their heartfelt and true contrition or conversion alone—with the condition that from that moment on they bear the cross of Christ and practice the aforementioned works [prayer, fasting, alms] (but not as imposed by anyone)."[31]

According to the rules of medieval disputations, the position of the opponent had to be reproduced correctly; otherwise, one would not speak to the

26 LW 31:93.
27 LW 31:90.
28 LW 31:92.
29 LW 31:93.
30 LW 31:94, 91.
31 TAL 1:61.

point and lose the debate. Since talking about "plenary indulgences" just refers to the punishments called for by divine justice, at least with most medieval theologians, one would imagine that Luther would have formulated a set of theses addressing this basic difference in understanding punishment from the outset, while in fact, he discusses in detail the relatively minor problem of whether canonical penalties can be transformed into purgatory in the aforementioned six theses from 8 to 13.[32]

In medieval theology, two aspects of punishment were distinguished: a *punitive* aspect, according to which punishment completes what is owed to God's justice for violating the divine order, and a *medicinal* aspect, which aims at changing sinners to help them not commit the same sin again. With respect to the first aspect, medieval theologians were convinced that someone else could perform the penitential work on behalf of the sinner; with respect to the second aspect, this was not possible.[33] If someone wished to get healthy again, he or she needed to take the medicine himself. The distinction was meant to make clear that indulgences and the remission of penalties do not make contrition superfluous. Whether this was plausible to contemporaries or not is hard to say.

Luther mocks this distinction: "Some of the new preachers have invented two kinds of sufferings: *Medicativae, Satisfactoriae*, that is, some suffering is for satisfaction and some for improvement. But, praise God, we have more freedom to disdain this kind of prattle than they have freedom to dream it up. For all suffering, indeed, everything God lays upon Christians is for their betterment and benefit."[34] So for Luther, punishments are no longer primarily seen as something negative that one would want to get rid of as soon as possible, but rather as something positive. Luther reduces medieval theologians' two aspects of punishment, the punitive and medicinal, to one, focusing only on the medicinal aspect. In this line, he declares at the very beginning of our treatise that the release of temporal punishment "in no way diminishes concupiscence and

32 TAL 1:61n25.

33 Cf. Thomas Aquinas, *On Sentences*, bk. 4, dist. 20, q. 1, a. 2, qc. 3 co.

34 TAL 1:62. Luther refers to theses 14 and 72 of Tetzel's "106 Theses against Luther"; see *Dokumente zur Causa Lutheri*, 323n23, 331. TAL 1:62n19 offers a quote from Thomas Aquinas about the punitive and medicinal aspects of punishment or satisfaction (*Quodlibet* bk. 2, q. 8, a. 2 ad. 3), but Thomas does not use the distinction "to a different end" than Tetzel; rather both agree that indulgences do not lift punishment in the medicative sense.

the infection of our nature. Neither does it increase charity or grant grace and interior virtue."[35] This is Luther's focus, and this focus is, surprisingly, an effective transformation of the person.

One might consider whether Luther's rejection of the concept of punishment due to God's justice is also based on his newly discovered understanding of the phrase "the righteousness of God" in Romans 1:16–17: not as, in a philosophical sense, the distributive righteousness with which God punishes the unrighteous but as the righteousness with which God makes sinners righteous.[36] But Luther nowhere in this debate refers to his new understanding of "righteousness of God."

2. Luther's Understanding of Purgatory and the Release from It through Indulgences

Focusing on the human person's sinful inner state and its healing, instead of on punishment, also shapes Luther's understanding of purgatory, which is different from the traditional medieval one. For the latter, divine justice demands a temporal punishment for every sin, but not all punishments can be met in people's lifetimes. Thus one has to assume a "place" after death where these remaining penalties can be expiated. This is purgatory. In this way, purgatory rests on the demands of divine justice. The claim of plenary indulgences is the remission of all penalties to be suffered either on earth or in purgatory. Remaining penalties hinder a soul in purgatory from entering heaven, but if they were to be remitted through a plenary indulgence, then the soul would immediately "fly up" to heaven. But Luther argues that even if such a remission were granted, indulgences would not affect the transformation of wicked human nature into something righteous and thus not open the gates of purgatory to heaven.

Luther answers the question of what hinders souls from leaving purgatory differently from medieval theologians. He interprets biblical authorities like "flesh and blood will not inherit the kingdom of God" (1 Cor 15:50) and "nothing defiled will enter" (Rev 21:27) in line with his understanding of the commandment to love God "with all your heart, and with all your soul, and with all your mind, and with all your strength" (Mark 12:30). This understanding is fundamental for Luther's concept of sin and grace. In the medieval

35 Wicks, *Luther's Reform*, 100.

36 LW 34:366–68.

understanding, God is loved by the will of a person, which can command (more or less) the person's own powers. By contrast, Luther insists on taking the biblical wording of the commandment of love for God seriously as calling for the dedication of the *whole* person to God, including all their desires, strivings, affections, and so on. Even if a person is directed to love God due to divine grace, nevertheless there are tendencies in the person that go in the opposite direction, loving created things more than the creator. This is concupiscence to be healed by divine grace, which can only happen in a lifelong process that will not even be finished when the person dies. The "healing agent" is infused grace, which is "an interior illumination of the mind and a kindling of the will. This is an eternal emanation into the soul like rays of the sun, and it does not become inactive after a plenary indulgence. This grace is necessary for the extirpation of concupiscence, until it is completely rooted out. This process is complete when a person is so filled with disgust for this life that he sighs longingly for God and finally breaks free from the body out of desire for God."[37] Luther's understanding of sin and concupiscence rests on his understanding of the commandment of love for God, focusing on the love of the whole person instead of focusing only or mainly on the will. This marks a difference from scholastic concepts. Thus the commandment of love is both the meeting point between Luther's and the scholastic understandings of sin *and* their point of divergence.[38]

Whether a person wholeheartedly loves God or not finally appears in the hour of death: Does a person willingly accept that it is God's will that they are about to die? If not, they will die as a sinner: "But the person did die in sin, since he did not love with his whole heart what God willed, but was unwilling, nor was 'his delight in the law of the Lord' [Ps 1:2]. Even though he outwardly obeyed the command, still his heart was not in it."[39] If a person cannot rise up to heaven because they did not die fully and wholly dedicated to God and thus remains in purgatory (understood in this way), the question concerning indulgences for the deceased is, Are indulgences able to help increase grace and love for God in the deceased? Luther compares the situation of a person in purgatory with the situation of a sinner before receiving grace: "The souls

37 Wicks, *Luther's Reform*, 100.

38 Cf. Theodor Dieter, *Der junge Luther und Aristoteles: Eine historisch-systematische Untersuchung zum Verhältnis von Theologie und Philosophie* (Berlin: De Gruyter, 2001), 80–136.

39 Wicks, *Luther's Reform*, 106.

in purgatory are related to subsequent grace, that is, to increase of grace and to its completion in glory, as a sinner is related to first grace or justification. For neither can merit grace, but both are able to receive it. This is true of one who has the first grace, even though he is no longer in this life, and of one who is still in this life, but without the prior grace."[40] According to Luther, as he expressed in theses 26 to 28 of the later so-called *Disputation against Scholastic Theology*, sinners completely depend on the operating of grace in order to be converted to God.[41] Even though persons in purgatory are understood as being in grace, nevertheless they are not in a position to merit the increase of grace; rather, they depend on God offering them grace anew in order to increase their grace. "Increasing in grace" does not mean that a person is now more justified than before. Rather, it indicates that grace permeates a person in a deeper and more comprehensive way in all aspects of their being. This is important, since God wills the complete dedication of our person. Since a deceased person is in purgatory because they died without wholehearted love to God, they can only leave purgatory if their love toward God increases, and this can only happen if God gives them grace upon grace. "One cannot so repent by natural power nor can the fire of purgatory free one from this sin without grace."[42]

If purgatory is understood as the "place" where people suffer from the punishments that they have not expiated in their lifetimes, it is indeed suffering the fire of purgatory that allows them to enter heaven after a certain time—or, of course, the remission of these penalties through indulgences applied to the deceased. But if a person is prevented from entering heaven (and thus is in purgatory) "due to the tinder and remaining earthly attachments" and being without "perfect love of God and longing for God,"[43] then release from purgatory will happen differently. Concerning indulgences for the deceased, this raises the question: "What good then are indulgences? Do they only serve to satisfy for actual sins? But how are souls saved when their actual sins are forgiven, but original or habitual sin remains?"[44]

In the treatise and in the *Ninety-Five Theses*, Luther thus develops an idea of purgatory that is different from the medieval one. It is based on the lack of

40 Wicks, 112.

41 LW 31:10–11.

42 Wicks, *Luther's Reform*, 106.

43 Wicks, 106.

44 Wicks, 105.

love for God and the corresponding fear, taking up First John 4:16: "There is no fear in love, but perfect love casts out fear; for fear has to do with punishment, and whoever fears has not yet reached perfection in love." In the *Ninety-Five Theses*, Luther states, "14. Imperfect purity or love on the part of the dying person necessarily brings with it greater fear. The smaller the love, the greater the fear. 15. This fear or horror is enough by itself alone (to say nothing of other things) to constitute the penalty of purgatory, since it is very near the horror of despair."[45] Can indulgences contribute to God's giving of new grace to people in purgatory? In our treatise, Luther makes a maximum assumption: "All the works and merits of Christ and the Church are in the hands of the pope and he can apply whatever good works are done through Christ in the Church."[46] For the deceased, this application is different from that for the living, "because the pope cannot absolve or forgive the departed, but only make intercession that God will forgive and absolve them." Thus indulgences for people in purgatory are not indulgences in the proper sense. Luther analyzes different aspects of the pope's intercession for the departed. The issue at stake is, Does the pope absolve people in purgatory "from the punishment due for their actual sins, or from the root-sin that they did not mortify or cure in life?" The latter can only happen through an infusion of grace. If this is so, then the pope does more for the departed than for the living. For the living, he only remits the penalties, while for the departed, he also intercedes for an infusion of grace.[47]

Another aspect is certitude about whether a soul is liberated from purgatory. The pope has no power over souls in purgatory; he can only intercede for them, but "God is free to decide to what extent, how, when, where, and for whom He hears the prayers of His Church. Who is certain that God accepts in the manner in which we make the petition?"[48] The freedom of God in receiving the Roman church's petitions is the reason it is inappropriate to state that paying the amount for an indulgence letter directly leads to freeing a soul from purgatory. Nevertheless, Luther goes on to mention the promises for praying, like "Ask and it will be given you" (Matt 7:7). From here, the trust and certainty arise that God will hear such prayers: "God does not turn back the prayer of his

45 TAL 1:36.

46 Wicks, *Luther's Reform*, 110.

47 Wicks, 111–12.

48 Wicks, 113.

Church, where Christ is praying with her."[49] Now Luther draws a very surprising conclusion:

> Since this is the case, the granting and gaining of indulgences is a most useful practice, in spite of the commerce and avarice which we fear is involved with them. Perhaps God wants to show greater mercy toward the departed in our day, since He sees them forgotten by the living. Also, more souls go to purgatory today than earlier, since Christians today are lazier than earlier. Thus many go there, but few work on their behalf, since both the departed and their survivors were and still are quite lazy. The pope comes to their aid at least in this manner.[50]

It is astonishing that for Luther, indulgences for the departed make more sense than for the living. Through indulgences, the living can get rid of the punishments imposed by the priests or the pope, while the departed might receive not only the remission of remaining penalties but, what is much more important, an increase of grace and love for God and a transformation of the inner state of their soul or heart.

In our treatise, Luther is also addressing the remission of penalties for the living. There is a certain tension and ambiguity in his statements. On the one hand, indulgences seem to be superfluous or insufficient because, for someone who is perfectly contrite, all punishments are taken away, for both actual and habitual sins, so that he or she can go to heaven without indulgences: "The perfectly contrite person goes to heaven without indulgences, but the imperfectly contrite person cannot go there even with indulgences. For God places no demands upon one who is perfectly contrite, neither for actual sins, nor for habitual, that is, for the tinder and 'original' sin." Faced with this aporia, Luther confesses his ignorance.[51] One should note that the aporia depends on Luther's understanding of purgatory, which is different from the scholastic one. On the other hand, Luther declares in his "maximum assumption" what indulgences for living could mean:

> The pope makes an application as satisfaction in the indulgences he grants to the living. The sense and intention of this is that if you have

49 Wicks, 113.

50 Wicks, 113.

51 Wicks, 105.

> sinned and then in sorrow for your sins want to make satisfaction, you then come to the pope saying, "Holy Father, I beg you to direct the works and prayers of the Church [to satisfy] for my sins." Then he answers, "Let it be as you ask." Then all who offer Mass, pray, fast, labor, or do any other work pleasing to God do this for you, so that you are freed from the labor of penance and satisfaction. This is a plenary indulgence.[52]

These highly surprising sentences are understood properly only when one realizes that Luther underlines that such a plenary indulgence is not all that one needs. Rather, his emphasis lies on the struggle against concupiscence. After having received remission of penalties, "then you must diligently crucify your members and mortify the source of sin, that is, your concupiscence. For just as it was the cause of the sins for which the indulgence was granted, so it will cause further sins, if you stand still in security."[53] While Luther does not reject indulgences for the living that remit only the punishments, in the *Ninety-Five Theses*, he addresses the challenge at stake much more strongly: "It is extremely difficult, even for the most learned theologians, to lift up before the people the liberality of indulgences and the truth about contrition at one and the same time."[54]

The *Tractatus* can be seen as a summary of Luther's early theology with respect to the question of indulgences. It is extremely interesting to observe his attempt to make sense of the institution and practice of indulgences based on the theological insights that he had gained in his theological development and that, conversely, also formed the basis for his criticism. He focuses on the inner state of the person "in grace" still shaped by concupiscence. Since indulgences for the living—remission of punishments imposed by a priest—do not help overcome concupiscence, they are of minor importance for Luther in the *Tractatus*; nevertheless, they have a limited meaning. Luther's understanding of concupiscence is based on his understanding of the commandment of love for God as total dedication of the whole person to God. This also determines Luther's concept of purgatory. It is not the unrepented punishments that make up purgatory, but it is concupiscence that characterizes the souls of the deceased even

52 Wicks, 110.

53 Wicks, 110.

54 TAL 1:39 (thesis 39).

after death and, as a lack of love for God, creates the fear that is the terror and torment of purgatory. Luther offers, so to speak, an existential interpretation of purgatory. The only way of getting out of purgatory is to increase love for God, which is only possible through grace given to the deceased by God. This again determines the understanding of indulgences for the deceased. They are prayers of the pope not for the remission of punishments, but for the increase of grace and love for God. Wholehearted love will end the time in purgatory. Therefore, indulgences for the deceased make more sense for Luther than indulgences for the living, because through the first type, the soul's concupiscence is addressed and attacked, while this is not the case for the living. As we have seen, Luther presupposes that there is no such thing as punishment due to divine justice. Even though he offers arguments against this concept as he understands it, he does not seem to be aware of its long tradition, which is fundamental for the medieval understanding of indulgences.

Luther's *Tractatus* shows a high degree of systematic coherence. Even though Luther quickly developed and changed his perception and evaluation of indulgences between 1517 to 1520, the *Tractatus* as a systematic treatment of the topic in 1517 remains an important source for identifying Luther's thinking in this year and background for interpreting his *Ninety-Five Theses*.

Freedom and Responsibility

Luther's Reformational Thinking in His Treatises of 1520 and Their Significance for Today

Irene Dingel

A half millennium ago, in 1520, Martin Luther published his great programmatic writings, among them *The Freedom of a Christian*. Freedom remains a relevant topic in all times, certainly also today. "All people strive for freedom," asserted *Zeit Online* in March 2018. "If there is one thing that most people in Western societies agree on today, it is probably the conviction that individuality, freedom, and self-determination are among the most important values."[1] Freedom has become a self-evident good, so that people hardly think about what freedom actually means. But now that everyone can freely and anonymously express what they think on the internet, including hate comments and other verbal incitement, the question of the limits of individual freedom has become virulent, increasingly burning.

What does *individual freedom* actually mean, and how far does it extend? The views on this seem to diverge. Our modern, secular concept of freedom goes back to the Enlightenment and is fed by the thinking of the English philosopher Thomas Hobbes, who understood freedom as freedom from external impediments or unrestrained coercion: "Free is he who can do what he wants and is not prevented from doing so by others. . . . Freedom is independence from external constraints."[2] But Martin Luther had already developed a concept

1 Tim Reiß, "Was heißt Freiheit?," *Zeit Online*, March 27, 2018, accessed March 1, 2020, https://www.zeit.de/2018/14/freiheit-werte-westen-geschichte.

2 According to Reiß.

of freedom that strikes highly modern chords. This concept of freedom, however, presumed not the secular human being but rather understood the individual as a spiritual and simultaneously temporal person, bound into an order of creation. Luther saw human beings placed in a relationship of tension between self-determination and responsibility. He developed his concept of freedom from this context. Responsibility, however, sets limits to a freedom understood as the absence of external coercion. It is worth considering his position in today's world.

With his "discovery" of a Christian concept of freedom, Luther gave not only theology but also European intellectual history in general a lasting impulse on which the Enlightenment could later build. To understand how and why, precisely in 1520, Luther began to think about the topic of freedom, one must consider the historical context. This essay will therefore (1) begin by assessing 1520 as the decisive year of the Reformation; (2) place the *Freiheitsschrift* (the tract on freedom) in the context of Luther's other major Reformation treatises, in which the decisive themes of the Reformation or the Protestant faith were discussed; and (3) evaluate what Luther wrote, followed by a brief perspective on the impact.

1. 1520 as the Decisive Year of the Reformation

After the celebration of the five-hundredth anniversary of the Reformation in 2017, one might think that 1517 was actually the decisive year for the Reformation. There is some justification for this. For we can indeed claim Martin Luther's *Ninety-Five Theses* as the initial spark for the process that unfolded after their publication. However, this should not obscure the fact that 1520 was another special climactic point in the development of the Reformation. In 1520, Luther outlined his entire theological program with four major Reformation writings, a program not substantially revised during his lifetime but at best fine-tuned and, depending on the context, given special accents. The year 1520 was also climactic because the events surrounding Luther's person came to a head. After the *Ninety-Five Theses* had been disseminated rapidly and widely through manuscript copies, reprints, and translations, the Dominican Order had brought charges of heresy against the rebellious Wittenberg professor in Rome in March 1518. Luther, who at first continued to present his ideas for discussion primarily in the academic milieu, was little impressed by this, for at the Heidelberg Disputation of April 1518, he unfolded for the first time in twenty-eight theological theses his *theologia crucis*.[3] This "theology of the cross" focused on God's encounter with his human creatures in the lowliness of the crucified one. At the same time, the canonical process against Luther got underway. In October 1518, he was summoned to an interrogation by the papal legate and cardinal Thomas de Vio from Gaeta, also called Cajetan. This interrogation took place in Augsburg, on the periphery of the imperial diet, which was just coming to a close. Cajetan was the most learned Dominican of his time, and his powers were far-reaching. A papal breve of August 23, 1518, had authorized him to place Luther under excommunication, since he was considered a *haereticus declaratus*, and to arrest him immediately, with the help of secular authorities if necessary. At the same time, he had the authority to admit the Wittenberg professor back into the church's fellowship if he showed remorse during the interrogation. The meeting between the two, however, brought no resolution: Luther did not recant his teachings and did not repent.[4]

On the contrary, at the Leipzig Disputation of 1519, where he appeared as an opponent of the Ingolstadt professor Johann Eck, he questioned the structure of the entire church—the hierarchical structure of ecclesiastical offices as well as the primacy of the papacy, the authority of the councils, and the derivation of this system from what was claimed to be divine law.[5] No wonder Eck pursued the resumption of the Roman heresy trial—the *Causa Lutheri*—which had been delayed by the imperial election after the death of Emperor Maximilian I in early 1519. Only in January 1520 did Pope Leo X take the initiative again. After deliberations at the Curia, a draft for a bull against Luther was in hand at the end of April 1520. This bull—*Exsurge Domine*, issued on June 15, 1520—mandated the capture and extradition of Luther to Rome and the destruction of all his writings if he and his followers did not repudiate their

3 Gerhard O. Forde, *On Being a Theologian of the Cross. Reflections on Luther's Heidelberg Disputation, 1518* (Grand Rapids, MI: Eerdmans, 1997).

4 On Cajetan, see Marcel Nieden, *Organum Deitatis. Die Christologie des Thomas de Vio Cajetan* (Leiden: Brill, 1997); Gerhard Hennig, *Cajetan und Luther. Ein historischer Beitrag zur Begegnung von Thomismus und Reformation* (Stuttgart: Calwer Verlag, 1966).

5 Markus Hein and Armin Kohnle, eds., *Die Leipziger Disputation, 1519* (Leipzig: Evangelische Verlagsanstalt, 2011); Mickey L. Mattox, Richard J. Serina, and Jonathan Mumme, eds., *Luther at Leipzig: Martin Luther, the Leipzig Debate, and the Sixteenth-Century Reformations* (Leiden: Brill, 2019).

positions within sixty days.[6] Now the fronts were clear, not only theologically, but also legally, even though Luther's excommunication did not take place until the bull *Decet Romanum Pontificem* was issued in January 1521. This escalation of the conflict with the Curia in Rome coincided with Luther's work on his formulations of the fundamental concepts of his reformational theology. In contrast to Melanchthon or (later) Calvin, he did not summarize them in dogmatic form but rather published them in individual treatises that arose out of specific situations and addressed current problems.

Luther received the news of his threatened excommunication while he was working on his *De captivitate Babylonica ecclesiae*. A little later, in October 1520, the opportunity for mediation between the fronts arose for the last time. Karl von Miltitz, a notary and chamberlain at the Roman Curia and at the same time papal nuncio, could not pass up the opportunity to make one last attempt to reconcile Luther with the pope, but in vain.[7] Their discussions prompted Luther to write a letter to Pope Leo X. He composed it in both Latin

6 Timothy Wengert has dealt with this treatise in "Luther's *Freedom of a Christian* for Today's Church," *Lutheran Quarterly* 28 (2014): 1–21; and his translation of the treatise, *The Annotated Luther* 1, ed. Timothy J. Wengert (Minneapolis: Fortress, 2015), 474–538. See also treatments in standard Luther biographies and in Irene Dingel, *Reformation—Zentren—Akteure—Ereignisse* (Göttingen: Vandenhoeck & Ruprecht, 2016), 56–63; and Dingel, "*Von der Freiheit eines Christenmenschen* (1520)—Historische und theologische Aspekte," in *Meilensteine der Reformation. Schlüsseldokumente der frühen Wirksamkeit Martin Luthers*, ed. Dingel and Henning P. Jürgens (Gütersloh: Gütersloher Verlagshaus, 2014), 122–31. See also Robert Kolb, *Luther's Treatise* On Christian Freedom *and Its Legacy* (Lanham, MD: Fortress Academic / Lexington, 2019).

7 Miltitz had journeyed to Saxony in September 1518 to bestow the "Golden Rose," a high papal honor, on the elector and at the same time to move him to cease protecting Luther and take measures against him. As a result, he met with Luther in January 1519 in order to solve this spreading controversy by diplomatic means. It was then that Luther declared his readiness to write nothing more on indulgences provided that his foes would no longer attack him for his views. See Heinrich Theodor Flathe, "Karl von Miltitz," in *Allgemeine Deutsche Biographie* 21 (1885): 759–60; Hans-Günther Leder, *Ausgleich mit dem Papst? Luthers Haltung in den Verhandlungen mit Miltitz 1520* (Stuttgart: Calwer Verlag, 1969); Armin Kohnle, *Reichstag und Reformation: kaiserliche und ständische Religionspolitik von den Anfängen der Causa Lutheri bis zum Nürnberger Religionsfrieden* (Gütersloh: Gütersloher Verlagshaus, 2001), 31–41.

and German, which makes it clear that he specifically wanted to include the non-academic public in this exchange. In this letter, Luther promised to remain silent in the future, provided that his opponents who had accused him of heresy in Rome would also remain silent and not take any further action against him.[8] Threatened with imprisonment, he attached his tract *The Freedom of a Christian*. Its thirty theses were a reaction to the bull threatening banishment, which wanted to constrain the reformer and his followers and curb their teachings. In contrast, the theses postulated freedom: freedom from canonical constraints and all spiritual opposition as well as freedom for faith and life. However, this did not change the fact that the bull threatening excommunication was distributed ever more widely, although not in all regions of the empire at that time. Luther maintained that the Antichrist was at work in the bull; it provoked him to identify the papacy with the Antichrist in two pamphlets, also from 1520.[9] In addition, as late as November 1520, shortly before the end of the official revocation period mentioned in the bull, he appealed to a Christian council committed to Holy Scripture. He asked the emperor, princes, and cities of the empire for support since he had not yet been able to testify before impartial judges. The year 1520 was thus a very turbulent and at the same time theologically productive year. The confrontation led Luther to apply to the papacy the concept of Antichrist that had been dominant since the late Middle Ages,[10] and at the same time, he sharpened the fundamental teachings of the Reformation in German and Latin writings.

2. *The Freedom of a Christian* in the Context of Luther's Programmatic Reformation Writings

Luther's reformational theology and the reform program associated with it found its most powerful formulation and concretization in the four programmatic writings of 1520.[11] Scholarly literature often speaks of three such writings,

8 WA 7:3–11, 42–49.

9 *Adversus execrabilem Antichristi bullam*, WA 6:597–612; *Wider die Bulle des Endchrists*, WA 6:614–29.

10 On the development of Luther's view, see Scott H. Hendrix, *Luther and the Papacy: Stages in a Reformation Conflict* (Philadelphia: Fortress, 1981).

11 See Dingel, "*Von der Freiheit*," 122–23.

but essentially, there were four programmatic treatises. In May 1520, Luther composed his treatise *On Good Works*.[12] Here he laid the theological foundations for his *Freiheitsschrift* by addressing the connection between faith and works. Beginning with the statement that the highest, noblest, and most pleasing work to God is faith in Christ, he placed the righteousness of faith in the center of his remarks, in contrast to all compulsion to do good works. Measured by this faith—according to Luther—the classification of all human works as good or less good, as pleasing to God or displeasing, must be assessed in terms of faith. Measured against the faith in Christ, it becomes pointless to distinguish between better, good, or less good works, let alone to rank their value for obtaining salvation. If human works please God, Luther thought, it is only because God accepts them for the sake of faith and lets them be considered good works.

With *On Good Works*, Luther had thus resolutely opposed all earlier piety based on works-righteousness. He not only questioned the usefulness of good works for salvation but had also reversed the relationship between justification and works: only the faith given by God to people motivates and liberates them to do unselfish, good works. The *Freiheitsschrift* built on this foundation and placed both justification and responsible human action under the perspective of freedom.

Luther was enormously productive in 1520. In June, he conceived his treatise *To the Christian Nobility of the German Nation on the Improvement of the Christian Estate*, which was printed a month later.[13] The first copies were available in August at the latest. In this treatise, Luther pursued a further reformational insight. His experiences had taught him that one could hardly expect the clergy of the time to take the initiative for measures to improve the state of the church—that is, to undertake necessary reforms in church and Christian life. Therefore, Luther turned to the Christian nobility, whose representatives he assigned responsibilities as *emergency bishops*. According to Luther, it was necessary to tear down three walls built by the Roman church, which had so far prevented reform. He called for the removal of (1) the division of

12 *Von den guten Werken*, WA 6:202–76.

13 *An den christlichen Adel deutscher Nation von des christlichen Standes Besserung*, WA 6:404–69, LW 44:123–217. See also Nicole Kuropka, "Über die Aktualität von Luthers Adelsschrift. An den christlichen Adel deutscher Nation von des christlichen Standes Besserung (1520)," *Luther* 91 (2020): 4–8.

society into a more highly valued spiritual class and a subordinate lay class; (2) the papal prerogative of authoritatively interpreting Holy Scripture; and (3) the power of decision to convene a council reserved to the pope. In contrast, Luther developed the idea of a general priesthood of all baptized persons—all believers—which pointed the way forward for the Reformation by emphasizing that all Christians are equally members of a truly spiritual state through baptism, the gospel, and faith.

Luther believed that access to Sacred Scripture was not reserved for specific individuals—namely, the pope and the clerical hierarchy—because of his conviction that all Christians were able to reach a correct understanding of Scripture through the Holy Spirit. The reformational emphasis on Bible translation and the general dissemination of the Bible are closely connected with this. Consequently, the biblical standards for assessing the prevailing grievances and developing necessary reforms had to be accessible to all Christians. Everyone had a responsibility to provide remedies, even if a council proved to be necessary.

Luther went even further with his treatise *De captivitate Babylonica ecclesiae*, which treated the sacramental activity of the church and thus its ritual activity, which was regarded as its theological center. As early as August 1520, Luther began work on this Latin treatise, which was addressed to learned, academically trained readers. Meanwhile, Rome was preparing his excommunication with the papal bull, dated June 15, 1520. In October 1520, *De captivitate* appeared in print.[14] The title is significant. In Luther's view, the church under the papacy had fallen into a veritable Babylonian Captivity, which had an effect especially on the understanding and practice of the sacraments. To free the church from this captivity, a captivity into which certainly the individual believer had also fallen, was Luther's concern. All should be enabled again to follow the gospel freely. To this end, Luther developed an understanding of the sacraments that broke away from traditional conventions and was exclusively derived from Holy Scripture. In his view, the characteristics of a sacrament were a sign instituted by Christ himself, a promise associated with it grounded in Holy Scripture and human faith, which on the one hand is awakened and strengthened by the sacramental action and on the other hand at the same time receives the divine promise. The consequence of this new definition was that

14 *De captivitate Babylonica ecclesiae*, WA 6:497–573, LW 36:11–126.

Luther only accepted as sacraments those ritual acts that could be attested by Holy Scripture. This reduced the traditional number of seven sacraments to only three: baptism, the Lord's Supper, and penance. Strictly speaking, even penance could hardly be considered a sacrament anymore, since a specific use of a sign instituted by Christ was not found in the Bible. Thus the churches of the Reformation limited themselves in the long term to the sacraments of baptism and the Lord's Supper. In *De captivitate* Luther had thus begun to question the foundations of the church's traditional understanding of salvation. He explained this in detail in the question of the Lord's Supper. He identified three Babylonian captivities imprisoning the Supper from which the church should now free itself: the withholding of the chalice from the laity, the doctrine of the transformation of the elements from bread and wine into the body and blood of Christ, and the understanding of the Lord's Supper as a sacrificial act.

At the time *De captivitate* appeared in print in early October, Luther was at work on his letter to Leo X and the *Freiheitsschrift*.[15] In *The Freedom of a Christian*, the reformer no longer was addressing a select target group—the Christian nobility or theological scholars—but all people in order to show what Christian life actually means and how it should be realized.[16] It is impossible to overestimate the impact of this treatise, for Luther was attempting no more and no less than the re-orientation of human life, a demonstration of the potential dimensions the individual's life as a meaningful life. This can be summarized under the theme, "freedom and responsibility." Basically, this phrase describes the entire Reformation doctrine of justification.

3. Justification as Freedom—Freedom as Responsibility

Like no other before him, Luther made freedom his theme. A priori, he was less concerned with social or political freedom and focused instead on a spiritual concept affecting the individual's life, the effects of which, however, penetrated into the spheres of society and politics. The Jena historian Georg Schmidt observes, "In Martin Luther, the historian comes across an author who

15 See also Georg Buchwald, *Luther-Kalendarium* (Leipzig: Egers & Sievers, 1929), 15–16.

16 WA 7:20–38. The German does vary, though relatively slightly, from the Latin text, which is the basis for the Wengert translation in TAL.

often spoke of 'freedom' at a time when this term was by no means part of the common property of political or even humanistic speech, at least not in the German-speaking world."[17] Luther's talking about freedom was unique in his time, even if the "gravamina of the German nation," the complaints regularly voiced by the political authorities at the imperial diet since the late Middle Ages, had periodically denounced the domination of the Roman Curia. The practices presented as "gravamina" were perceived as servitude for the Germans. The diets also criticized similar domination by the emperor, "a Spanish servitude," and demanded "liberty" in the face of it. Ulrich von Hutten also propagated "German freedom" in order to mobilize the imperial knighthood in opposition to the emperor.[18] His was a passion for a form of political freedom. In contrast, for Luther, freedom became a central theological theme. In his German writings, published between 1517 and 1530, there are no less than five thousand examples of appeals for this freedom.[19]

Perhaps Luther's examination of the topic of freedom was so fundamental because his own experiences since 1517 had had a decisive influence on his work. Attempts had been made to place demands on him, both theological as well as those based on canon law, to follow requirements to which he no longer felt able to comply. Both the church's teaching and its juridical process confronted him, just as had his earlier spiritual struggles, pressing from within and without. Therefore, *The Freedom of a Christian* focused on the question of what makes human beings free and righteous before God so that they are able to turn to other people in freedom and unselfishness in everyday life. Luther developed his answer on the basis of Paul's statement in First Corinthians 9:19: "For though I am free from everyone, yet have I made myself a servant to everyone, that I might gain many of them." At the beginning of his treatise, he placed two theses that at first appear to be contradictory: "A Christian is a free lord over all things and subject to no one," and "A Christian is a servant of all people and subject to everything."[20] These two theses correspond to the two perspectives

17 Georg Schmidt, "Luthers Freiheitsvorstellungen in ihrem sozialen und rhetorischen Kontext (1517–1521)," in *Martin Luther—Biographie und Theologie*, ed. Dietrich Korsch and Volker Leppin (Tübingen: Mohr Siebeck, 2010), 9.

18 Schmidt, 13–22.

19 Anja Lobenstein-Reichmann, *Freiheit bei Martin Luther. Lexikographische Textanalyse als Methode historischer Semantik* (Berlin: De Gruyter, 1998), 18.

20 WA 7:21.1–4.

on which Luther based his theological development of the topic. The human person—the "Christian," in Luther's formulation—exists on the one hand in relationship to God and on the other hand in relationship to the world and fellow human beings. In these distinct but overlapping existential locations, the Christian person is free and bound at the same time, bound specifically in concrete, responsible actions for the benefit of neighbors.

Luther explains his first thesis, "A Christian is a free lord of all things and subject to no one," with the statement that it is not external living conditions that give rise to a person's righteousness and freedom. The origin of human righteousness and freedom lies rather in God, who freely grants both to a person. This, according to Luther, takes place through God's word—that is, God's address to human beings. In both the Old and the New Testament, this address of God occurs as a demand or expectation and as a promise: law and gospel.[21] This double perspective of God's word as law and gospel became decisive for the overall structure of Luther's theology. In his *Freiheitsschrift*, he addressed the belief that God's law, with all its demands and requirements for human beings, actually presupposes that human beings can act as righteous, free persons, since only under this condition would they actually be able to meet the expectations or commandments of God. But human beings could not become righteous, free persons of themselves without the righteous and liberating action of God, Luther maintained.[22] The Augustinian hermit monk Luther had experienced this himself in his search for a merciful God. His reformational discovery thus underwent a deeper development as the author formulated his doctrine of justification in the *Freiheitsschrift*. It can be summed up in the following short formula: in the gospel, God promises human beings the righteousness and freedom that they, despite all sincere efforts, could never acquire for themselves under the demands and requirements of the divine law.

At the same time, Luther attached great importance to linking this reformational doctrine of justification with Christology. He therefore explained how closely this promise of God was linked to the person of Jesus Christ. According to Luther, trust in God, who became human in Christ, and faith in him as the mediator of righteousness along with freedom binds believers to Christ in a relationship like that which exists between two lovers, between

21 WA 7:23.24–25.4. See also Reinhard Schwarz, "Luthers Freiheitsbewußtsein und die Freiheit eines Christenmenschen," in *Martin Luther—Biographie*, 31–68.

22 WA 7:26.13–31.

bride and bridegroom, so that a kind of community or exchange of goods takes place. Drawing on medieval bridal mysticism, he described this as a "happy exchange."[23] He used this image—so alien to us today—to describe the justification of human beings as God's self-identification as God incarnate in Jesus Christ, who assumed human guilt and destroyed it through his righteousness. Christ transfers his righteousness to human beings, effecting that transfer through faith, which unites the two partners like a bridal ring.[24] This delivered the fundamental freedom from the requirements of ecclesiastically determined good works or requirements for satisfaction. This also meant there was a direct relationship between God and human beings that none had dared to think of in the Middle Ages. According to Luther, those thus united in faith with the Son of God are able to come directly before God without the mediation of other church authorities. They are endowed with a priestly dignity that enables them to intercede for themselves and others.[25] With that, also here in the *Freiheitsschrift*, Luther called into question the hierarchical distinction between clergy and laity. Above all, the role of the many saints who stood as actors between God and human beings, as mediators in every need, disappeared.

Luther's statements about freedom, which he grounded in Christology, were profound theological reflections, even if he dressed them in simple words for the common people. What he unfolded here became a central statement of the Reformation par excellence, which he tried to make accessible to the people of his time with fresh theological expressions: faith in God, who turns lovingly to human beings,[26] is not only liberation from the compulsion to justify themselves with their own works—the compulsion to confirm their status in relation to God and to focus totally on themselves in everything they do and worry about.[27] This faith is also the only appropriate fulfillment of the

23 WA 7:25.34. See also Oswald Bayer, *Martin Luther's Theology: A Contemporary Interpretation*, trans. Thomas H. Trapp (Grand Rapids, MI: Eerdmans, 2008), 225–30.

24 WA 7:25.34–26.4.

25 WA 7:26–29.7.

26 WA 7:26.13–31.

27 On Luther's concept of "turned into oneself," see Paul Althaus, *The Theology of Martin Luther*, trans. Robert C. Schultz (Philadelphia: Fortress, 1966), 144–50; see also Bayer, *Martin Luther's Theology*, 182–84.

First Commandment: you are to have no other gods. For Luther, the root of all sin (original or inherited) was the continual effort to build up one's own righteousness and the attempt to base one's identity on this humanly constructed righteousness.[28]

This way in which human beings have become "free masters of all things" has implications for human action in everyday contexts because it can be free from self-centered, selfish striving.[29] Luther was not at all opposed to individual self-realization or to the personal development of the individual. Rather, what he opposed was the unrelenting effort to make one's own identity dependent on what one has "acquired" or on one's own performance. It is this inner freedom that makes possible an unselfish commitment in the service of others and thus gives one the freedom to shape the world. In this sense, however, "a Christian is also a servant of all things and subject in everything." This accentuates a sense of responsibility because, in secular contexts, Luther also considered good works and activities that meet temporal needs to be beneficial: "Therefore, a person's thinking should be free in all works and should be directed only to serve and benefit others; a person should keep in mind nothing else but what is needful for others: that is truly Christian living."[30] This is the way the reformer intended to interpret *bondage*. Luther also explained this in a highly theological way in his *Freiheitsschrift*: the faith that freed people from the compulsion to perform in God's sight motivates them to act on behalf of others as God acted himself through Christ—namely, in free, unselfish commitment.[31] This bondage meant "to become a Christ to others," to turn to them in loving care.[32] In this way, Luther made faith not only an impulse but also an important presupposition and foundation for unselfish love and unselfish action in the world. To "become a Christ to others" meant nothing other than a caring acceptance of others and, in a larger dimension, activity on behalf of others in shaping the world. For Luther, the prerequisite for this to take place free from striving for power and self-interest, guided by sincerity and a sense of responsibility, was an intact relationship with God. The bondage that Luther placed at the center of his second thesis is therefore not to be understood as enslavement or abject

28 See also Luther's *Large Catechism*, first commandment, BSELK 930–47, BC 386–92.

29 WA 7:29.31–38.15.

30 WA 7:34.29–32.

31 WA 7:35.20–26.10.

32 WA 7:35.28–36.2.

submission but as the voluntary acceptance of the responsibility that results from a needs-based organization of human coexistence.

This conception of freedom in the human relationship with God thus also included the bonding acceptance of responsibility in human coexistence and in the shaping of the world. That has absolutely timeless validity. However, to understand this, it is necessary to recall which ecclesiastical conditions and pious expectations defined the pious life in Luther's time. Only then does it become clear what explosive power the *Freiheitsschrift* exercised and how radical Luther's argument was. All the many works—mostly institutionalized by the church—for acquiring righteousness, such as almsgiving and repetitious praying of the Lord's Prayer, were called into question at a stroke. But Luther also admonished the proper use of Christian freedom. He did not simply abolish everything in the sphere of churchly activities thoughtlessly, without reflection.[33] According to Luther, concern for the common good—the practical appropriateness and impact of efforts in behalf of the community—was in no way to be neglected. With rationally governed consideration, Luther advocated, for example, for freedom in dealing with rites and ceremonies. Since, in the reformational view, these were only outward forms and exercises of piety without any worth in acquiring salvation, decisions about their retention or abolition could also be freely made in responsible consideration to specific situations.[34]

Conclusion: Significance and Impact

Luther's *Freiheitsschrift* has properly been categorized as one of his most important theological writings. In it, he worked out in an especially clear way the central position of the doctrine of justification within reformational theology. It

33 WA 7:36–38.

34 This was especially important for Luther's dispute with Karlstadt over his rigorous abolition of established ritual practices and substitution of reformational forms. Against this, Luther appealed for freedom in dealing with rites and ceremonies, with sensitivity to those who could not and would not accept this reform and innovation so quickly (the shielding of the weak). See Luther's "Invocavit Sermons of March 1522," WA 10 III:1–64. See also Helmar Junghans, "Freiheit und Ordnung bei Luther während der Wittenberger Bewegung und der Visitationen," *Theologische Literaturzeitung* 97 (1972): 95–104; James S. Preus, *Carlstadt's* Ordinaciones and *Luther's Liberty: A Study of the Wittenberg Movement 1521–22* (Cambridge, MA: Harvard University Press, 1974).

shows us how the justification of sinners before God enables individuals to turn their gaze away from themselves and to assume responsibility in the temporal sphere unselfishly and with a sense of the common good. In Luther's doctrine of justification, therefore, salvation takes shape in a full relationship with God and the world and thus takes on the character of freedom.

The *Freiheitsschrift* considerably strengthened Luther's impact, which had already attained European dimensions before 1520. For example, the *Freiheitsschrift* was translated into various European national languages. Even in the Netherlands—where the papal nuncio Aleander had successfully distributed the bull of excommunication and then launched repressive measures on behalf of the Habsburgs—Luther's writings were translated or reprinted.[35] In Italy, too, where the Reformation met with little response, translations of Luther's *Freiheitsschrift* were circulated, albeit mostly anonymously or under a different name.[36]

To this day, freedom from religiously charged constraints and the freedom to act responsibly in political, social, and economic contexts is a major, much-discussed issue. In his *Freiheitsschrift*, Luther developed an understanding of "freedom" that for the first time placed the individual in an existentially experienced field of tension between freedom and responsibility. Freedom from spiritual enslavement and freedom to assume responsibility became maxims that shaped the intellectual history of Europe in the long term. It is worth recalling repeatedly that this individual freedom must not be at the expense of others and the environment but should lead to responsibility for others and the world. This is among the most relevant topics of our time.

Translated by Robert Kolb

35 In Antwerp, for example, where the Augustinian cloister belonged to Luther's Saxon Congregation and its monks were in contact with Luther, efforts were made in 1520 and 1521 to publish by some of its brothers, among them the prior, Jacob Praepositus, who had matriculated at the University of Wittenberg between 1516 and 1520. They had gotten to know Luther personally and became his disciples. Reprints of his works also appeared in Leiden and Zwolle. See Irene Dingel, "Luther und Europa," in *Luther Handbuch*, ed. Albrecht Beutel, 3rd ed. (Tübingen: Mohr Siebeck, 2017), 240–52, esp. 242–43; C. Ch. G. Visser, *Hollands Lutheraner. Geschichte und Gegenwart* (Erlangen: Luther-Verlag, 1991), 12–13.

36 Dingel, "Luther und Europa," 251; Manfred E. Welti, *Kleine Geschichte der italienischen Reformation* (Gütersloh: Mohn, 1985), 22.

Philip Melanchthon (1497–1560) and Urbanus Rhegius (1489–1541)

Scott Hendrix

The German reformers Philip Melanchthon and Urbanus Rhegius have scarcely, if ever, been compared directly. This is understandable, as they had very different relationships with Martin Luther and the course of the Reformation. On the one hand, it is well known that Luther and Melanchthon lived and worked closely together in Wittenberg for almost forty years. The correspondence between them is extensive. On the other hand, less has been known about Rhegius and Luther. Their correspondence is much sparser, and we have no records of Rhegius visiting Wittenberg or seeing Luther more than twice.

The first personal encounter between Rhegius and Luther took place in August 1530 after Rhegius was recruited by Duke Ernest of Braunschweig and Lüneburg to move north and lead the effort to make his large territory Lutheran. Rhegius accepted the offer and, in August of 1530, headed north with his family. The party stopped first in Nuremberg, where he was wined and dined. Afterward, they proceeded to the castle at Coburg where the outlawed Luther was sheltered throughout the Diet of Augsburg. The next day with Luther was for Rhegius the visit of a lifetime. His exuberance can be seen in an excerpt from a letter sent in 1534 to friends in Augsburg.

In this letter, Rhegius claimed that words could not convey how great Luther was. As a theologian for the entire world, he was without equal, and no scholar was worthy of passing judgment on him.[1] Another letter of admiration

1 Walter König, *Der Reformator Urbanus Rhegius: Chronik einer Familie zwischen Langenargen and Finkenwerder* (Museum Langenargen, 2006), 57–59.

was sent by Rhegius to Luther in 1537 after they met for the second and last time. It was a meeting of Lutheran theologians who gathered in the town of Smalcald to sign Luther's *Smalcald Articles* and Melanchthon's *Treatise on the Power and Primacy of the Pope*. During the meeting, the group was shaken by Luther's nearly fatal bout with kidney stones. On his way home, Rhegius expressed his joy at Luther's recovery and recalled how one cry of agony from Luther had pierced his own heart. "In his remote part of Saxony," Rhegius wrote, "churches and their pastors were praying that Luther would remain with them for many years to come."[2]

THE ROAD TO AUGSBURG (1530)

Rhegius and Melanchthon probably met for the first time in 1530 at the Diet of Augsburg. They could have met in 1529 at the Marburg Colloquy where both Luther and Melanchthon were present, but Rhegius was too sick to attend. However, even before 1530 they had opportunities to correspond. Months before the colloquy started, Melanchthon sent a letter to Caspar Aquila in Saalfeld advising him not to be drawn into worldly matters but to concentrate on his ministry. Melanchthon added that he was waiting for a reply to a letter he had written to Rhegius.[3]

By that time, Rhegius knew how important Melanchthon was to the Reformation and to Luther. And Melanchthon had learned about Rhegius through the southern German humanists. In 1521, Rhegius proudly published a dialogue in which he named the humanist-theologians with whom he felt connected: Erasmus, Melanchthon, Oecolampadius, Beatus Rhenanus, Hutten, Karlstadt, and Hummelberger.[4] Letters written by him before 1522 show that he was in contact with most of them and others like Zwingli. In June 1519, a letter from Ulrich Zasius to Thomas Blaurer paid respect to "Urbanus Rhegius

2 Urbanus Rhegius, letter to Martin Luther, Braunschweig, April 18, 1537, WA Br 8:72–73.

3 Philip Melanchthon, letter to Caspar Aquila in Saalfeld, Weimar, ca. February 23, 1529, MBWR 1:756.

4 Hellmut Zschoch, *Reformatorische Existenz und konfessionelle Identität: Urbanus Rhegius als evangelischer Theologe in den Jahren 1520 bis 1530* (Tübingen: Mohr, 1995), 33–34.

and even more so to Philip."[5] It was an early assessment of two rising academics whose scholarship was a common feature.

Rhegius was eight years older than Melanchthon, but their early lives and educations unfolded along similar paths. Both were born in southern Germany but miles away from each other. Melanchthon grew up in Bretten, a small town between Stuttgart and Karlsruhe. Both he and Rhegius lost their fathers at early ages. Philip was soon enrolled in a popular Latin school, where he excelled in Greek. After one year, his progress was recognized, and his mentor, the well-known scholar Johannes Reuchlin, presented to him a Greek grammar and changed Philip's last name, Schwartzerdt, to its Greek equivalent, Melanchthon.[6]

In the fall of 1509, Melanchthon enrolled at Heidelberg and was awarded a bachelor of arts degree at the earliest date allowed. He continued his studies in Tübingen, where the master's degree he earned qualified him to teach. He was seventeen years old and only three years away from being called to teach Greek at Wittenberg. From 1518 to 1530, he followed the typical busy path of a young professor—except, of course, walking into the beginning of the Reformation and gaining the trust of its initiator. He also earned a degree in theology without being ordained and, at Luther's advice, married the daughter of the mayor of Wittenberg. While Luther was exiled in 1522, Melanchthon corresponded with him and then worked face-to-face with Luther as they introduced the changes that made Wittenberg an evangelical town.

Rhegius did not earn his master's degree until early 1516 in Ingolstadt. He was twenty-seven years old and was required to teach onsite two more years. Rhegius started his education at the Latin school in Lindau on the shore of Lake Constance, very near his hometown of Langenargen. The school was well respected and boasted that its top graduates attended prominent universities. Rhegius attended the school from 1503 to 1508, and centuries later, in 1928, a publication of the school described him "as one of the theologians who in 1530 distinguished himself at the Diet of Augsburg."[7]

5 Traugott Schiess, ed., *Briefwechsel der Brüder Ambrosius und Thomas Blaurer 1509–1548* (Freiburg, 1910), 2:225.

6 Heinz Scheible, *Philipp Melanchthon der bedeutendste Sohn der Stadt Bretten*, in *Geschichte der Stadt Bretten von den Anfängen bis Zerstörung 1689*, ed. Alfons Schäfer (Bretten: Kommissionsverlag G. Braun,}1977), 263–65.

7 König, *Reformator Urbanus Rhegius*, 19.

From Lindau, he enrolled at Freiburg, the traditional university of the Counts of Montfort who occupied the castle in Langenargen and supported Rhegius's mother.[8] By the time he was ready to graduate, his favorite professor was Johann Eck. However, Eck found himself entangled in a theological dispute so bitter that he left Freiburg for Ingolstadt. Rhegius followed, and after earning the master's degree, began to make his name known by joining a cadre of humanists who shared poetry and history with one another.[9]

From that point on, Rhegius's life became a roller coaster. It started on a high point in 1517, when Emperor Maximilian crowned Rhegius Poet and Orator Laureate. He then earned a doctorate at the university in Basel and later took holy orders for the priesthood. In 1520, Rhegius was chosen to become the primary preacher at the Cathedral in Augsburg. It was not long before the new position required him to read the bull that threatened Luther with excommunication. He complied, but at the same time, Rhegius was beginning to appreciate Luther more and more. Within the next year, his sympathy for Luther became public, and under growing pressure, he was dismissed.

The next four years, 1521 to 1525, promised to be his hardest, but instead, they were the beginning of a new life. After more travel, reading, and preaching, Rhegius landed back in Augsburg as a follower of Luther and co-priest to Johannes Frosch at the St. Anna Church. On June 16, 1525, Frosch presided over Rhegius's marriage to Anna Weissbrücker, whose father was a wealthy gold merchant and supporter of Lutherans in the town. Watching the marriage of a priest and the offer of bread and wine to all present must have bolstered hopes for a growing Lutheran presence.

THE DIET OF AUGSBURG (1530)

By 1527, Urbanus, Anna, and their children had settled in the parsonage that was built onto one side of the church, called the Wunderhaus. The mother of Rhegius was part of their household, and it might have been an ideal arrangement if Augsburg had not been the center of religious turmoil. Catholics and Lutherans were by no means the only believers in town. The followers of Ulrich

8 Karl Heinz Burmeister, review of *Der Reformator Urbanus Rhegius*, by Walter König, *Montfort* 60, no. 3 (2008): 234–36.

9 König, *Reformator Urbanus Rhegius*, 21; Maximilian Liebmann, *Urbanus und die Anfänge der Reformation* (Münster: Aschendorff, 1980), 98–99.

Zwingli, the reformer in Zurich, were well-represented and benefitted from having a popular preacher of their own. Prominent leaders of Anabaptist clusters were outlawed, but they circulated pamphlets and made clandestine visits to maintain the faith of the brethren. The contacts Rhegius had with both Anabaptists and followers of Zwingli did not enhance his standing with either of them.

The Diet of Augsburg was called by Emperor Charles V to prevent Catholics and Protestants from splitting his empire and, specifically in Germany, to reunite both under papal authority. Melanchthon arrived in Augsburg on the second day of May with a sizable amount of what became the *Augsburg Confession*, but it was not yet fully woven into a document. First, it had to be discussed by all the Lutheran scholars present, including Rhegius, who could walk to the meetings from home.

Rhegius soon gravitated toward the cluster of theologians from Wittenberg. In a letter to Luther on May 21, he reported that he spoke daily with Melanchthon, Jonas, Agricola, and Spalatin and that, if Luther were present, his own joy would have been complete. At the same time, he stayed connected with Reformers in southern Germany and Philip of Hesse, who invited him to dinner. For two hours, they discussed the Lord's Supper. The year before, Philip had hoped that the Marburg Colloquy, which Rhegius had missed, would bring Zwingli, Luther, and their followers to an agreement on the Lord's Supper. Now Philip wanted to try that again with Rhegius.[10]

In the meantime, Rhegius convinced Philip of Hesse that the Lutherans were right and persuaded him to sign the *Augsburg Confession*.[11] The diet was also the longest time that Melanchthon and Rhegius spent together. If both could talk today, they might agree their time together came at exactly the right moment for shared conversation and cooperation.

Different Paths

Why Rhegius decided to accept the offer of Duke Ernest and move north that year is not clear. He left the diet before it was over, and he, Anna, and the children left Augsburg at the end of August. Perhaps he had no stomach for the religious turmoil in town, or perhaps it was an opportunity to work with a duke

10 Rhegius to Luther, Augsburg, May 21, 1530, WA Br 5:334–35.

11 Zschoch, *Reformatorische Existenz*, 349–50.

whose goal coincided with Rhegius's own. His mother had died, and by moving away he had little to lose. That was not true for Anna. She might never see her family again, and the family was deprived of watching her children grow up. Her father might have taken it the hardest. Anna was his only daughter. She did return home in 1543, but it was after her father died, when she came to collect a large inheritance.[12]

When Rhegius and his family arrived in Celle, they had to accustom themselves to a strange town and to the Low German language of northern Germany. After a brief time in Celle, Rhegius agreed to become superintendent of the clergy in the town of Lüneburg and briefly moved his family there. Facing resistance in this role he soon realized he could accomplish little in the entire territory to which he had been sent.[13] After returning to Celle, he promised Duke Ernest he would never again move away. Ernest gave the family a new two-story house and made Rhegius the general superintendent of clergy throughout the territory.[14] At that point, Rhegius had only eight years to live, but by preaching, writing, and traveling, he achieved at least part of the agenda that Duke Ernest had envisioned for him.

For Melanchthon, life after the diet was also different. Because Melanchthon lived nineteen years longer than Rhegius, he experienced more of the aftermath of the Reformation. Controversies abounded, and while maintaining his obligations in Wittenberg, Melanchthon traveled to an astounding number of colloquies, conferences, and one diet. He also received offers to move to England, France, and Tübingen, and if the communication were better, he would have made an appearance at the Council of Trent.

Through all that, Melanchthon found time to devote to his Greek, not only as a professor in his early days at Wittenberg but also throughout his life. He advocated for the study of Greek in Germany, wrote about prominent figures in ancient Greek and Greek literature, and used theologians like the Cappadocians as a foil, both positive and negative, to articulate his own views

12 König, *Reformator Urbanus Rhegius*, 43.

13 Richard Gerecke, "Urbanus Rhegius als Superintendent in Lüneburg 1532–1533," in *Reformation vor 450 Jahren: Eine Lüneburgische Gedenkschrift*, ed. G. Körner (Museumsverein für das Fürstentum Lüneburg, 1980), 91–93.

14 König, *Reformator Urbanus Rhegius*, 66–67.

on theological topics.[15] His own theology was of course Lutheran, but there was plenty of disagreement among Lutherans for him to seek a middle ground. Sometimes, his willingness to find agreement was more of a problem than a solution, but despite the disputes, he always considered himself to be a scholar and theologian.

During his last years, Rhegius was also a theologian. He had the same qualifications as Melanchthon, but he never taught at a university longer than the two years required after his master's degree. As far as we know, in Lüneburg he did no formal teaching. However, at the Augsburg diet, he was clearly a theologian beside other theologians, and the same applied in 1537 when he signed the *Smalcald Articles*. In the preface to the *Book of Concord* (1580), the "very profitable works" of Rhegius are named along with those of Melanchthon, Brenz, Bugenhagen, and others.[16]

His writings after 1530 that can be classified as theological are *An Explanatory Commentary on Obadiah* (1535), *Dialogue between Urbanus Rhegius and His Wife Anna Based on the Sermon Jesus Delivered to the Young Men on the Road to Emmaus* (1536), *A Formal Inquiry into the Abysmal and Scandalous Words against Us concerning Christian Doctrine, for Young Ministers of the Word in Lüneburg* (1536), *How to Recognize and Seize False Prophets* (1538), and *A Sermon on the Good and Bad Angels* (1538). Rhegius was also a theologian as he wrote a new constitution for the churches in Hanover and Lüneburg. The *Dialogue* is especially interesting. Rhegius would choose a passage from the Old Testament and explain to his wife how that passage was a prophecy of Christ. We do not know if Hebrew words were used, but Anna had studied Hebrew in Augsburg, and Melanchthon called her clever and knowledgeable. She lived in Celle until 1569, twenty-eight years after the death of her husband.

Both Rhegius and Melanchthon had always been theologians, but in their last years, they revealed a difference between them. The difference was not in their theologies but in the way their theologies were expressed and employed. As he always did, Melanchthon expressed his views mainly like a scholar, whether he was writing, teaching, or debating. Conversely, Rhegius expressed

15 H. Ashley Hall, *Philip Melanchthon and the Cappadocians: A Reception of Greek Patristic Sources in the Sixteenth Century* (Göttingen: Vandenhoeck & Ruprecht, 2014); Asaph Ben-Tov, *Lutheran Humanists and Greek Antiquity: Melanchthonian Scholarship between Universal History and Pedagogy* (Leiden: Brill, 2009).

16 BC 11.

his theology like a missionary. Between 1533 and 1537, he traveled with Duke Ernest to convents in order to convert the nuns to Lutheranism. It was not an easy task.[17] Outside Lüneburg, he wrote rebuttals and advice to towns that were threatened by Anabaptists, sects, and the Münster uprising. Neither Melanchthon nor Rhegius thought he was competing with the other. Instead, whether they realized it or not, they were exercising the gifts each had in order to protect and solidify the Lutheran Reformation.

17 Adolf Wrede, *Die Einführung der Reformation in Lüneburgschen durch Herzog Ernst der Bekenner* (Göttingen, 1887), 205–27.

"What the Fathers Thought"

Melanchthon and Oecolampadius on the Eucharist

Amy Nelson Burnett

In his studies of the relationship between Philip Melanchthon and Erasmus of Rotterdam, Timothy Wengert has stressed the subtleties of humanist rhetoric and warned against a superficial reading of their letters.[1] The same caution is necessary when examining the published exchange between Melanchthon and the Basel reformer Johannes Oecolampadius. The latter's 1530 *Dialogue: What the Fathers, Both Greek and Latin, Thought about the Eucharist*, reprinted and responded to Melanchthon's *Statements of Certain Ancients concerning the Lord's Supper, Related in Good Faith*.[2] At first glance, both works seem straightforward, although they differ significantly in format and approach. Melanchthon's *Statements* is short and sweet; Oecolampadius's *Dialogue* is long and rambling. Melanchthon quoted at length from a few selected Fathers; Oecolampadius cited a large number of authorities and alluded to many others.

---

1 Timothy J. Wengert, *Human Freedom, Christian Righteousness: Philip Melanchthon's Exegetical Dispute with Erasmus of Rotterdam* (New York: Oxford University Press, 1998), 21–27; Timothy J. Wengert, "Famous Last Words: The Final Epistolary Exchange between Erasmus of Rotterdam and Philip Melanchthon in 1536," *Erasmus of Rotterdam Society Yearbook* 25 (2005): 18–38. This essay is dedicated to Tim in remembrance of stimulating summertime conversations in Wolfenbüttel about Oecolampadius's dialogue.

2 Johannes Oecolampadius, *QVID DE EVCHARISTIA VETERES TVM Graeci, tum Latini senserint, Dialogus, in quo Epistolae Philippi Melanchthonis et Ioannis Oecolampadij insertae* (Basel: Froben, 1530); Philipp Melanchthon, *Sentenciae Veterum aliquot scriptorium, de Coena Domini, bona fide recitatae*, CR 23:731–52; prefatory letter to Friedrich Myconius in MBWT 4/1:46–50, nr. 863.

There is an important underlying similarity, however, in that both publications demonstrate the rhetorical skill of their authors. Neither work should be taken at face value but must be read with an awareness of how its author presented his arguments in the wake of the Marburg Colloquy. A detailed comparison of the two publications would be beyond the scope of this essay, but by drawing attention to their historical context and describing the rhetorical strategies of each reformer, it lays the foundation for such a study.

Melanchthon's *Statements*

The claim that the Church Fathers supported one's understanding of the Eucharist was as old as the eucharistic controversy itself. Ulrich Zwingli cited Tertullian, Origen, and Augustine in his earliest works on the Lord's Supper, but the interpretation of the Fathers gained new importance with the publication in the summer of 1525 of Oecolampadius's scholarly treatise, *On the Genuine Exposition of Christ's Words, "This Is My Body," according to the Oldest Authorities*.[3] The interpretation of patristic sources was an important component of Oecolampadius's published debate with the Nuremberg humanist Willibald Pirckheimer over the course of 1526 and 1527.[4] Melanchthon's *Statements of Certain Ancients*, published in early 1530, was the Wittenberg reformer's long-awaited first contribution to the debate and a challenge to Oecolampadius, his former friend and mentor.

Although it is not immediately obvious, Melanchthon structured his collection of patristic citations as a forensic oration. The prefatory letter to the Gotha preacher Friedrich Myconius served as the introduction or exordium, although Melanchthon varied the usual format somewhat by placing the *propositio*, or central argument, in the opening sentence of the letter: the Fathers "believed the same as we believe, i.e. that the body and blood of the Lord are truly present in the Lord's Supper."[5] He then explained his decision to present

3 Johannes Oecolampadius, *DE Genvina Verborum domini, Hoc est corpus meum, iuxta uetutissimos authores expositione, liber* (Strasbourg: Knobloch, 1525).

4 Amy Nelson Burnett, "'According to the Oldest Authorities': The Use of the Church Fathers in the Early Eucharistic Controversy," in *The Reformation as Christianization. Essays on Scott Hendrix's Christianization Thesis*, ed. Anna Marie Johnson and John A. Maxfield (Tübingen: Mohr Siebeck, 2012), 373–95.

5 MBWT 4/1:46. Translated by Amy Nelson Burnett.

the simple and clear statements of the Fathers without comment by contrasting it with the way others gathered together a large number of citations "in which much is ambiguous or obscure"—indirect criticism of the way Oecolampadius had cited and then explained the Fathers in his earlier publications.[6] Melanchthon also mentioned several patristic authors whom he would not cite in the body of the work: Origen, Jerome, Gregory of Nazianzus, Basil the Great, and John of Damascus. As the *narratio*, or background, necessary to understand the issue being debated, Melanchthon turned to the origin of the controversy, which he blamed on Andreas Karlstadt, a "savage" who was inspired by his hatred of Luther. Melanchthon also dismissed the teachings of John Wycliffe, which contained many errors. In contrast, Melanchthon praised the authority of the early canons of the church, particularly those adopted by the councils of Nicaea and Ephesus and the synod of Gangra.[7]

The *confirmatio* began with the actual text of the treatise. It consisted of citations from the works of seven Fathers, presented with virtually no comment or explanation: Cyril of Alexandria, John Chrysostom, Theophylactus (whom Melanchthon, like Erasmus, referred to as Vulgarius), Hilary, Irenaeus, Cyprian, and Ambrose.[8] Melanchthon intervened only to introduce one of the Cyprian citations and describe the Ambrose citation.[9] The *confutatio* was a long discussion of a passage attributed to Augustine in both the *Decretum* and the *Sentences* of Peter Lombard that the Swiss reformers had used to argue that

6 Willibald Pirckheimer had criticized Oecolampadius more directly for twisting and distorting the meaning of passages he cited. Amy Nelson Burnett, *Debating the Sacraments: Print and Authority in the Early Reformation* (New York: Oxford University Press, 2019), 158–77.

7 MBWT 4/1:48–50.

8 The *Sententiae* reprinted two passages from Cyril on John 6 and one on John 15:1; one citation each from Chrysostom's homilies on John 6:41 and Matthew 26:26–28, and *De dignitate sacerdotum*; Theophylactus's explanation of the words of institution in Matthew and Mark from the Bulgarian bishop's gospels commentary; a lengthy citation from Hilary's *De trinitate* VIII.13–17; a passage from Cyprian's *Ad Caecilium* and from the treatise *De caena Domini* attributed to Cyprian; two passages from Irenaeus's *Contra haereses* IV.18.5, V.2.2; and references to two works attributed to Ambrose, *On the Mysteries* and *On the Sacraments*, with a brief quotation from the latter.

9 CR 23:733–44.

Christ's body could be in only one place.[10] Melanchthon criticized those who placed more reliance on reason than on God's command and who insisted that "this is my body" should be understood figuratively. It was not safe, he concluded, for consciences in temptation to depart from the clear testimonies of both Scripture and the Fathers.[11] In the *peroratio*, Melanchthon asserted again that there was no reason Christ could not be truly present in the sacrament, which was instituted by God to arouse minds to faith.[12]

By dividing his treatise into a prefatory letter and a presentation of patristic texts without commentary, Melanchthon very cleverly highlighted the words of the Fathers. As the rhetorical structure suggests, Melanchthon did not intend his audience to read the quotations from the Fathers without having first read the prefatory letter. Putting the introduction and narration in the form of a letter, however, allowed him to emphasize the Fathers cited in the body of the work—the confirmation and confutation of his overall argument.[13]

Melanchthon structured the *Statements* so that the Fathers fell into three categories.[14] In a memo submitted to the *landgraf* of the Marburg Colloquy, Philip of Hesse, the Wittenberg reformers cited Hilary, Chrysostom, Cyprian, Irenaeus, Cyril, Ambrose, and Theophylactus as supports for their position.[15] These were the Fathers cited at length in the *Statements*, and Melanchthon

10 The Augustine passage in Emil Friedberg, ed., *Corpus Iuris Canonici*, 2 vols. (Leipzig: Tauchnitz, 1879–81), 1:1330; IV.d. 10, c. 1.

11 CR 23:744–50.

12 CR 23:750–52.

13 The impact of this strategy can be seen in the edition of the *Sentenciae* in the *Corpus Reformatorum*, which reproduces only the treatise and not the prefatory letter. The reader is first presented with several columns of patristic quotations before Melanchthon's own voice is heard.

14 For a detailed discussion of Melanchthon's patristic citations in the *Sentenciae*, see Gottfried Hoffmann, *Kirchenväterzitate in der Abendmahlskontroverse zwischen Oekolampad, Zwingli, Luther und Melanchthon: Legitimationsstrategien in der inner-reformatorischen Auseinandersetzung um das Herrenmahl*, Oberurseler Hefte, Ergänzungsbände 7 (Göttingen: Edition Ruprecht, 2011), 199–214.

15 MBW nr. 823, MBWT 3:583–89 nr. 823; see also, Melanchthon's notes at Marburg, MBWT 3:580–82, nr. 822, where he cited Hilary, Cyril, Cyprian, Ambrose, and Vulgarius and conceded that only Augustine seemed to support their opponents. This list differed somewhat from the five Fathers Luther had discussed in his 1527 *Das diese Wort Christi fest stehen wider die Schwarmgeister*: Augustine, Tertullian, Irenaeus, Hilary, and Cyprian. WA 23:209–43; LW 37:104–24.

provided two or three quotations from most of them. Some of these passages had long been part of the debate. Oecolampadius had first discussed passages from Hilary's *On the Trinity*, Irenaeus's *Against Heresies*, Chrysostom's homilies on John 6 and Matthew 26, and Cyril's homilies on John 6 in his *Genuine Exposition*. Pirckheimer challenged the Basler's interpretation of the first three authors in his 1526 *Response to Johannes Oecolampadius*, while Luther addressed the passages from Hilary and Irenaeus in *That These Words of Christ Still Stand Firm against the Fanatics*. Earlier Lutheran writers had also pointed out that Oecolampadius now rejected the position of Theophylactus, whose commentary on the Gospels the Basler had translated.[16] Melanchthon's most important new contributions were from Cyril's homily on John 15:1 and an excerpt from Chrysostom's *On the Dignity of the Priesthood*.[17]

The remaining quotations from Ambrose and Cyprian were more problematic. Pirckheimer had also cited *On the Sacraments* and *On the Mysteries*, both attributed to Ambrose, but Oecolampadius had rejected Ambrose's authorship when debating the work with Pirckheimer. In referring to these books, Melanchthon glossed over the question of authorship by stating that they were "not greatly dissimilar to other writings of Ambrose."[18] Similarly, Oecolampadius and Pirckheimer had debated the authorship of the sermon on the Lord's Supper attributed to Cyprian; Melanchthon left the question open, saying only that "whoever the author of this work is, it apparently is not a recent writing."[19] Whatever the status of these passages, however, the overall impression left by this bloc of citations was strong patristic support for the Wittenberg position.

The second group consisted of the Fathers Melanchthon named in the prefatory letter as untrustworthy, ambiguous, or generally supportive. By

16 On Oecolampadius's translation of Theophylactus, see Ernst Staehelin, "Die Väterübersetzungen Oekolampads," *Schweizerische Theologische Zeitschrift* 33 (1916): 57–91, esp. 64–66. Johannes Brenz, Urbanus Rhegius, and Willibald Pirckheimer had all used Theophylactus's comment on Matthew 26:28 against Oecolampadius. Burnett, "According to the Oldest Authorities." Melanchthon printed the original Greek and then gave his own translation rather than using that of Oecolampadius. CR 23:739.

17 Cyril's homily on John 15 was cited for the first time at Marburg. MBWT 3:582, 587, nr. 822. I have not found an earlier reference to Chrysostom's *De dignitate sacerdotum*.

18 CR 23:743.

19 CR 23:742.

relegating these Fathers to the introduction, Melanchthon avoided discussion of citations taken from their works by his opponents. Both Zwingli and Oecolampadius had cited Origen frequently at the beginning of the controversy, but Melanchthon dismissed that Father as uncertain because of his use of allegory. The Swiss reformers had also often cited Jerome. Melanchthon countered this by writing that although Jerome did not necessarily support the Wittenberg position, neither did he support its opponents.[20] According to Melanchthon, Gregory of Nazianzus provided no clear statement on the Supper, while Gratian's *Decretum* included a passage from Basil the Great that, Melanchthon wrote, "is not opposed to our view." Last but not least, Melanchthon counted John of Damascus as a strong defender of his position, and he mentioned with approval the many authors cited by Cardinal Bessarion in his treatise on the sacrament.[21] These later writers demonstrated the church's continuous belief in the presence of Christ's body in the Supper.

The final category consisted of Augustine alone, although one might also include those Fathers important to the prior debate whom Melanchthon chose not to mention. As the man who quite literally wrote the textbook on rhetoric, the Wittenberger certainly knew that the *confutatio* must be a refutation of the opponents' arguments. His very limited focus on only one passage from Augustine is therefore all the more striking, since citations from Augustine were far and away the most numerous in all previous discussions, including those at Marburg. At the colloquy, Melanchthon had conceded that Augustine provided more support for his opponents than for the Wittenbergers, which explains his unwillingness to discuss the bishop of Hippo.[22] Melanchthon's silence concerning Tertullian is just as significant because much ink had been spilled over the proper interpretation of this particular North African Father in the earlier debate.

---

20 This was not a recent conclusion. At the beginning of 1526, Justus Jonas reported to Johann von Dolzigk that he and Melanchthon had examined Jerome's discussions of the Eucharist and concluded that that Father wrote "very carelessly (*fast vnfleissg*) about it." Gustav Kawerau, ed., *Der Briefwechsel des Justus Jonas* (Halle, 1884–85; repr. Hildesheim: Olms, 1964), 97–98, nr. 96.

21 MBWT 4/1:47. Melanchthon was referring to Bessarion's *De Sacramento Evcharistiae, & quibus uerbis Christi corpus perficiatur* (Nuremberg: Petreius, 1527).

22 Gerhard May, ed., *Das Marburger Religionsgespräch 1529*, Texte zur Kirchen- und Theologiegeschichte 13 (Gütersloh: Gütersloher Verlagshaus, 1970), 32.

The single passage from Augustine that Melanchthon did address, concerning the location of Christ's body, had an important place both in the earlier debate and at Marburg. In his exchange with Pirckheimer, Oecolampadius had tried and failed to locate the original text in Augustine's writings. Melanchthon explained the reason for this difficulty: it was actually a pastiche taken from several of Augustine's works. He asserted that when one looked at the various statements in their original context, it was apparent that they did not pertain to the sacramental reception of Christ's body and blood. The last clause in particular, "For the body in which he arose must be in one place, but his truth is diffused everywhere," had nothing to do with the Lord's Supper, and Augustine certainly did not mean to bind Christ's body to only one location.[23]

This discussion suggests that Melanchthon's use of the Fathers in the *Statements* was not as simple and straightforward as it seems. His strategy of citing "certain ancients" without comment, downplaying others, and entirely omitting discussion of some of the most frequently cited passages left readers with the impression that the Church Fathers all supported the Wittenberg position. This was the impression that Oecolampadius tried to dispel with his *Dialogue*.

OECOLAMPADIUS'S *DIALOGUE*

In view of the *Dialogue*'s full title, it is rather surprising that discussions of the work treat it simply as a presentation of the Basel reformer's own theology and say little about his use of the Fathers.[24] As we shall see, however, Oecolampadius skillfully interwove his own views with those of the authors he cited.

23 CR 23:744–45. On earlier discussions of this passage, see Burnett, "According to the Oldest Authorities," 379–80, 388.

24 Ernst Staehelin, *Das theologische Lebenswerk Johannes Oekolampads*, Quellen und Forschungen zur Reformationsgeschichte 21 (Leipzig: Heinsius, 1939), 607–11; Walther Köhler, *Zwingli und Luther: Ihre Streit über das Abendmahl nach seinen politischen und religiösen Beziehungen*, vol. 2, *Vom Begin der Marburger Verhandlungen 1529 bis zum Abschluß der Wittenberger Konkordie von 1536*, Quellen und Forschungen zur Reformationsgeschichte 7 (Gütersloh: Bertelsmann, 1953), 204–7. Ralph Walter Quere, *Melanchthon's Christum Cognoscere. Christ's Efficacious Presence in the Eucharistic Theology of Melanchthon* (Nieuwkoop: De Graaf, 1977), 310–39, refers almost in passing to Oecolampadius's use of the Fathers to support his own view, although he devotes more attention to the Basler's interpretation of

Another overlooked aspect of Oecolampadius's response to Melanchthon is the Basler's decision to present his arguments in the form of a conversation. The work was the only Latin dialogue written specifically as a contribution to the eucharistic controversy.[25] The unusual format of the *Dialogue* reflected the agreement reached at the Marburg Colloquy to refrain from further polemic. Melanchthon's *Statements* was influenced by that agreement as well, for with the exception of the attack on Karlstadt, it did not name any opponents of the Wittenberg position, although the work was certainly understood as a challenge to Oecolampadius. Because a direct response to Melanchthon would have been perceived as violating the Marburg agreement, Oecolampadius chose to reprint his correspondence with Melanchthon from the spring of 1529, as well as the *Statements of Certain Ancients*.[26] This was followed by a friendly discussion between Oecolampadius and the somewhat doubting but open-minded Nathanael—a name that called to mind the initially skeptical "Israelite in whom there is no deceit" who came to acknowledge that Jesus was the Son of God (John 1:45–51). The dialogue format allowed Oecolampadius to point out Melanchthon's "errors" without attacking the Wittenberger directly.

The *Dialogue* was not aimed at Melanchthon alone, however. At the beginning of their conversation Nathanael characterized Oecolampadius's Catholic opponents as "slanderers rather than theologians," and he criticized the virulence of Luther's books. In contrast, he described Erasmus and Melanchthon, who "once were among Oecolampadius's friends," as more desirous of peace, and he praised their eloquence and authority.[27] Erasmus's most direct

---

the patristic passages used by Melanchthon. Only Hoffmann, *Kirchenväterzitate*, 66–75, 94–114, discusses Oecolampadius's use of the Fathers at length.

25 The only other comparable dialogues were the 1525 printing of John Wycliffe's *Trialogus* and Johannes Cochlaeus's 1529 *Septiceps Lutherus*, written against the visitation instructions for Electoral Saxony and which included a section on the sacrament.

26 That correspondence was initiated with a letter from Oecolampadius to Melanchthon, March 31, 1529 (MBWT 3:466–70, nr. 766). Melanchthon's answer was printed as *Epistola . . . ad Iohannem Oecolampadius, de Coena Domini* (MBWT 3:487–95, nr. 775), to which Oecolampadius responded (MBWT 3:557–65, nr. 812). Only the latter two letters were printed in the *Dialogus*.

27 In Oecolampadius, *Dialogus*, a4v–a5r Nathanael says, "Rofenses, Clichthouaeos, Fabros, et multos alios magis maledicos quam theologos"—a reference to the works attacking Oecolampadius by John Fisher, Josse van Clichtove, and Johann Fabri. It

contributions to the eucharistic controversy were his Latin pamphlets responding to Konrad Pellikan and Leo Jud published in 1526. As Oecolampadius mentioned in the *Dialogue*, the Dutch humanist had also discussed the topic in his letters, a volume of which had appeared in 1529.[28] More immediately, however, in the spring of 1530, Erasmus published Alger of Liège's *On the Truth of the Lord's Body and Blood in the Eucharist*.[29] It was prefaced with a letter to Balthasar Merklin, the bishop of Constance, in which Erasmus praised both Alger and Guitmund of Aversa for their opposition to Berengar of Tours and their knowledge of "the old Doctors of the church, Cyprian, Hilary, Ambrose, Jerome, Augustine, Basil and Chrysostom." Erasmus acknowledged that these learned men sometimes wrote obscurely or seemed to contradict each other, but he argued that they had always agreed that the "real substance of the Lord's body and blood is present in the Eucharist." This teaching also had "the constant approval of synods and the general agreement of Christian people."[30] The preface could thus be seen as a challenge to Oecolampadius's interpretation of the Fathers, and the Basler's *Dialogue* was a response to Erasmus as well.[31]

continues, "Lutherus a suis libris me nonnihil alienauit. At qui tibi tuisque refragantur, sediatiore animo sunt et pacis ubique cupidissimi uidentur. . . . De Erasmo et Melanchthone loquor, quorum in genijs nihil uiuidius, quorum facundia nhil luculentius, quorum autoritate nihil plausibilius habetur, & ij quidem olime inter amicos numerarabant, nunc uero etiam scriptis si non tibi, certe causeae tuae aduersantur."

28 Oecolampadius, a6r. Amy Nelson Burnett, "'Things I Never Said or Thought'? Erasmus' Exegetical Contribution to the Early Eucharistic Controversy," in *Collaboration, Conflict and Continuity in the Reformation. Essays in Honor of James M. Estes on His Eightieth Birthday*, ed. Konrad Eisenbichler (Toronto: Centre for Reformation and Renaissance Studies, 2014), 275–95.

29 Alger of Liège, *De ueritate Corporis & sanguinis dominici in Eucharistia* (Freiburg: Faber, 1530).

30 Erasmus's dedicatory preface (1530) to *Opus epistolarum Des. Erasmi Roterdami*, ed. P. S. Allen et al. (Oxford: Clarendon, 1906–58), 8:377–82, nr. 2284; see also in the same collected works, 16:218–25. Augustinus Marius, the cathedral preacher in Basel until the city abolished the mass in 1529, had just published Guitmund of Aversa's *De ueritate Corporis et Sanguinis Christi in Eucharistia* (Freiburg: Faber, 1530).

31 Oecolampadius also briefly responded to arguments in Luther's two eucharistic treatises of 1527 and 1528, but with the exception of the Wittenberger's use of Hilary and Irenaeus mentioned below, these did not concern the use of the Fathers.

The model for Oecolampadius's dialogue was probably Martin Bucer's vernacular *Dialogue* [. . .] *on the Agreement of Dr. Luther and His Opponents on Christ's Supper*, published in 1528. Throughout that pamphlet, Bucer highlighted the spiritual communion of Christ's body and blood received by believers in sacramental communion, and he claimed that the differences between the two parties were not as great as they seemed.[32] In his own *Dialogue*, Oecolampadius would rephrase these points to argue at greater length that the sacrament did convey something to believing recipients and to assert that the two sides disagreed not on the presence or absence of Christ but rather on the mode of Christ's presence—an argument that would play a prominent role in later debates over the Supper.[33] Bucer's dialogue was irenic in tone, in conscious opposition to the invective of Luther and others, and throughout the work, both speakers deplored Luther's harsh attacks on his opponents. Oecolampadius likewise avoided polemic in his *Dialogue*, although there was more than a little bitterness underlying his comments about the Wittenbergers' conduct at Marburg. The Basler also acknowledged the impact of Melanchthon's *Statements* as a defense of the Wittenberg position. At the beginning of the *Dialogue*, he told Nathanael to read Melanchthon's publications with care and warned him not to be swayed by respect for their author.[34]

Oecolampadius's own work was a carefully crafted piece of rhetoric, made even more complex by the inclusion of both the correspondence and Melanchthon's *Statements*. The *Dialogue* was a much longer work than the *Statements*, but it too followed the basic structure of a forensic oration. Oecolampadius opened the work with a letter to the reader in which he justified its publication. As in his earlier exchanges with Pirckheimer, he presented his party as blameless and attacked in an unworthy way by their opponents. It was not pride but rather the need to defend the truth that provoked him to respond. Oecolampadius aligned himself with Christ, Paul, and the Church Fathers in opposing those who erred. The Wittenbergers misunderstood his position, and so it was

32 *Vergleichung D. Luthers und seins Gegentheyls vom Abentmal Christ, Dialogus. Das ist eyn Freundlich gesprech, Bucer Deutsche Schriften* (Gütersloh: Mohn, 1960) 2:305–83; see also Burnett, *Debating the Sacraments*, 237–40.

33 Oecolampadius, *Dialogus*, e1r–v.

34 Oecolampadius, a5v–a6v.

necessary for Oecolampadius to clarify what he believed.[35] The assertion that the two parties initially misunderstood each other had been introduced at Marburg as part of a possible agreement on the Supper, and it would become a prominent part of Bucer's later interpretation of the history of the controversy.[36] To claim that the Wittenbergers still misunderstood the Swiss after three days of debate in Marburg was disingenuous, however, and the claim must be seen as an appeal to Oecolampadius's readers rather than to Melanchthon himself.

The opening scene of the dialogue served as an exordium, and the inserted correspondence and Melanchthon's *Statements* functioned as the *narratio*.[37] Returning to the dialogue format, Oecolampadius stated the *propositio*: "We do not say this bread is a bare sign in the Supper, but is in some way efficacious, by the working of the Holy Spirit in the gathering of the faithful, so that it becomes a kind of more noble and holy body, as we are joined in one body to Christ the head."[38] He then responded point by point to the arguments of Melanchthon's letter to Myconius, among other things justifying the need to explain the meaning of the Fathers rather than simply presenting the bare text.[39] With regard to those Fathers named but not discussed by Melanchthon, he argued that Origen, Jerome, Gregory of Nazianus, and Basil all supported his side. Although he did not say so in the *Dialogue*, he had cited passages from all of them in his *Genuine Exposition*, and his discussion was thus a response to Melanchthon's implicit criticism of that work. Oecolampadius also cited specific passages from other authors Melanchthon did not mention: Tertullian, Athanasius, and Bede the Venerable, whose commentary on Luke was a paraphrase of Jerome.[40] The Basler dismissed Gratian, Guitmund, and Lanfranc as mere compilers who drew from more recent authors, and he relativized Melanchthon's references to John of Damascus, Bessarion, and Theophylactus by

35 Oecolampadius, a2r–a4r; cf. MBWT 3:558: "Nostrum de eucharistia sententiam nondum habuisse perspectam"; MBWT 3:561: "Quod nondum tibi satis innoteuerit nostra sententia."

36 Burnett, *Debating the Sacraments*, 292.

37 Oecolampadius, *Dialogus*, a6r–d8v.

38 Oecolampadius, d8v–e1r.

39 Oecolampadius, e2v–e3r.

40 While Oecolampadius had cited passages from Origen, Jerome, Basil, and Tertullian in *De Genvina . . . expositione*, the citations from Athanasius, from Gregory of Nazianus's *Sermo de baptismo*, and from Bede's commentary on Luke were new to the debate.

comparing their views to other more recent authors, beginning with the early scholastics and continuing through contemporary Catholic theologians who had written against Oecolampadius.[41] Implicit in this criticism was the charge that Melanchthon was as mistaken in his understanding of the Supper as those who upheld transubstantiation.

The *confirmatio* fell into two parts. In the first part, Oecolampadius cited those patristic authorities who supported his position.[42] These included the decrees of the Council of Nicea concerning baptism and the Eucharist as well as passages from Chrysostom, (pseudo-)Dionysius the Areopagite, Augustine, Hesychius, and Jerome.[43] All of these passages illustrated the distinction between externals and the spiritual benefit they signified, and Oecolampadius used them to argue that believers were to move from the earthly things they perceived with their senses to the heavenly and intelligible things they saw with the eyes of their minds. As if to demonstrate his superior knowledge of Greek, Oecolampadius provided the original of all Greek quotations, along with his own translation. He also quoted the section of Chrysostom's sermon on Matthew 26:26–28 that immediately preceded that given by Melanchthon as a way of casting doubt on the younger man's good faith in selecting patristic support for his position.

The second part of the *confirmatio* was an account of the Fathers' discussion of the Eucharist in response to various heretics. This historical approach to the church's response to heresy may well have been inspired by Heinrich Bullinger's *On the Origin of Error in the Business of the Eucharist and Mass*, written sometime in 1526 and published in early 1528 with Oecolampadius's encouragement. In that work, Bullinger described "how the western church accepted the mass and transubstantiation." He placed this development after

41 Oecolampadius, *Dialogus*, e3r–e8v; Oecolampadius specifically mentioned Anselm, Guitmund of Aversa, Lanfranc, Paschasius and Alger of Liège, whose works had all recently been published, as well as John Fisher, Josse Clichtove, Johann Fabri and Johann Eck.

42 Oecolampadius, f1r–g5r.

43 Oecolampadius cited Augustine's *De doctrina Christiana*, (pseudo-)Dionysius's *Celestial Hierarchy*, Jerome's letter *ad Hebidiam* and his commentary on Matthew 26:28, and several passages from Hesychius's commentary on Leviticus. As a counter to Melanchthon's citation from Chrysostom's homily 82.5, Oecolampadius cited homily 82.4, first in Greek and then in his own translation. Oecolampadius, f5v–f6r.

the reign of Charlemagne and associated it especially with the controversy over Berengar's teaching. Bullinger blamed Hildebrand / Pope Gregory VII for introducing the error of transubstantiation, which was then propagated by the books of Lanfranc, Guitmund, and others and eventually incorporated into both the *Decretum* and Lombard's *Sentences.*[44]

Oecolampadius's historical account began much earlier, with a discussion of the fourth-century heresies of the Euchites or Messalians and the Anthropomorphites, then focusing at greater length on Cyril of Alexandria and the Council of Ephesus against the Nestorians and Eutychians. The Basler also quoted a section of Leo I's letter to the Council of Chalcedon and criticized Lanfranc's "distorted" citation of it in his treatise against Berengar. The Berengarian controversy was discussed at length. Here too Oecolampadius drew on the treatises of Lanfranc and Berengar's other opponents, although the Basler dismissed their arguments as frivolous. He also discussed the dispute between Abelard (whom he called Adelhard) and Bernard of Clairvaux, interpreting the latter to highlight the distinction between sacramental and spiritual manducation.[45]

Having discussed those patristic sources that supported his view, Oecolampadius turned to a refutation of Melanchthon's *Statements*. His *confutatio* was also twofold. The first section addressed the specific passages contained in the *confirmatio* of Melanchthon's treatise. The Basler not only gave his own understanding of the passages but also introduced statements from other Fathers—including Augustine, Hesychius, and Tertullian—that supported that understanding. Oecolampadius devoted the greatest attention to Irenaeus and Hilary, whose works had played a central role in the debate over the patristic understanding of the Eucharist from the beginning. Here the Basler explicitly rejected Luther's interpretation of each Father in *That These Words Still Stand Firm against the Fanatics.*[46] Oecolampadius defended his translation of Theophylactus by saying the commentary contained much that was good, but with regard to the Eucharist, Theophylactus was "less practiced." The Basler also highlighted the dubious attribution of Melanchthon's citations from Ambrose

44 Heinrich Bullinger, *De Origine Erroris, in Negotio Evcharistiae ac Missae* (Basel: Wolff, 1528), c6r–d6r; on dating, see Heinrich Bullinger, *Theologische Schriften. Werke. Dritte Abteilung* (Zurich: Theologischer Verlag, 1983–), 2:136.

45 Oecolampadius, *Dialogus*, g5v–k2r.

46 WA 23:229–39; LW 37:115–20.

and Cyprian and offered further statements from both authors that were genuine and supported his own position.[47]

The second section of the confutation concerned Melanchthon's discussion of the passage cobbled together from Augustine. It also addressed Melanchthon's other arguments concerning the location of Christ's body and the interpretation of "this is my body." Augustine's statements about the location of Christ's body could not be separated from his beliefs about the Eucharist, as Melanchthon tried to do. Oecolampadius rejected the accusation that he wrongly separated Christ's divine and human natures; it was his opponents who confused the properties of the two natures. Responding to Melanchthon's statement that "this is my body" should be understood literally, Oecolampadius asserted that Jerome, Augustine, and Fulgentius all understood the words figuratively, and the Scripture verse that provided the best parallel was "the rock was Christ," not "this is my beloved Son," as the Wittenbergers had maintained at Marburg. Last but not least, citing Augustine and Fulgentius on First Corinthians 10:17 ("we who are many are one bread"), Oecolampadius emphasized the mystical union in which Christians were joined together as Christ's body.[48] In the very brief *peroratio*, Nathanael stated that he was satisfied with Oecolampadius's arguments and bemoaned the hard-heartedness of the Wittenbergers, who had cut off fellowship with their opponents, while Oecolampadius stated his willingness to give an account of his faith to anyone who asked.[49]

As this analysis demonstrates, Oecolampadius used the Church Fathers in a different way than Melanchthon. They served as supports for his own understanding of the Eucharist rather than as testimony that the Fathers believed Christ's true body and blood were present in the Supper. The Basler was as much concerned with the purpose and meaning of the sacraments in general as he was with the relationship between bread and Christ's body, and indeed, his answer to the first question shaped his answer to the second. Oecolampadius brought out the Neoplatonic presuppositions of many of the Fathers, which fit more comfortably with his own Erasmian Neoplatonism than they did with the nominalist presuppositions of the Wittenbergers.

47 Oecolampadius, *Dialogus*, k2r–m6v.

48 Oecolampadius, m6v–o5v. The reference to Luther's use of "this is my beloved Son" at Marburg can be found at k6r–v.

49 Oecolampadius, o5v–o6r.

The broad range of patristic sources cited in Oecolampadius's *Dialogue* is testimony to his ongoing involvement with patristic scholarship in Basel in the later 1520s. In 1528, Andreas Cratander published a three-volume edition of Latin translations of the works of Cyril. Oecolampadius contributed several translations, including Cyril's book against Julian the Apostate and the letter *Ad reginas de recta fide*, both works he cited in his *Dialogue*.[50] He also included citations from other patristic editions produced in Basel during this time, such as Hesychius's commentary on Leviticus and a collection of works by John Chrysostom and Athanasius, both published in 1527.[51] The following year, Lanfranc's treatise was printed in Basel together with the *Catalogue of Heresies* of Philastrius, the fourth-century bishop of Brescia.[52] The treatises of Alger and Guitmund published in Freiburg in 1530 by men who left Basel after the Reformation were both a continuation of this scholarship. Oecolampadius's use of these publications in his *Dialogue* merits further study.

Another important question deserving more attention is the impact of Oecolampadius's *Dialogue* not only on Melanchthon but also on the development of the broader Reformed tradition.[53] Toward the end of his work, the

50 Staehelin, "Väterübersetzungen," 66–68. In the dedication to the Cyril edition, Oecolampadius defended his understanding of the sacrament and his faithfulness in translating the Fathers against his Catholic critics. Ernst Staehelin, ed., *Briefe und Akten zum Leben Oekolampads, zum vierhundertjährigen Jubiläum der Basler Reformation* (Leipzig: Heinsius, 1927–34), 2:203–25, esp. 213–20.

51 *Isychii Presbyteri Heirosolymorvm, in Leviticvm Libri Septem*, ed. Johannes Sichard (Basel: Cratander, 1527); *Divi Ioannis Chrysostomi . . . & divi Athanasii . . . lucubrationes aliquot*, ed. Erasmus (Basel: Froben, 1527).

52 *Philasterii Episcopi Brixiensis Haereseon catalogus. Cui adiectus est erudissimus libellus Lanfranci Episcopi Canthuariensis de Sacramento Eucharistiae*, ed. Johannes Sichard (Basel: Petri, 1528).

53 On the discussion of Oecolampadius's influence on Melanchthon, see Tobias Jammerthal, *Philipp Melanchthons Abendmahlstheologie im Spiegel seiner Bibelauslegung 1520–1548* (Tübingen: Mohr Siebeck, 2018), 8–10, 114–15. Hoffmann, *Kirchenväterzitate*, concluded that there was no significant change in Melanchthon's use of the Fathers between 1527 and 1531 but suggested that Melanchthon's study of Oecolampadius's treatises may have provided a new understanding of the Church Fathers evident at the end of 1534. Quere, *Melanchthon's Christum Cognoscere*, 341–52, saw Oecolampadius's influence in Melanchthon's discussion of sacramental efficacy and incorporation into Christ. His discussion is theological rather than historical, and it is distorted by his neglect of Bucer (and of Oecolampadius's

Basler summarized his understanding of the Eucharist, explaining the relationship between the external eating of bread by which the body was fed and the internal eating by which the soul was refreshed. The Basler asserted that "the true body, and not a figure of the body, is offered to the mind drawn beyond sensible things, and accordingly is communicated to the faithful by the working of the Holy Spirit."[54] This was not the "symbolic memorialism" of Zwingli, who emphasized the importance of the Eucharist chiefly as a public testimony of praise and thanksgiving. It is closer to Bullinger's "symbolic parallelism," but it differs in the Basler's insistence that spiritual and sacramental eating were connected by the working of the Holy Spirit.[55] Oecolampadius betrayed a small but important difference with the Zurichers early in the *Dialogue* when he said that "spiritual eating is effected by faith"—in other words, it was not faith itself, as Zwingli taught.[56] As Oecolampadius's frequent references to the need to move from external to internal imply, the relationship between sacramental and spiritual eating was dynamic, not static. External sacramental communion was the starting point for, and not simply the visible representation of, internal spiritual communion. This connection between external and internal also distinguished Oecolampadius's position from that of Caspar von Schwenckfeld, who posited a sharp separation between sacramental and spiritual eating.[57] It has greater similarity with the position of Martin Bucer, who cited Oecolampadius's *Dialogue* repeatedly in his negotiations with Melanchthon and Gregor Brück at the Diet of Augsburg.[58] Any discussion of the negotiations for eucharistic concord

influence on Bucer) and his use of the term *Zwinglian* to describe both reformers, although there were significant differences between Zwingli on the one hand and Bucer and Oecolampadius on the other regarding these two issues.

54 Oecolampadius, *Dialogus*, n6r.

55 On the terms *symbolic memorialism* and *symbolic parallelism*, see Brian A. Gerrish, "The Lord's Supper in the Reformed Confessions," *Theology Today* 23 (1966): 224–43, reprinted as Brian A. Gerrish, "Sign and Reality: The Lord's Supper in the Reformed Confessions," in *The Old Protestantism and the New: Essays on the Reformation Heritage*, ed. Johannes Gerber (Chicago: University of Chicago Press, 1982), 118–30.

56 Oecolampadius, *Dialogus*, f5r.

57 Burnett, *Debating the Sacraments*, 277–80.

58 See the letters from July–August 1530, *Correspondence de Martin Bucer* (Leiden: Brill, 1979) 4:201–19, 220–28.

through the first half of the 1530s should therefore take account of Oecolampadius's influence, both direct and indirect, on all participants.

Neither Oecolampadius nor Melanchthon was engaged in a dispassionate study of "what the Fathers thought." Each claimed that the Fathers agreed with him, not that he agreed with the Fathers.[59] The very fact that both authors could make this assertion demonstrates that what the Fathers thought was not so readily apparent. As Erasmus admitted, the Fathers' writings could indeed be obscure and contradictory. For that reason, both reformers used all the rhetorical tools at their disposal to make their case. Those who ignore the role of rhetoric in the theological debates of the sixteenth century do so at their own peril.

59 For instance, Oecolampadius, in MBWT 3:562, states, "I am most sure that the orthodox ancients stand on our side."

Joachim Mörlin, Architect of Concordist Theology

Robert Kolb

Philip Melanchthon and Johannes Bugenhagen once regarded Joachim Mörlin as their "amicus carissimus."[1] Mörlin called Melanchthon his "carissime domine praeceptor."[2] Tilemann Heshusius labeled Mörlin a "γνήσιος discipulus Lutheri"[3] and viewed him as an "excellent theologian, with outstanding merits in God's church, burning with more pious zeal than many others . . . endowed with the most faithful, most eloquent gifts and outstanding zeal."[4] Cast into a number of disputes over proper formulations of Luther's and Melanchthon's legacy, Mörlin did not live to experience the final drive toward the resolution of the controversies that involved him during the course of his ministry, but at key points in those controversies, he played a critical role in determining the agenda addressed in the *Formula of Concord* and laying the groundwork for the solutions it proposed. The dissolution of two friendships marked the distinctive paths that he took as he pursued the defense of what he understood to be Luther's teaching.

Born in Wittenberg as the son of an instructor on the arts faculty—Jodok (Jodocus) Mörlin (ca. 1490–1550)—Joachim grew up in Westhausen, a village in the Franconian part of the electorate of Saxony.[5] His impoverished family had moved there when his father became pastor in 1521. Jodok had studied

1 From a letter dated March 25, 1553, MBWR 7:47, § 6771; CR 8:52–53, nr. 5352.

2 On November 12, 1555, MBWR 7:362, nr. 7631.

3 *Explicatio epistolae Pavli ad Romanos* (Jena: Huttich, 1571), (*)7a.

4 *Commentarius in secvndam Pavli epistolam ad Timotheum* (Helmstedt: Lucius, 1586), A3b.

5 Jürgen Diestelmann's *Joachim Mörlin, Luthers Kaplan—"Papst der Lutheraner"* (Neuendettelsau: Freimund, 2003) gives a thorough overview of Mörlin's life, unfortunately without any scholarly apparatus.

at the Universities of Freiburg and Leipzig before beginning teaching in Wittenberg in 1510. Because of his large family and perhaps his drinking habit, Pastor Mörlin had no money to send his sons to Wittenberg for education. Thus until funding appeared, Joachim learned the trade of a potter. After preparatory study in Marburg and Constance, Joachim made his way in 1532 to Wittenberg, where the son of a former colleague naturally had open doors welcoming him. In 1536, he earned his master of arts degree, served several parishes briefly, and returned to the university in 1539, receiving his doctorate a year later.[6]

His professors recommended him to Count Günther von Schwarzburg, patron of the church of the Thuringian town of Arnstadt, as the town's ecclesiastical superintendent. His zeal led him into conflict with the municipal leadership over usurious practices and neglect of the town hospital. The city council removed him from office in 1543 after he had criticized the count for executing a man for stealing fish. The city of Göttingen quickly called him to serve as its ecclesiastical superintendent. He taught in the Latin school in addition to his pastoral duties.

Following the introduction of the Augsburg Interim and the revelation of the text of the Leipzig Proposal in 1548, Mörlin was in correspondence with Anton Corvinus, general superintendent of the duchy of Braunschweig-Calenberg-Göttingen. Corvinus sharply criticized Melanchthon's role in formulating the proposed religious policy for electoral Saxony, expressed in the Leipzig Proposal, to keep imperial armies out of Saxony in the wake of Charles V's defeat of Evangelical forces in the Smalcaldic War.[7] Although Mörlin seems to have shared Corvinus's convictions, his muted criticism seems not to have alienated him from Melanchthon at this point. In late 1550, however, Duke Erich II of Braunschweig-Calenberg-Göttingen, who had sided with Emperor Charles V after the Smalcaldic War, pressured Göttingen to remove Mörlin from office because of his sharp criticism of the Augsburg Interim. Mörlin's attacks from the pulpit on the town council's readiness for compromise with the duke led to

6 WA 39 II:124–44.

7 *Der Briefwechsel des Anton Corvinus*, ed. Paul Tschackert (Hannover/Leipzig: Hahn, 1900), nr. 248–51, nr. 286; 251–52, nr. 287. See Philip Julius Rehtmeyer, *Historiae ecclesiasticae inclytae urbis Brunsvigae Pars III. Oder: Der beru[e]hmten Stadt Braunschweig Kirchen-Historie Dritter Theil* [. . .] (Braunschweig, 1710), 210.

his exile.[8] Erich's mother, Duchess Elisabeth of Brandenburg, who opposed her son's religious policy, arranged temporary refuge for Mörlin and recommended him to her son-in-law, Duke Albrecht of Prussia. In September 1551, Albrecht welcomed Mörlin to Königsberg as pastor of its chief church.

There, his dispute with his colleague Andreas Osiander reaffirmed his positive relationship with Melanchthon, for Mörlin found Melanchthon to be a faithful disciple of Luther on the subject of justification. Mörlin set the agenda of the Osiandrian controversy over justification and Christology in 1551–52 after he abandoned attempts to mediate the dispute when he became convinced of Osiander's serious errors. He joined with other former Wittenberg students, including Martin Chemnitz, in rejecting key ideas in Osiander's teaching on justification. Mörlin attempted to reconcile his fellow exile from Nuremberg with those who also held to what Luther had taught Mörlin. These attempts foundered on Osiander's clarification of his belief: that God's word of absolution of sinners created only a legal fiction and that true human righteousness could only be restored to sinners through Christ's divine nature coming to dwell in them. Osiander's instruction at the University of Ingolstadt by Johannes Reuchlin, the foremost Hebrew scholar in German-speaking lands at the time, had shaped the student's presuppositions in the worldview of the Kabbala, the Neoplatonic contours of which prevented him from understanding Luther's teaching on the creative and re-creative power of God's word. As Martin Stupperich observes, Osiander's ability to use his opponents' language without realizing that it undermined his own position undercut his ability to engage Wittenberg thinking forthrightly.[9] Their initial friendship dissolved as Mörlin came to understand what Osiander intended to teach.[10] Alongside his concern regarding Osiander's misrepresentation of his mentors' understanding of the justifying power of God's absolving word, Mörlin recognized that his opponent's teaching regarding the communication of attributes between Christ's divine and human nature directly undermined Luther's emphasis on the hypostatic union of the two natures in Christ. The ducal librarian Martin Chemnitz picked up this argument and dedicated much of his patristic research

8 Johannes Meyer, "Mörlins Entlassung aus Göttingen," *Zeitschrift der Gesellschaft für niedersächsische Kirchengeschichte* 34/35 (1929/1930): 37–65.

9 Martin Stupperich, *Osiander in Preussen, 1549–1552* (Berlin: De Gruyter, 1973), 116.

10 Stupperich, 110–54.

to this issue.[11] Mörlin's public criticism of his colleague's understanding of justification, both from his pulpit and at court, climaxed in clashes in autumn 1551.[12] While admonishing his congregation to obey the ducal government in all secular matters, he encouraged refusal to accept Albrecht's mandate enforcing Osiandrian doctrine on his church. This led to Duke Albrecht's dismissal of Mörlin on February 14, 1552. Despite advice from some of his councilors and a demonstration on the streets by women and children from Mörlin's congregation, Albrecht remained determined to keep Mörlin from his lands, refusing his request to visit his critically ill wife.[13] Mörlin fled to nearby Danzig. Melanchthon recommended him as a candidate for the leadership of the church in Lübeck,[14] but a call from the town council of Braunschweig reached him in May in Danzig, and he accepted the office of ecclesiastical superintendent there.[15]

Mörlin continued to refute Osiander's teaching as his followers defended it in Prussia under Albrecht's tutelage. He engaged leading advocates of Osiander's position and modified forms of it throughout the following decade.[16] In his critiques, Mörlin set forth positions on justification by faith and the person of Christ that foreshadowed the teaching of the *Formula of Concord*. His relationship with Chemnitz, developed as both were rebutting Osiander's teaching, played a decisive role in the lives of both and of the wider Wittenberg circle. Mörlin's direct influence on Chemnitz, who became his coadjutor in Braunschweig from 1554 to 1568 and then his successor as superintendent, constituted a vital element in the construction of the *Formula*'s teaching, since Chemnitz was one of its chief authors. He had already begun challenging Osiander's rejection of the imputation of Christ's righteousness as the cause of justification before Mörlin moved from mediator to critic of Osiander in 1552.

---

11 Theodor Mahlmann, *Das neue Dogma der Lutherischen Christologie. Problem und Geschichte seiner Begründung* (Gütersloh: Gütersloher Verlagshaus, 1969), 99–109, 115–22, 205–38; cf. Erich Roth, "Ein Braunschweiger Theologe des 16. Jahrhunderts: Mörlin und seine Rechtfertigungslehre," *Jahrbuch der Gesellschaft für niedersächsische Kirchengeschichte* 50 (1952): 59–81.

12 Timothy J. Wengert, *Defending Faith. Lutheran Responses to Andreas Osiander's Doctrine of Justification, 1551–1559* (Tübingen: Mohr Siebeck, 2012), 16–21.

13 Stupperich, *Osiander*, 154–65, 212–15, 224–43, 311–22, 359–62.

14 See Melanchthon's letter to Sebastian Ersam of Lübeck, April 25, 1553, MBWR 7:47, nr. 6771; CR 8:52–53, nr. 5352.

15 Roth, "Braunschweiger Theologe," 80.

16 Wengert, *Defending Faith*, 154–56, 161–62, 173–84, 424–30.

Mörlin's stance in opposition to Osiander placed him in a broad front of individuals from all corners of the Wittenberg circle, including Philip Melanchthon, whose strong repudiation of the Königsberg favorite echoed those of other friends of Mörlin, including Matthias Flacius Illyricus.[17] Osiander accused Mörlin of leading other Wittenberg theologians astray,[18] while others in the Wittenberg circle issued defenses of Mörlin's position.[19] In 1554, Melanchthon asked his colleague Paul Eber to give Tübingen professor Jakob Beurlin either his own or Bugenhagen's copy of Mörlin's *Historia* of the Osiandrian controversy.[20]

Mörlin's critique of Osiander's argument addressed several issues in a keenly analytical fashion; the distinctive characteristic of his approach, Wengert has argued, was his pastoral concern for comforting afflicted consciences.[21] His devotion to Luther led him to reject decidedly any representation of his mentor's teaching that he considered false.[22] Osiander's Neoplatonic foundations led him not just to distinguish the Creator from creatures but also to separate them so definitively that he could not grasp Luther's understanding of the hypostatic union of the divine and human natures of Christ and the communication of their attributes with each other in this union, in which the natures remained distinct but were inseparably united. Mörlin attacked Osiander on this point.[23] Mörlin, with others, further rejected Osiander's definition of saving righteousness as Christ's indwelling righteousness rather than the freedom from sin and the restoration of God's favor accomplished through the death

17 Wengert in *Defending Faith*, 101–4, indicates that with Flacius and his comrade in Magdeburg at this time, Nikolaus Gallus, Mörlin wrote a third of the ninety treatises against Osiander by Wittenberg-trained theologians and their professors.

18 Gerhard Müller and Gottfried Seebaß, eds., *Andreas Osiander der Ä. Gesamtausgabe* (Gütersloh: Gütersloher Verlagshaus, 1997), 10:427, 6–15; Wengert, *Defending Faith*, 273.

19 Anton Otto, *Wider die tieffgesuchten vnd Scharffgespitzten aber doch nichtigen Vrsachen Osianders, darmit er den Artikel von der Gerechtikeit lestiget vnd verkeret kleglich* (Magdeburg: Rödinger, 1552); Wengert, *Defending Faith*, 287–88.

20 See his letter of May 24, 1554, MBWR 7:197, nr. 7190; CR 8:294, nr. 5609.

21 Wengert, *Defending Faith*, 189–90.

22 On Mörlin's devotion to Luther, see Robert Kolb, *Martin Luther as Prophet, Teacher, and Hero: Images of the Reformer, 1520–1620* (Grand Rapids, MI: Baker, 1999), 159–61, 190–94; see also Wengert, *Defending Faith*, 315–16.

23 Kolb, 103–4.

and resurrection of Christ. He insisted, following Luther's *theologia crucis*, that in the proclamation of the foolishness of the cross (1 Cor 1–2), God redeems sinners; he found that Osiander's understanding of justification lacked anchoring in Christ's redemptive work in cross and resurrection.[24]

Mörlin's relationship with Melanchthon apparently continued; the preceptor sent him greetings when writing to Chemnitz in 1555. Melanchthon trusted Mörlin enough to allow him to attempt mediation between himself and Matthias Flacius, who had become Melanchthon's sharpest critic, thus earning the latter's bitterest recriminations as a result of their differing perspectives on the Leipzig Proposal of 1548. On January 14, 1557, a group of Lower Saxon pastors met in Braunschweig to formulate a basis for discussion between Flacius and Melanchthon, along with certain supporters.[25] Mörlin headed a delegation that brought Flacius and several of his protégés to the town of Coswig, less than ten miles from Wittenberg. While Chemnitz remained at Melanchthon's side, Mörlin headed a small group carrying messages from Flacius's group in Coswig and the Wittenberg responses back and forth. In the end, a solution evaded them. Melanchthon wrote a conciliatory letter to Mörlin and the other leaders of the effort, but the attempt at reconciliation failed because Flacius and his colleagues were more concerned with rejecting compromise on vital issues of the faith and Melanchthon still held some bitterness over the harsh criticism he had received from his former students.[26]

Later in 1557, however, the relationship between Melanchthon and Mörlin crumbled. Emperor Ferdinand I hoped to reconcile the Evangelical churches in his lands with the papal party and called for a religious colloquy at the diet in Worms that summer. Melanchthon had urged that a representative from the city of Braunschweig be among those considered as a member of the Evangelical team; Mörlin as superintendent was the most obvious candidate. He was suggested by name for the team by Erasmus von Minkwitz, who was the chancellor of Elector Ottheinrich of the Palatinate. Against the opposition of Duke Christoph of Württemberg, whose sympathies lay personally if not doctrinally with

24 Kolb, 108–12, 150–51.

25 *Unschuldige Nachrichten von Alten und Neuen Theologischen Sachen* (Leipzig, 1702), 634–35.

26 *Unschuldige Nachrichten*, 678–83.

Osiander,[27] Mörlin was chosen to be among the negotiators.[28] Early in the Evangelical participants' planning, Mörlin tried to play a conciliating role,[29] but he left little doubt that his voice would support the "Gnesiolutheran" positions of the ducal Saxon delegation, led by Viktorin Strigel, as he worked together with them on position papers during the colloquy.[30] Although he expressed common interests with the ducal Saxons in his personal conversation with Melanchthon in the early days of the colloquy,[31] serious differences were emerging. Mörlin took a leading role in opposing the Württemberg delegation's reluctance to condemn Osiander, while Melanchthon strove to avoid such public condemnations.[32] In the end, Mörlin joined Erasmus Sarcerius from Mansfeld and other ducal Saxon theologians in leaving the colloquy in protest at the beginning of October.[33] His involvement with the leadership of ducal Saxony, both ecclesiastical and political, deepened over the years. In 1569, after Duke Johann Wilhelm assumed rule of the duchy, the new sovereign attempted to gain Mörlin as a professor at the University of Jena.[34]

In 1559, Mörlin participated, at least as a reviewer, in the drafting of the ducal Saxon *Book of Confutation*, a confession designed to clarify doctrinal controversies within the Wittenberg circle with clear rejections of false teaching. When it appeared in print in 1559, its condemnations of Georg Major's proposition that "good works are necessary for salvation," of synergistic affirmation of a role for the human will in conversion, and of the compromises of

27 Wengert, *Defending Faith*, 191–220.

28 Benno von Bundschuh, *Das Wormser Religionsgespräch von 1557 unter besonderer Berücksichtigung der kaiserlichen Religionspolitik* (Münster: Aschendorff, 1988), 239–242; Bjorn Slenczka, *Das Wormser Schisma der Augsburger Konfessionsverwandten von 1557: Protestantische Konfessionspolitik und Theologie im Zusammenhang des zweiten Wormser Religionsgesprächs* (Tübingen: Mohr Siebeck, 2010), 79, 84–93.

29 Bundschuh, 273–74.

30 Bundschuh, 421, 425, 459; Slenczka, *Schisma*, 217, 246–49, 259, 285–86, 302, 331, 374.

31 Bundschuh, 361–62.

32 Bundschuh, 347–52, 419.

33 Bundschuh, 454–62.

34 Daniel Gehrt, *Ernestinische Konfessionspolitik. Bekenntnisbildung, Herrschaftskonsolidierung und dynastische Identitätsstiftung vom Augsburger Interim 1548 bis zur Konkordienformel 1577* (Leipzig: Evangelische Verlagsanstalt, 2011), 311.

the Leipzig Proposal all offended Melanchthon, as did its standing as an alternative to the Frankfurt Recess, which had been the electoral Saxon proposal for uniting Wittenberg adherents.[35]

Later in 1559, the breach widened between Melanchthon and Mörlin when the Preceptor attacked Tilemann Heshusius for insisting on using Luther's language regarding the Lord's Supper. Shortly after the collapse of the colloquy at Worms, Melanchthon had complained of Mörlin's use of ἀρτολατρεία (veneration of the bread)[36] in his defense of Luther's insistence on the true presence of Christ's body and blood in the Lord's Supper. In Melanchthon's critique of Heshusius's teaching, written for Elector Friedrich III of the Palatinate, he had dismissed Mörlin's saying, "You dare not say, 'mum, mum,' but say what the priest has there in his hand," as "papist" teaching.[37] Mörlin's published response to Melanchthon's attack on Heshusius held that communicants receive Christ's body and blood through the mouth and rejected "Zwinglian arguments" maintaining that only the "power" of Christ's body is present in the Lord's Supper because Christ's human body ascended to heaven. Mörlin rejected the papists' position that outside the use of the sacraments, the elements enclose Christ's body and blood and should be adored and paraded through the streets. The elements are "the true essential body and blood of Christ," as Christ's words of institution state. Thus both believers and unbelievers receive Christ's body in the consecrated elements. Mörlin denied that he taught a local inclusion of the body in the bread and the omnipresence of Christ's body. Melanchthon's focus on the benefits of the Supper rather than its nature seemed to Mörlin to

35 "Brevis narratio de controversia inter Flacium etc. et Victorin. Strigelium et Hugelum," Herzog August Bibliothek, Wolfenbüttel, Guelf. Helmst 64.2:244; Caspar Heldelin, *Eine Christliche predigt vber der Leiche des . . . Matthiae Flacij . . .* (Ursel: Heinrich, 1575), Bb1–Bb2a, assigned authorship of the *Book of Confutation* to Joachim's brother, Maximilian Mörlin, superintendent in Coburg; Johann Stössel, superintendent in Heldburg; and Simon Musaeus, professor at Jena, with further revisions by Johann Aurifaber, court preacher in Weimar, Flacius, and Joachim Mörlin and Erasmus Sarcerius. See Gehrt, *Konfessionspolitik*, 129–65; Friedhelm Gleiß, *Die Weimarer Disputation von 1560: Theologische Konsenssuche und Konfessionspolitik Johann Friedrichs des Mittleren* (Leipzig: Evangelische Verlagsanstalt, 2018), 44–56.

36 In a letter to Albert Hardenberg, September 18, 1558, MBWR 8:268, nr. 8730; CR 9:616–17, nr. 6601.

37 CR 9:961–62, nr. 6861B; MBWR 8:408, nr. 9119.

separate the reception of the Supper from its benefits.[38] In the last days of his life, Melanchthon complained bitterly of Mörlin as an associate of his archenemy Flacius.[39] The alienation of the Preceptor and this disciple, like many others, was complete.

As early as 1555, a dispute with a layman in Braunschweig, Henning Klod, over the true presence of Christ's body and blood in the Lord's Supper had sharpened Mörlin's sensitivity to that issue.[40] As a leader among the *ministeria* of the Lower Saxon Circle, Mörlin was becoming enmeshed in the tensions plaguing Braunschweig's sister Hanseatic city Bremen. This dispute between two pastors of Dutch origin, Johann Timäus and Albert Hardenberg, arose over Christ's presence in the Lord's Supper.[41] Melanchthon and Hardenberg had become close friends in the last decade of the Preceptor's life, but the latter's spiritualizing understanding of the sacramental presence of Christ offended those faithful to Luther's teaching. Mörlin visited Bremen in late 1556 to negotiate with the parties; he joined Flacius, pastor Joachim Westphal of Hamburg, and others in a delegation that presented concerns of the Lower Saxon *ministeria* to Elector August of Saxony and King Christian III of Denmark in 1557. The Bremen city council consulted Mörlin regarding the calling of a new superintendent in late 1559 and followed his advice, placing Tilemann Heshusius in that office.[42] The matter came to a head in February 1561, when under pressure from the Danish court, the Bremen council removed Hardenberg from office. At a meeting of the Lower Saxon *ministeria* in Lüneburg, Hardenberg's interpretation of Christ's sacramental presence was treated along with other controverted issues at the time. Mörlin, with Chemnitz's assistance, drafted a confession, the Lüneburg Declaration, subscribed by fifteen pastors

38 *Auff den Bericht vnd Radtschlag / So vnter dem namen des Herrnn Philippi Melanthonis zu Heidelberg gedruckt vnd ausgangen ist / Antwort vnd Bericht* [. . .] (n.p., 1560), A2a–B2b.

39 In letters to Jakob Runge, April 14, 1560, MBWR 8:468f., nr. 9296, CR 9:1094f., nr. 6974; and to Duke Albrecht of Prussia, April 15, 1560, MBWR 8:469, nr. 9297, CR 9:1095ff., nr. 6975.

40 Rehtmeyer, *Historiae*, 225–29.

41 Mahlmann, *Dogma*, 44–61.

42 Wim Janse, *Albert Hardenberg als Theologe: Profil eines Bucer-Schülers* (Leiden: Brill, 1994), 74, 78–80; Rehtmeyer, *Historiae*, 238–45.

from Lübeck, Bremen, Hamburg, Rostock, Magdeburg, Braunschweig, Lüneburg, and Wismar.

This document reflects the situation of the Wittenberg circle in the early 1560s in three ways. It rejects decisively papal authority and the authority of the Council of Trent, which was in recess but nonetheless a powerful papal weapon. It presents the Gnesio-Lutheran rejection of errors attributed to the Wittenberg faculty and its supporters. It addresses the divisive battle between Timäus and Hardenberg, affirming Timäus's teaching of Luther's concept of the true presence of Christ's body and blood in the sacrament without mentioning his defense of that concept: a Christological argument based on Luther's use of the attributes of Christ's divine and human natures and their communication.[43] The Declaration also reflects the tensions raised by Elector Friedrich III's attempt six months earlier at a diet of Evangelical princes in Naumburg to affirm the *Confessio Augustana Variata*, with its article on the Lord's Supper that was open to misinterpretation and so permitted him to pursue a spiritualizing doctrine of Christ's presence in the Lord's Supper.

Mörlin's Lüneburg Declaration focused on five pressing topics under dispute within the Wittenberg circle: justification (regarding Osiander), Georg Major's proposition that "good works are necessary for salvation," the Lord's Supper, adiaphora, and the freedom of the will. The controversy over the freedom or bondage of the will had erupted in public exchanges since the composition of the Frankfurt Recess three years earlier. The Lüneburg Declaration's brief statements of proper teaching (most often citations from the *Augsburg Confession* or the *Apology*), along with statements of false teaching to be rejected, anticipated the resolution of these disputes in the *Formula of Concord*, albeit in quite condensed form. Like the review of the controversies dividing the Wittenberg circle composed at this time by Martin Chemnitz and first published thirty years later, after his death,[44] the Lüneburg Declaration prefaced its treatment of the

43 Mahlmann, *Dogma*, esp. 82–93. Mörlin consistently avoided the Christological argumentation in defense of the true presence of Christ's body and blood in the Supper; see his letter of April 26, 1566, in Inge Mager, *Die Konkordienformel im Fürstentuim Braunschweig-Wolfenbüttel* (Göttingen: Vandenhoeck & Ruprecht, 1993), 470.

44 *De controversiis quibusdam, quae superiori tempore, circa quosdam Augustanae Confessionis Articulos, motae & agitatae sund; Iudicium*, ed. Polycarp Leyser (Braunschweig: Simon Gronenberg, 1594).

controversies with an explication of its *corpus doctrinae* in the Wittenberg sense of a rule of faith (*analogia fidei*).[45] This treatment of the primary authority of Scripture and the secondary authority of other documents set a pattern for the *Formula of Concord*'s determination that "the binding summary, basis, rule and guiding principle by which all teaching is to be judged according to God's Word."[46] The Lüneburg Declaration followed the form of teaching set forth in the "prophetic and apostolic writings of the Old and New Testaments" and the well-tested ancient creeds together with the *Augsburg Confession* of 1530. To combat corruptions and contrary opinions that had crept into the churches of the *Augsburg Confession*, the "Declaration" used the *Apology*, the *Smalcald Articles*, and "finally the catechisms and other writings of Luther" "to interpret God's Word."[47]

The positions taken by the Lüneburg Declaration on the five controverted topics it treated foreshadowed the solutions proposed by the *Formula of Concord*. Osiander's doctrine of justification by the indwelling divine nature of Christ was rejected; the Declaration repeated Mörlin's earlier defense of the forensic nature of God's pronouncement restoring righteousness on the basis of the reconciling satisfaction of the law's demand through Christ's death. Trusting in Christ brings true consolation. Ambrose as well as the *Augsburg Confession*, its *Apology*, and the *Smalcald Articles* were cited, affirming the biblical teaching of the necessity of good works as a result of the unconditional salvation effected by faith in Christ, a rejection of Georg Major and his followers. According to the Lüneburg Declaration (repeating the teaching of the three earlier Wittenberg confessions), in the Lord's Supper the sacramental bread and wine are Christ's body and blood. Against the acceptance of the *Confessio Augustana Variata* at the Naumburg diet earlier in the year, the Declaration insisted on the *Invariata* of 1530. Regarding adiaphora, it affirmed article 15 of the *Augsburg Confession* in allowing considerable freedom in ecclesiastical practice, rejecting the right of bishops to dictate that certain practices are necessary for salvation. However, in a time of persecution, concessions in adiaphora may not be made, as a number of Bible passages make clear (1 Cor 7:18f., Rom 14:6, Gal 2:4f., 14, 4:10f., 5:1, 13). The Lüneburg Declaration rejected several phrases that Melanchthon

45 Irene Dingel, "Melanchthon and the Establishment of Confessional Norms," in *Philip Melanchthon: Theologian in Classroom, Confession, and Controversy*, by Irene Dingel et al. (Göttingen: Vandenhoeck & Ruprecht, 2012), 161–79.

46 BSELK 1308–17; BC 526–29.

47 *Erklerung*, B3a–B4a.

and his disciples had used that seemed to attribute some power of the human will to turn itself from sin toward God, citing Augustine and article 18 of the *Augsburg Confession* to bolster its argument. Mörlin asserted that while God does not draw sinners to salvation as if they were blocks of wood, the Lord does make the unwilling willing, even though apart from God's grace sinners have no more ability on their own to accept Christ and his gospel than does a block of wood.

The Lüneburg Declaration enjoyed the support of the secular governments of Lower Saxony, but they also were navigating the treacherous waters of imperial politics. Therefore, in an August 1561 meeting in Lüneburg, local theologians issued a mandate that demanded the preaching of pure doctrine but forbade harsh critique of theological opponents in preaching and print. Mörlin joined a number of other pastors in the area in condemning this new Lüneburg Mandate.[48] He continued to comment in print on the proper interpretation of the Wittenberg legacy. In 1565, a claim of Heidelberg theologians—that Luther had himself rejected his early insistence on the presence of Christ's body and blood in the sacrament—provoked Mörlin to rebut this assertion.[49]

On occasion, Mörlin demonstrated his own independent thinking in sharply criticizing colleagues whose teaching of specific topics departed from what he viewed as biblical teaching. Anton Otto had defended Mörlin against his Prussian critics in 1552. In 1556, Otto—along with Andreas Poach, Nikolaus von Amsdorf, and a few others—rejected the decision of a synod in ducal Saxony that, while "good works are not necessary for salvation," proper biblical teaching does hold that good works are necessary for salvation in the doctrine of the law. Mörlin argued, ignoring Luther's distinction of twofold righteousness and the passive nature of the righteousness of Adam and Eve, that before the fall the law represented the path to salvation. In a private exchange that finally broke into print, he sharply criticized Otto and Poach, with whom Mörlin had worked together to oppose Viktorin Strigel's teaching on the role of the human will in conversion in 1562. Mörlin feared a diminution of the necessity of faith's producing good works, following Melanchthon's lead in securing a sense of human responsibility that flows from taking God's law seriously.[50]

48 Rehtmeyer, *Historiae*, 245–47.

49 *Wider die Landlu[e]gen / der Heidelbergischen Theologen* (Eisleben, 1565).

50 *Dispvtationes tres. Pro tertio vsv legis contra fanaticos* (n.p., 1566). Cf. Matthias Richter, *Gesetz und Heil: Eine Untersuchung zur Vorgeschichte und zum Verlauf*

In the years following, Mörlin and Chemnitz also broke with their long-time ally Matthias Flacius over Flacius's definition of original sin as the Aristotelian substance of sinners. On December 1, 1567, Mörlin warned his fellow pastors against Flacius's corruptions of the truth. He addressed several issues that Flacius and other Gnesio-Lutherans had raised in their criticism of Melanchthon. He did not abandon his earlier critique of his preceptor, but he did reject errors he found in the positions of Gnesio-Lutheran friends, repudiating certain instances of what he considered their unfair treatment of Melanchthon. Three years later, he and Chemnitz joined Johannes Wigand and Tilemann Heshusius—who had also supported Flacius in his earlier criticism of the Leipzig Interim and Georg Major and Viktorin Strigel's positions on good works and freedom of the will—in rejecting Flacius's use of the Aristotelian concept of substance in defining original sin. Mörlin distinguished the image of God, which sinners have lost, from the substance of the human creature created by God in body and soul, with mind, will, and heart or emotions. He posited that the poison of sin has totally infected and corrupted this human substance, citing Luther six times in opposing Flacius's use of Luther's "essential sin" and the sinner as "in the image of the devil."[51]

Mörlin's final words to his colleagues in Braunschweig in December 1567 also rejected those like Andreas Musculus and Anton Otto who opposed the third use of the law. He dismissed Nikolaus von Amsdorf's revival of Luther's phrase "good works are detrimental to salvation" (without acknowledging its origin in Luther's writings). In addition to repudiating Flacius's definition of original sin, he also criticized Flacius for unfairly interpreting Melanchthon's explanation of the concept of Christ as Logos and for oversimplifying the preceptor's definition of the gospel as both repentance and the forgiveness of sins (a definition that Flacius thought obscured God's pure grace preached in the gospel). Flacius's rejection of the use of the words *regeneration* and *vivification* as synonyms for *justification* also seemed hypercritical to Mörlin. Flacius's description of the action of the will in conversion as "coerced" offended Mörlin as well, as did his refusal to acknowledge any natural knowledge of God. Just

---

des sogenannten Zweiten Antinomistischen Streits (Göttingen: Vandenhoeck & Ruprecht, 1996), 176–202.

51 *De peccato originis scripta qvaedam contra Manichaeorum delirium. Quod Peccatum Originis sit Substantia. D. VVigandi. D. Heshvsii. D. Morlini. D. Kemnicii* (Jena: Ritzenhan, 1571), K8b–L8a.

as friendship with Melanchthon did not prevent the Braunschweig theologians from criticizing their preceptor, so it did not keep them from confuting the false teachings of their friend Flacius.[52]

These statements reflect positions that Mörlin and Chemnitz had incorporated into a new confessional standard for the duchy of Prussia in spring 1567.[53] Duke Albrecht turned to his earlier bête noire, Mörlin, and his *Vademecum*, Chemnitz, to fashion this *Corpus doctrinae* to bring peace to his church. Mörlin and Chemnitz had created such a *Corpus doctrinae* for the city of Braunschweig in 1564. That collection had contained Bugenhagen's Ordinances of 1528, the *Augsburg Confession*, the *Apology*, the *Smalcald Articles*, and the Declaration of 1561. The *Corpus doctrinae Prutenicum* addressed the topics of God, the two natures of Christ, the law, original sin and free will, justification by faith, good works (including the third use of the law), the sacraments in general, the Lord's Supper, and the pastoral office. Mörlin and Chemnitz thus expanded the agenda of the earlier controversies—over adiaphora, justification, the necessity of good works for salvation, freedom of the will, and the Lord's Supper—to include related Christological questions, original sin, and the third use of the law. In 1573, Jakob Andreae adopted their list of critical issues to be resolved among the adherents of the *Augsburg Confession* in his *Six Christian Sermons*, thereby setting the agenda of the drive toward concord, which culminated in the *Formula of Concord*.[54] Mörlin did not live to see that day, but his role in shaping the *Formula*'s agenda and substance was decisive.

52 Rehtmeyer, *Historiae*, Beilagen, 111–16.

53 It was published with these other documents and separately as *Repetitio corporis doctrinae ecclesiasticae Oder Widerholung der Summa vnd Inhalt der rechten / allgemeinen Christlichen / Kirchen Lehre wie dieselbige aus Gottes Wort / in der Augspurgischen Confession / Apologia / vnd Schmalkaldischen Artickeln begriffen / Vnd von Fu[e]rstlicher Durchleuchtigkeit zu Preussen etc. Auch allen derselbigen Getrewen Landtstenden vnd Vnterthanen / Geistlichen vnd Weltlichen / im Hertzogthumb Preussen / Einhellig vnd bestendiglichen / gewilliget vnd angenomen / Ku[e]rtzlich zusammen verfasset* (Eisleben, 1567, published with the other confessions, Königsberg, 1567).

54 On texts in the further development of the Solid Declaration of the *Formula*, see *BSELK*, vol. 2: *Die Konkordienformel.*

Albert Hardenberg, Philip Melanchthon, and the "Openly Hostile" Preachers of Bremen

A Cautionary Tale

Hans Wiersma

The essay at hand revolves around the reformer Albert van Hardenberg and his fourteen-year tenure as a preacher in Bremen. This story relates to the process of confessionalization that determined a complex set of outcomes for Europe in the second half of the sixteenth century and beyond. In particular, this narrative lies at the heart of the Second Sacramentarian Controversy, which precipitated the need for various evangelical clarifications regarding the Lord's Supper—clarifications that culminated in the *Formula of Concord*, article 7 and, relatedly, article 8. Although this story has been told and retold in German publications over the centuries and has received progressively deeper scrutiny, English-language Reformation scholarship concerning this story remains scant.[1] In general, Hardenberg scholarship focuses upon the intricacies

---

1 For the most recent, most thorough Hardenberg scholarship, see Wim Janse, *Albert Hardenberg als Theologe: Profil eines Bucer-Schülers*, Studies in the History of Christian Thought 57 (Leiden: Brill, 1994). The first scholarly biographical treatment of Hardenberg is Daniel Gerdes, *Historia motuum ecclesiasticorum in civitate Bremensi sub medium seculi XVI. a. 1547–1561 tempore Alberti Hardenbergii suscitatorum* [. . .] (Groningen: Spandaw & Rump, 1756). The first German-language

of the theological debates in which he was engaged.[2] This essay will focus instead upon the story of Hardenberg's relationship with his colleagues and how events transpired in consequence of those relationships. The story is worth telling because (1) it's a good story, (2) it sheds light on the everyday, human concerns that can drive a community toward a confessional tipping point, and (3) it can serve as a cautionary tale. Before commencing with the story proper, an outline of the historical developments that bookend Hardenberg's time in Bremen is in order.[3]

The Reformation(s) in Bremen

Luther-style preaching arrived in Bremen in November 1522, when Hendrik van Zutphen, a Wittenberg-trained Netherlander, came to town.[4] At the time of his arrival, Zutphen was in the process of an escape from Antwerp, where he served as prior of the Augustinian monastery. Post–Edict of Worms persecutions in Antwerp precipitated Zutphen's escape. His plan was to travel to Wittenberg and take sanctuary there. However, when his Bremen hosts invited

biography is Elard Wagner, *Doctor Albert Hardenberg sim Dom zu Bremen gefüretes Lehramt und dessen nächste Folgen* (Bremen: Meier, 1779). For readers of German interested in an engaging, readable example of nineteenth-century popular scholarship, see Bernhard Spiegel, *D. Albert Rizäus Hardenberg: Ein Theologenleben aus der Reformationszeit* (Bremen: Müller, 1869).

2 About one-fifth of Janse's impressive tome is devoted to "Hardenbergs Biographie" (*Albert Hardenberg*, 5–113). By contrast, the major sections focus upon "Hardenbergs Theologie" (118–252) and "Die Dogmengeschichtliche Stellung der Theologie Hardenbergs" (256–479).

3 Some elements of the telling of this story were first presented in my paper titled "'Openly Hostile' Preachers: The Fall of the Lutherans and the Rise of the Reformed in Bremen, 1547–1580," presented at the Sixteenth Century Society & Conference in Geneva, Switzerland, on May 29, 2009.

4 For the purposes of this essay, *the Netherlands*, *Low Countries*, *Lowlands*, and related terms will denote the seventeen provinces of the Habsburgian Netherlands inherited in 1506 by the future Charles V. These provinces currently correspond with territory outlined by the modern-day Netherlands, Belgium, and Luxembourg, as well as northerly slices of the Hauts-de-France and Grand Est regions of modern-day France. For a detailed and engaging rendition of events surrounding the six-year-old Charles's ascension as heir, see Geoffrey Parker, *Emperor: A New Life of Charles V* (New Haven, CT: Yale University Press, 2019), 3–23.

"Brother Henry" to preach in the evangelical style, his sermon made such an impression that the city council appointed him pastor of the city's St. Ansgar Church.[5] Bremen's Reformation had begun. In 1524, the city council requested two additional pastors be sent from Wittenberg; subsequently, Jacob Probst and Johann Timann were appointed to Bremen's St. Mary Church and St. Martin Church, respectively. The reason for Bremen's preference for preachers from the Low Countries is mainly due to the similarity at the time of Middle Dutch and the Middle Low German (Plattdeutsch) spoken in Bremen.

In 1534, Probst and Timann drafted a new church order for Bremen's congregations, a guiding document delivered to Wittenberg, where it was vetted and approved by Melanchthon and Johannes Bugenhagen.[6] Then, as if to demonstrate their thoroughgoing Lutheranness, Bremen's clergy and city council punctuated the newly crafted church order with an addendum titled "A Mandate from the City of Bremen against the Desecrators of the Sacrament."[7] The church order and its addendum were then published together. Finally, in 1537, Bremen attested its commitment to the Wittenberg movement by sending Timann to join talks being held in Smalcald, two hundred miles to Bremen's south.[8] Interestingly, accounts of the Smalcaldic League's formative meetings indicate that there was major disagreement over the wording of the "Concerning the Sacrament of the Altar" section of the *Smalcald Articles*. One of the main sticking points was this phrase: "The bread and the wine in the supper are the true body and blood of Christ."[9] Ten years later, these words would

5 For Luther's assessment of Zutphen's life and death, see "The Burning of Brother Henry," LW 32:261–86. For an assessment of Luther's assessment, see my article "The Death of Brother Henry van Zutphen: The Story of a Lowlands Martyr as Chronicled by Jacob Probst and Martin Luther," *Luther-Bulletin* 15 (2006): 50–60.

6 See J. Friedrich Iken, *Bremische Kirchen-Ordung von 1534* (Bremen: Müller, 1891). For an exploration of the church order's *theologia crucis*, see my "A Theology of the Cross in the 1534 Bremen Church Order," *Lutheran Quarterly* 30 (2016): 181–92.

7 In *Angenamen de Ordeninge Van der Ouericheit. Sampt einem Mandate der Stadt Bremen Wedder de Sacrament Schender* (Magdeburg: Michael Lotter, 1534) a iiii–[a viii]. In this essay, all English translations of text originally in published in German, Dutch, and Latin, are my own (see note 1).

8 Timann's name appears in the list of signers, *Smalcald Articles*, BC 328. Timann was also present at the Colloquies of Worms (1540) and Regensburg (1541).

9 "Editors' Introduction to the Smalcald Articles," BC 296.

become one of the main points of conflict for Timann and others in Bremen's very own Sacramentarian Controversy.

The Smalcaldic portent aside, one would have been hard-pressed to find another major German city that was as unanimously Lutheran as Bremen was in the year of Luther's death, 1546. As 1547 dawned, the only thing left to do, really, was to reopen Bremen's shuttered cathedral and put a Lutheran in its pulpit. Ironically, the preacher invited to fill that pulpit would introduce the first crack in Bremen's Lutheran unanimity.

Skip ahead to 1580. In that year Bremen's city council invited Christoph Pezel, a Calvinist, to come to Bremen for a brief stay. The purpose of Pezel's stay was to help settle an outbreak of the Lord's Supper dispute among the city's preachers.[10] The result was the removal from office of Bremen's last remaining Lutheran pastor. The council invited Pezel to preach in his place. In 1581, the city council went a step further, officially appointing Pezel as pastor of not one but two of Bremen's parishes. During his long tenure in Bremen, Pezel would replace Luther's *Small Catechism* with his own, establish a high school (*Gymnasium Impresse*) in which students read Calvin's writings, removed all art from Bremen's church buildings, and published the *Consensus of the Pastors of Bremen's Churches*—a document that was steadfastly Reformed in orientation.[11]

Jürgen Moltmann, in one of his little-known early works, described what happened in Bremen under Pezel as a "Second Reformation"—a term that eventually came into use to describe those areas of Germany that confessionalized along the lines of Calvin's doctrine.[12] Recognizing that there are problems with the term, it can nevertheless be asserted that, if there was such a thing, Bremen's

10 Ironically, this dispute was likely occasioned by Lutheran attempts at consensus-building ultimately represented in 1577's *Formula Concordiae*.

11 "Pezel, Christoph," in *The New Schaaf-Herzog Encyclopedia of Religious Knowledge*, vol. 9 (1911; repr. Grand Rapids, MI: Baker, 1977), 3–4. The name of the Lutheran removed from office in 1580 is Jodocus Glanaeus. Pezel was meant to debate Glanaeus in the presence of Bremen's city council. When Glanaeus failed to show up for the debate, the council found him to be in contempt and dismissed him. See also "Der *Consensus ministerii Bremensis ecclesiae* von 1595," in *Bremisches Jahrbuch* 10 (Bremen: Müller, 1878), 84–105.

12 Jürgen Moltmann, *Christoph Pezel (1539–1604) und der Calvinismus in Bremen*, Hospitium Ecclesiae 2 (Bremen: Hauschild, 1958).

Second Reformation was underway well before Christoph Pezel arrived on the scene.[13]

What had happened? What took place *before* Pezel's arrival that set the stage for his welcome, for the ready acceptance of his able leadership and, consequently, for Bremen's eventual full embrace of the Reformed confessions?

The answer involves a series of events that, in turn, requires the description of a variety of players involved in those events. If the question is, "What happened?" then an honest answer is, "It's complicated." Nevertheless, when accounting for the fall of the Lutherans and the rise of the Reformed in Bremen from the years 1522 to 1580, the story of Albert van Hardenberg's tenure (1547–61) is, as shall be seen, a critical place to start.

Albert van Hardenberg

As one of the eleven original members of the Smalcaldic League, Bremen was pledged to join its German allies when, in 1546, Emperor Charles V's armies were mobilized under the command of Fernando Álvarez, the Duke of Alba. The Smalcaldic alliance sustained loss after loss as the empire's forces advanced deep into German lands. In May 1547, Wittenberg fell without a fight. However, on May 23, the league's armies emerged victorious at the Battle of Drakenburg, ending the siege of Bremen.[14] Bremen's fighters and at least one field pastor returned to the city as heroes. The name of the field pastor: Albert van Hardenberg.

Hardenberg was born around 1510 in the village of Hardenberg, twenty-five miles east of Zwolle, in what is today the Netherlands' province of Overijssel.[15] Hardenberg's school years—his early *Bildung*—took place in a "progressive" milieu informed by the *Devotia moderna*, Humanist learning, and time spent in a school run by the Brothers of the Common Life. At age twenty, Hardenberg moved to Leuven, where he enrolled in the controversial *Collegium Trinlingue*

13 For a discussion of the problems with the term *Second Reformation*, see *Die Reformierte Konfessionalisierung in Deutschland: Das Problem der "Zweiten Reformation,"* ed. Heinz Schilling (Gütersloh: Mohn, 1986).

14 See Helmut Lucke, *Bremen im Schmalkaldischen Bund, 1540–1547* (Bremen: Staatsarchiv, 1955), esp. "Die Belagerung und Befreiung Bremens," 72–105.

15 As a child and youth, I (see note 2) spent many summer months at my paternal grandparent's home in Zwolle.

co-founded by Erasmus. During the next decade, Hardenberg was drawn to Reform-oriented student circles, despite the risk of opposition from Leuven's conservative theological faculty. In 1539, two events transpired that profoundly impacted Hardenberg. The first: on a trip to Mainz, Hardenberg met Johannes a Lasco (Jan Laski), initiating a long, but not lifelong, friendship. Second, upon an inquisition initiated by certain members of Leuven's theology faculty, Hardenberg was arrested and imprisoned as part of a sweep of students suspected of heterodox belief.[16]

After paying a fine and obtaining his release, Hardenberg left Leuven and returned to the northern Netherlands, taking up residence near the Frisian city of Groningen. Here, he remained in frequent contact with Lasco, who had since moved to nearby Emden. It was during this period that Hardenberg began corresponding with Melanchthon.[17] At Melanchthon's behest, Hardenberg commenced a short period of study in Wittenberg. During his time in Wittenberg—which ended in March 1544—Hardenberg attended lectures delivered by Melanchthon and Luther. Hardenberg later reported that he often discussed the Lord's Supper with Luther during this time. Upon Melanchthon's recommendation, Hardenberg served as a theological consultant at the 1544 Diet of Speyer. This official "gig" led to a series of "church business" sojourns in an impressive number of locales, including Strasbourg, Basel, Bern, Zurich, Saint Gallen, Constance, and Augsburg. During these sojourns, he met a variety of Reformers, including Martin Bucer, who would become determinative in Hardenberg's theological development. After his time bouncing between southern German and Swiss cities, Hardenberg spent time in the lower Rhineland, including stays in Cologne and Kempen, near Düsseldorf. According to Bucer, it was in Kempen that "thousands" came to hear Hardenberg preach. Finally, with Germany embroiled in the Smalcaldic War, and as imperial forces neared Bremen, Hardenberg enlisted as a field pastor ministering to those on the evangelical side.[18]

Hardenberg was wounded during the Battle of Drakenburg on May 23, 1547. The scars from his wounds would remain visible for the rest of his

16 Janse, *Albert Hardenberg*, 3–13.

17 Janse lists 128 examples of correspondence between Hardenberg and Melanchthon during the years 1543–60. Of these letters, 120 were written during Hardenberg's fourteen years in Bremen.

18 Janse, 13–31.

life.[19] The wounded Hardenberg entered Bremen among the victors. Before long—upon the recommendation of Count Christoph of Oldenburg and the support of Timann, Probst, and the rest of Bremen's clergy—Hardenberg was appointed as preacher to the newly reopened St. Peter Cathedral, the first evangelical *Domprediger*. Hardenberg began preaching in June or July and, according to reports, was an immediate hit. Whether out of jealousy for the popular newcomer or concerns for orthodoxy, it did not take long for the first sign of trouble in the clergy ranks to present itself.[20]

Open Hostilities

Curiously, the rift began in the homes where Timann and Hardenberg were invited to dinner. It seemed that when the two preachers were put in the same room together, they could not keep from arguing—nor, apparently, from hurling kitchenware. Why? It may be that "Timann's strict, narrow orthodoxy" led him to be suspicious of "Hardenberg's more open attitude." Or it may be that Hardenberg alarmed Timann with statements that appeared to differ substantially from the approved doctrine outlined in Bremen's 1534 church order. Whatever the reason, in mid-autumn, in the home of a councilman, Hardenberg and Timann were in the process of an escalating argument concerning the Lord's Supper. At one point, Hardenberg quoted Augustine quoting Socrates. Timann blurted out, "See! He's an arch-*Schwärmer*! A Zwinglian! He cites a pagan!" Hardenberg responded by leaping across the table, thumping his chest, and making threats. In addition, around this time, Hardenberg had raised Timann's ire after the latter heard the former lecture on John 6 and its connection to Jesus's words at the Last Supper. Consequently, Timann and another preacher, Johann Selst, lodged a complaint with the city council. The council did not take action to resolve the complaint. Still, the stage was set for a long period of hostilities among Bremen's preachers.[21]

19 Spiegel, *D. Albert Rizäus Hardenberg*, 79.

20 Carl Rottländer, *Der Bürgermeister Daniel von Büren und die Hardenbergischen Religionshänder in Bremen (1555–1562)* (Göttingen: Kästner, 1892), 8.

21 Rottländer, 10; Janse, *Albert Hardenberg*, 32–33. For the details about the kitchenware—a pot, actually—and the fight in the councilman's home, see Wilhelm Klose, "Jacobus Spreng, genannt Probst," in *Zeitschrift für die historische Theologie*

Soon after the turn of the new year 1548, in a sermon explaining the "sign of circumcision" mentioned in Romans 4:11, Hardenberg apparently employed language indicating that he understood the bread and wine of the Lord's Supper as "signs." Word of this trespass traveled quickly in Bremen. Hardenberg once again found himself the object of an official complaint from the other preachers. This time, the city council requested that a statement of faith concerning the Lord's Supper be written—a request Hardenberg obliged by mid-month. Hardenberg's *Abendmahlsbekenntnis* assured his adjudicators that "the entire Christ, God and human, with all his possessions" were materially and substantively designated in the Lord's Supper. This *Sententia de praesentia* (Opinion concerning the [real] presence) was forwarded to Wittenberg for approval. Melanchthon responded, giving Hardenberg's *Sententia* high marks, noting the "measured and godly" writing. Melanchthon also admonished the other pastors to exercise forbearance in their judgments and to avoid conflict. After the dust settled, Hardenberg reported the incident to Lasco in Emden. Lasco wrote back, observing, "Once again, a fight is stopped by a word from Melanchthon."[22]

Despite Melanchthon's successful intervention, concern about Hardenberg's confessional loyalties persisted among Bremen's clergy. Hardenberg's ties with Lasco didn't help.[23] At first, Lasco had received a warm welcome from Bremen's clergy when visiting Bremen in 1549 and 1550. It was even apparently tolerated when, on one occasion, Probst gave Lasco the sacrament and Lasco brought the host to his mouth in the Reformed manner. In 1552, Lasco published a tract that clarified his Zwinglian understanding of the Lord's Supper. With Lasco's "true colors" verified, Bremen's pastors "scolded" Hardenberg for providing hospitality to Lasco when the latter traveled through Bremen again in December 1553. Writing about these events afterward, Hardenberg focused

30 (Gotha: Perthes, 1860), 297; see also Spiegel, *D. Albert Rizäus Hardenberg*, 122–23.

22 Janse, *Albert Hardenberg*, 33. The chronologies and summaries of events in this and the following paragraphs are based on Janse's work and, where indicated, by supporting sources. For a condensed version of the story of Albert van Hardenberg's tenure in Bremen, see Hanns Engelhardt, "Der Irrlehrestreit zwischen Albert Hardenberg und dem Bremer Rat 1547–1561," in *Hospitium Ecclesiae* 4, ed. Bodo Heyne and Hans Jessen (Bremen: Schünemann, 1964), 29–52.

23 Janse cites sixty examples of correspondence between Lasco and Hardenberg during the years 1540–55. Janse, 504–18.

some of his ire on Probst.[24] Up until the scolding, Probst—who was superintendent of pastors—had been a frequent guest in Hardenberg's home. After the scolding, with Probst's actual opinion of Lasco made known, Hardenberg surmised that Probst had come "over to eat and to treat me in a fatherly way . . . in order to draw me out and entrap me." Because of this suspicion, Hardenberg stopped inviting Propst for dinner, at which point "the old, childish" Probst became "openly hostile."[25] As 1554 dawned, the lid was ready to blow.

The complaints about Probst notwithstanding, Hardenberg's main opponent in Bremen's full-blown *Abendmahlstreit* would prove to be Timann. However, before Timann went on the offensive, Hardenberg played a bit of defense. Hardenberg was aware that his hospitality to Lasco at the end of 1553 brought the question of his Lutheran bona fides under deeper suspicion. Hardenberg also knew that his own Bucerian doctrine concerning the Lord's Supper differed from Lasco's Zwinglian views. Finally, Hardenberg understood that supporting Wittenberg's foothold in East Frisia would make it more difficult for his colleagues to accuse him of contra-Wittenberg leanings. These three considerations help explain Hardenberg's (surprising) plan to align East Frisia more clearly with Wittenberg.

In July 1554, Hardenberg traveled to Wittenberg to discuss the plan with Melanchthon. The plan had two parts. First, Hardenberg would work with a Lutheran pastor in Emden to replace the Emden Catechism of 1546—which leaned Reformed—with one that corresponded with the more "moderate" views of Wittenberg. Second, Hardenberg would aid efforts to fill Emden's vacant superintendency with a candidate approved by Wittenberg. Concerning this second part of the plan, Hardenberg supported a proposal that *Melanchthon himself* fill the vacancy. Melanchthon declined. When Lasco returned from London, where he had been working to support exiled Reformed communities,

24 Janse, 34.

25 Janse, 34n24. Janse's work includes an abundance of quotations from Albert van Hardenberg, *D. Hardenbergii Autographum De Controversia Sacramentaria Bremensi* (Bremen: n.p., 1560). As the title suggests, the *Autographum* represents Hardenberg's "side of the story" concerning Bremen's *Abendmahlstreit*.

he was understandably horrified to learn of Hardenberg's subversion. The friendship was at an end.[26] Soon afterward, Lasco left Emden for good.[27]

The Doctrine of Ubiquity and the Dismissal of Hardenberg

Two months before the Hardenberg-Melanchthon scheme was hatched, Timann had begun work on what would become his *Farrago sententiarum consentientium* (A collection of agreed-upon opinions). Timann's *Farrago* was aimed at the teachings of Lasco and, more broadly, at the Swiss Reformers—Zwingli, Calvin, and Bullinger—and their formulations of the Lord's Supper.[28] Although Timann refrained from referring to Hardenberg by name in this writing, the subtext of Timann's publication was the conflict with Hardenberg. This subtext becomes clearer when one appreciates Timann's introduction of Luther's "almost forgotten ubiquity doctrine" in his argument against Lasco and the Swiss. Indeed, Hardenberg later reported that Timann had openly declared that "if we allow a fanatic [Swarmero] to teach against ubiquity, the foundation will be completely shaken." Hardenberg's complaint indicates his understanding that Timann's introduction of the concept of the omnipresence of Christ's inseparable divine and human bodies was intended to sideline Hardenberg's own position: namely, that in the bread and wine, Christ is bodily present via a

26 Janse, *Albert Hardenberg*, 43–45; Wilhelm Neuser, "Hardenberg und Melanchthon: Der Hardenbergische Streit (1554–1560)," *Jahrbuch der Gesellschaft für Niedersächsische Kirchengeschichte* 65 (1967): 151–53.

27 Lasco moved to London in April 1555, where he continued work supporting expatriated Reformed communities. See Andrew Pettegree, "The London Exile Community and the Second Sacramentarian Controversy, 1553–1560," *Archiv für Reformationsgeschichte* 78 (1987): 223–52. See also Christoph Strohm, ed., *Johannes a Lasco (1499–1560): Polnischer Baron, Humanist, und Europäischer Reformator* (Tübingen: Mohr Sieback, 2000).

28 Johann Timann, *Farrago Sententiarvm consentientivm in vera et catholica doctrina, de Coena Domini, quam firma assensione, & uno spiritu, iuxta diuinorum uocem, Ecclesiae Augustanae confessionis amplexae sunt, sonant & profitentur* (Frankfurt: Brubacher, 1555).

union of God's word, outward sign, and divine gift, effected by the Holy Spirit and received in faith.[29]

Throughout 1555, well before the *Farrago* was published, Timann made the ubiquity of Christ's physical presence the theme of many of his sermons. According to Hardenberg, Timann railed against "the Zwinglians, Enthusiasts, Nestorians, and other heretics who separated, divided, and completely tore apart the two natures of Christ." Hardenberg understood that Timann's polemical sermons—and the related heralding of the doctrine of ubiquity—was aimed at him. Consequently, Hardenberg began preaching against ubiquity and in favor of his own, more "moderate" position—the same position described in his Melanchthon-approved *Sententia de praesentia* from seven years before. In fact, as Hardenberg understood it, his doctrine rather than Timann's complied with the Wittenberg Concord of 1536. Timann—by insisting upon the ubiquity of Christ's presence as the defining characteristic of the authentic (Gnesio-) Lutheran position—had moved the goalposts.[30]

Timann's *Farrago* finally appeared in published form on November 1, 1555. In early 1556, Superintendent Probst and the rest of Bremen's preachers—excluding Hardenberg—officially endorsed the doctrines set forth in Timann's *Farrago*. This move essentially made Timann's distinctions around ubiquity the litmus test for orthodoxy in Bremen. Hardenberg reciprocated, charging that those who supported the ubiquity doctrine were themselves heretics and betrayers of the teachings of Luther. The conflict among Bremen's preachers had once again boiled to the surface to the degree that the city's leaders were moved to address the resulting civic unrest. During Lent, Probst and Hardenberg were called to appear before the city council to account for the dissension in the ranks. Hardenberg insisted that his views were in line with

---

29 See Janse, *Albert Hardenberg*, 194–225, for a highly detailed investigation of the development and clarification of Hardenberg's *Abendmahlslehre*; see Janse, 250–52, for an eleven-point summary of Hardenberg's doctrine of the Lord's Supper. According to Janse's understanding of Hardenberg's position, "The *Gift* [*Gabe*] is the entire Christ as substance of the sacrament. The gift is not spiritual [geistig] but ministerial [geistlich]: the communion is restricted neither to Christ nor to the human spirit, so that the qualification 'spiritualistic' [spiritualistisch] does not apply to Hardenberg's teaching on the Lord's Supper." Janse, 251 (emphasis in original).

30 Janse, 45–46.

the *Augsburg Confession*, the *Apology*, and the Wittenberg Concord, even more so with the witness of Scripture. On the Tuesday before Easter, the council called Probst and Hardenberg to appear again, this time with Timann present as well. Hardenberg brought with him a copy of Timann's *Farrago*, commended its contents to the council, and asked to be left alone. Despite the implied symbolism of Hardenberg's gesture ("They can have their doctrine, let me have mine"), fiery sermons for and against the ubiquity doctrine continued. Hardenberg's opponents called him out by name; Hardenberg did the same. Bremen's citizens took sides, as did members of the city council. For example, Daniel van Büren, a councilman for nearly twenty years, thought Timann's stridency was off-putting. Other council members reported annoyance with Hardenberg.[31]

In the hope of stemming the still-rising tide of acrimony, the council requested a consensus statement from Bremen's preachers. A brief document titled "The Confession of the Preachers of Bremen concerning the Supper of Jesus Christ" was presented on October 21, 1556. Timann, Probst, and most of the rest of Bremen's preachers subscribed; the document was submitted with the understanding that it awaited Hardenberg's signature.[32] Clearly, the document had the intention of putting Hardenberg on ice. In November, Hardenberg wrote to the city council that he could not sign the "Confession," since it was grounded upon the notion of Christ's ubiquity rather than upon the witness of Scripture described in the *Augsburg Confession*. In response to his colleagues, Hardenberg produced his own *confessio* of eighteen *Articles against Ubiquity* (*Themata adversus Ubiquitatem*).[33] In December 1556, Hardenberg traveled to Wittenberg to once again enlist the support of Melanchthon. The trip paid off. Hardenberg obtained from Melanchthon an official opinion, the *Wittenberger Gutachten* of January 1557. Melanchthon's judgment allowed Hardenberg's position and sideline the "ubiquity" position espoused by Timann. Although the fallout of the "Wittenberg Opinion" had consequences well beyond

31 Janse, 45–50.

32 The articles survive in Tilemann Heshusius, *Das Jesu Christi warer Leib und Blut im Heiligen Abendmal gegenwertig sey wider den Rottengiest zu Bremen Doc. Albert Hardenberg* (Magdeburg: n.p., 1560), Diiij^{b}–Ei^{b}. Heshusius's publication appeared in a variety of editions. Each edition included a version of the 1556 document representing the position of Bremen's preachers.

33 Janse, *Albert Hardenberg*, 51–54.

Bremen's city limits, its effect in Bremen was in fact a recess of hostilities of sorts.[34] Once again, it appeared that Melanchthon's intervention was able to calm the waters. At the very least, the *Gutachten* demonstrated that, whatever concerns there might have been about "Philippism" at the start of 1557, Melanchthon and Wittenberg still held some sway over the leaders, preachers, and citizens of Bremen.

The Melanchthon-engineered peace held for several years. Timann's death that same year and Probst's increasing frailty no doubt contributed to the decrease in open hostilities. However, as before, the controversy merely simmered. In 1560, an organized group of pastors and city council members renewed their efforts to remove Hardenberg. With the looming resignation of the old man, Probst, the anti-Hardenbergers in Bremen and beyond began to plot a replacement for Timann's pulpit *and* Probst's superintendency. Tilemann Heshusius—recently stationed in Heidelberg, a doctor of theology, and an impassioned preacher—was considered the man for the job. Heshusius responded that he would come to Bremen under the condition that there would be public debate that settled the Lord's Supper controversy, if not once and for all, then at least for Bremen. Heshusius imagined that the disputation would include Calvin, Bullinger, and Lasco—an ambitious vision that did not materialize. In a letter dated December 21, 1559, Hardenberg reported to Melanchthon that Heshusius had arrived in Bremen.[35]

As plans for the "showdown" were discussed, Melanchthon again pledged to support Hardenberg.[36] Melanchthon's death on April 19, 1560, therefore, devastated Hardenberg. Alas, Melanchthon would not be able to step in and save the day this time. Hardenberg's attempts to solicit support from others in Wittenberg fell flat. The disputation opened in Bremen on May 23, 1560. Like Timann before him, Heshusius attacked Hardenberg and proclaimed the

34 For a broad treatment of the effect of the publication of Melanchthon's *Wittenberg Opinion* and the beginning stages of Germany's Second Sacramentarian Controversy, see Janse, 63–77.

35 Wilhelm Heinrich Neuser, "Hardenberg und Melanchthon. Der Hardenbergische Streit 1554–60," *Jahrbuch der Gesellschaft für niedersächsische Kirchengeschichte* 65 (1967): 185.

36 There are eight extant letters from Melanchthon to Hardenberg dated between the arrival of Heshusius in December 1559 and March 31, 1560. Hardenberg's letters to Melanchthon during this time are not extant. Janse, *Albert Hardenberg*, 526–27.

doctrine of ubiquity (die Ubiquität).[37] Hardenberg was labelled a Zwinglian. When councilman Büren rose to defend Hardenberg, Heshusius retorted with insults, calling Büren a "gray ass and a booby bird."[38] Heshusius also took to the pulpit, breaking "loose against Hardenberg like a violent clap of thunder." In a sermon on Sunday, June 1, Heshusius went so far as to call into doubt Hardenberg's orthodoxy concerning baptism.[39]

As a result, many council members began to suspect Hardenberg of being an Anabaptist. Consequently, in June, the city council began the process to investigate and dismiss Hardenberg from the office he had held for thirteen years. One conspicuous opponent of the process was Büren, now openly friendly with Hardenberg and—not so incidentally—now also one of Bremen's four revolving mayors. At the same time, curiously, Heshusius appears to have taken the council's decision to take action against Hardenberg as a signal that his work in Bremen was done; soon after, he accepted a new post as superintendent in Magdeburg. His time in Bremen had lasted less than a year.[40] Heshusius's going-away gift to Hardenberg was the publication of a lengthy polemic, *That Jesus Christ's Real Body and Blood Are Present in the Holy Supper, against That Corrupting Spirit [Rottengeist] of Bremen, Doctor Albert Hardenberg.*[41]

The legal process against Hardenberg—which included the involvement of a council headed by the regional bishop—slowly wound its way to its inevitable conclusion. The Bremen preachers drafted one last confession of faith aimed at Hardenberg's perceived heterodoxy. As before, Hardenberg's subscription was expected. When Hardenberg refused to sign, the cathedral chapter handed Hardenberg his "notice"—the notice being in fact a strongly worded ban. On February 18, 1561, escorted by a large crowd of supporters, Albert van Hardenberg left Bremen never to return. Not long after, Hardenberg wrote

37 For a provocative take on Heshusius's ideas on the ubiquity of Christ—that Heshusius's conception was closer to Calvin's doctrine in certain respects—see David Steinmetz, "Calvin and His Lutheran Critics," *Lutheran Quarterly* 4/2 (Summer 1990): 179–94. The title of the article is misleading; Steinmetz deals solely with Heshusius.

38 In German, "grauer Esel" and "Tölpel." Janse, *Albert Hardenberg*, 82.

39 Janse, 77–83.

40 Janse, 82–83.

41 Tilemann Heshusius, *Das Jesu Christi warer Leib und Blut im Heiligen Abendmal gegenwertig sey wider den Rottengiest zu Bremen Doc. Albert Hardenberg* (Magdeburg: Kirchner, 1560).

down his own reflections of the process that led to his dismissal; he concluded these recollections with Gamaliel-like wisdom: "If it's from God, it will remain; if not, then God will see that it will soon fail."[42]

DIVINE INTERVENTION(?) AND DENOUEMENT

With the departure of Albert van Hardenberg from Bremen, one would assume that the cause was won for the Gnesio-Lutheran ubiquity side.[43] But that would be incorrect. Heshusius's replacement, Simon Musaeus, was even more stridently anti-Hardenbergian than Heshusius. After arriving and settling in, Musaeus began to lead the work of drafting a new church order for the city of Bremen. This new church would clarify and entrench the pro-ubiquity position required for the city's preachers. In addition, the draft included language that provided for the excommunication of all who supported false teaching, including the teaching of Hardenberg. This provision mandated that all of Bremen's parishioners would be interviewed for the purpose of determining the state of each person's orthodoxy. This unprecedented inquisitorial authority was clearly aimed at rooting out those who supported Hardenberg, including Mayor Büren. Understandably, a sizeable portion of Bremen's citizens, Büren among them, were alarmed by what the new church order would entail.[44]

At just this point in time—when things were looking bleakest for the non-Gnesio-Lutheran position in Bremen—it was Büren's turn to take his

42 Janse, *Albert Hardenberg*, 84–89; Rottländer, *Bürgermeister Daniel von Büren*, 64. Note: Spiegel's 1869 biography includes a portrait of Hardenberg that precedes the title page. Below it are printed the words of Hardenberg's citation of Acts 5:38–39, in Plattdeutsch: "Jck spreke mit dem Gamaliel: Jsset van gade, so wert idt wal bliven, wo nicht, soe geve got dattet in balde under gaë. Amen."

43 For a summary report of the eighteen months that preceded Hardenberg's ouster, see Hanns Engelhardt: "Das Irrlehreverfahren des Niedersächsischen Reichs-Kreises gegen Albert Hardenberg 1560/61," in *Jahrbuch der Gesellschaft für niedersächsische Kirchengeschichte* 61 (1963): 32–62.

44 The main source for the descriptions provided here and the remaining paragraphs outlining the post-Hardenberg history of Bremen's "troubles" is Rottländer, *Bürgermeister Daniel von Büren*, 64–88 ("6. Capitel. Reaction in Bremen zu Gunsten der Orthodoxie und die Revolution vom January 1562"). A major portion of Rottländer's original sources can be found in the first two volumes of *Beiträge zur Bremische Kirchengeschichte*, ed. Johann Kohlmann, 4 vols. (Bremen: Heyse, 1844–52).

constitutionally prescribed term as presiding mayor (talk about deus ex machina!). On January 9, 1562, as providence would have it, Büren assumed the presidency of the city council. Bremen's constitution gave the council ten days to replace Büren. Büren's strategy was to broadcast far and wide what life under Musaeus's inquisition would be like. Musaeus, in response, led his supporters in prayer, beseeching God for a new mayor. As the time limit approached, a groundswell of support for Büren arose. This support was not so much a result of sympathy for Büren as it was a result of a growing awareness among Bremen's citizenry regarding the potential theocratic despotism represented by the new church order.

On January 19, the day of the deadline for Büren's ouster, the situation on Bremen's streets was unstable. The other three mayors—each of whom supported Musaeus—found themselves under siege, their houses surrounded by angry mobs. Bremen's pastors were similarly threatened. The riotous gatherings persisted even when the January 19 deadline to oust Büren had passed. On January 22, Büren played a strong hand—a very strong hand. In order to restore public peace, the council would need to allow the existing church order, the 1534 church order drawn up by Timann and Probst, to remain in effect. In addition, the council would agree to dismiss Musaeus as superintendent and ban him from the city. Finally, and perhaps most significantly, Büren demanded that the council draft legislation that prevented it from establishing a new church order without the approval of Bremen's citizens.

Rather than acquiesce, the response of the other three mayors—as well as a large portion of council members, Musaeus, and many other clergy—was a walkout. Included in the list of reasons for their flight from Bremen were (1) they had been threatened with death if they did not consent to Büren's demands, (2) the civil and churchly authority had been compromised beyond repair, and (3) they continued to suffer ridicule and fear.

With his many opponents gone from the scene, Mayor Büren, with the support of the remnant councilmen and clergy, was free to fill the empty council seats and pulpits with people more to his liking. Perhaps recognizing that they had snatched defeat from the jaws of victory, many of the preachers and councilmen that left the city never returned. In the span of a single day, Bremen flipped from a stronghold of Gnesio-Lutheranism to a home for Lutheran moderation. Here is how one partisan chronicler of Bremen's church history concluded his account of these events: "In this way Bremen endured the difficult period until the Agreement of Verden (February 25, 1568), where the dispute was decided to the disadvantage of the walkouts. They could return to the city, but now, relieved of their offices, they were deprived of all influence. From January 19, 1562, onward, Bremen remained free of spiritual Tyranny."[45]

Conclusion

What lesson might be learned from the story of Albert van Hardenberg and the openly hostile preachers of Bremen? In the middle of the last century, pastor and theologian Hermann Sasse contended "that every dissension concerning the Gospel necessarily expresses itself in a dissension over the Lord's Supper." Sasse allowed, however, that "the reason for such controversies may be found in a lack of love, as seems to have been the case in Corinth."[46] Sasse's observation shows that even when Lutherans disagree about something as serious and as central as the word and the sacraments, the divide is due to or at least worsened by the lack of love. Certainly, the ever-simmering, often escalating open hostility between the preachers in Bremen betrayed a relative lack of the kind of Christian love that is patient and kind rather than envious, boastful, arrogant, rude, irritable, or resentful. What if disputes among Lutherans were marked by opponents who did not immediately insist on their own way or rejoice in wrongdoing but instead rejoiced in the revealing of the truth? And if this question applies in the midst of conflict about the essentials of word and sacrament, how much more does it apply in the midst of arguments about adiaphora?

Whatever the case, the story of Albert van Hardenberg and the openly hostile preachers of Bremen serves as a cautionary tale. When a lack of love and charity—coupled with an abundance of stridency and a refusal to entertain compromise—cause a group, a congregation, or a church to force others out (or to walk out themselves), then beware! In the end, both the enforcers and the walkouts may gain their purity but lose their influence and maybe even their relevance.

---

45 Rottländer, *Bürgermeister Daniel von Büren*, 88.

46 Hermann Sasse, *This Is My Body: Luther's Contention for the Real Presence in the Sacrament of the Altar* (Minneapolis: Augsburg Fortress, 1959), 3.

Part 2

Reading and Interpreting Texts in the Reformation

The Lectures on Judges

A Witness to Transitions in the Reformation Movement in Wittenberg

Volker Leppin

A great achievement was made for Luther research when Georg Buchwald published what he estimated to be Luther's lectures on Judges in 1884.[1] The text was found in a manuscript of the *Ratsschulbibliothek* in Zwickau, a library with some treasures from the early Reformation era collected by the sixteenth-century Zwickau counsel secretary Stephan Roth. Even though the index of the manuscript itself ascribed the text to Luther,[2] the manuscript tradition is anything but stellar.[3] The manuscript does not give Luther's own text nor even a student's immediate notes from the lecture. It is, at best, a later copy. Furthermore, as Theodor Kolde highlighted, the lecture not only ends with chapter 18 (which might be the result of not completing it in the classroom) but comments on fragments of Judges rather than the book as a whole.[4] Additionally, taking seriously the manuscript's identification of Stephan Roth as the author,[5] the index names another unidentified writer,[6] making the ascription to Luther quite insecure, to say the least.

This means that we neither have a direct witness of the lecture nor know by evidence that this really is Luther's. Further, we do not know who was the first to think it was Luther's, neither do we know the lecture's supposed date.

1 Georg Buchwald, ed., *Dr. Martin Luthers Vorlesung über das Buch der Richter* (Leipzig: Drescher, 1884).

2 L. M. Blankenheim, "Die Richtervorlesung Luthers," *Archiv für Reformationsgeschichte* 51 (1960): 1.

3 See WA 4:527.

4 Theodor Kolde, "Review of Martin Luthers Vorlesung über das Buch der Richter," *Theologische Literaturzeitung* 9 (1884): 557–61, 559.

5 WA 4:VIII.

6 Blankenheim, "Richtervorlesung," 1.

Most scholars are in agreement about dating it to the early years of the Wittenberg movement. This could be true, based on a quotation from Erasmus's *Paraclesis* (one of his prefaces to the *Novum Instrumentum* of 1516),[7] which might serve as a terminus a quo for the lecture. Further dating must depend on an evaluation of the content. Some scholars over the years have clearly denied Luther being the author, while others still maintain it. In any case, one must at least admit that there is no other evidence of Luther having given lectures on Judges, especially during a time when he remembered lecturing on Titus.[8]

1. Who Is the Author?

The clearest evidence of Luther being the author is a nearly word-for-word parallel between a part of the lecture and a phrase in Luther's *Decem praecepta Wittenbergensi praedicta populo* (Sermons on the Ten Commandments), dealing with the priest's obligation to preach the gospel and the very poor state of such preaching in the congregations.[9] Gustav Kawerau pointed to the fact that this text was based on a sermon from September 21, 1516, not only to prove the authenticity of the lectures but also to date them.[10] However, the editorial history of the *Decem praecepta* is quite complex. These texts were indeed based on sermons held at Wittenberg, but the sermon here in question (at least in its reported version) does not cover the passage picked up in the lecture.[11] Thus this paragraph might have been added to the *Decem praecepta* at any time between 1516 and 1518; it does not provide an exact date of the lecture before the later date. Further, there is also the possibility that someone—whether the first reporter or a later writer—inserted it into the lectures from the printed version of the *Decem praecepta*, slightly revising it.

7 Cf Anon., *Praelectio in librum Iudicum*, WA 4:569.7–11; see Erasmus von Rotterdam, *Paraclesis*, in *Werke*, ed. Werner Welzig (Darmstadt, 1995), 3:16. See also Erasmus, letter to Nicolaus Everardi, May 15, 1524 (OPVS EPISTOLARVM | DES. ERASMI ROTERODAMI [. . .]; Basel: Froben, 1529), 810, referred to in WA 4:569 n1 and page VIII.

8 WA TR 3:477.19, nr. 3644c; WA TR 4:223.33, nr. 4323.

9 Cf. Anon., *Praelectio in librum Iudicum*, WA 4:538.6–17, with Luther, *Decem praecepta*, WA 1:445.16–26.

10 WA 4:528.

11 Luther, *Sermo Die sancti Matthaei*, WA 1:85–87.

Even more, the very same passage suggests a person other than Luther as a possible author. The paragraph discusses the need of parishioners to attend worship, which was debated around 1517. On November 13 of that year, Pope Leo X announced in the breve *Intelleximus quosdam*, "Believers who attend the mass on Sundays or Feasts outside their parish church in congregations of the mendicant orders fulfill the ecclesiastical precepts regarding mass attendance."[12] With this, the pope took a clear position in an ongoing debate between Caspar Schatzgeyer and Johann von Staupitz. Staupitz, despite being a mendicant himself, argued in a treatise of 1500 for the need to attend the parish worship service.[13] Schatzgeyer then attacked him in a treatise pleading for the right to join the mendicants' services.[14] If the lectures on Judges referred to this very question and even considered it further, then this seems to indicate that the lecturer had some common interest with Staupitz. This might be the case with Luther, but it could also be true of others. The fact that the question had become current again at the end of 1517 might also suggest the origin of the lecture can be dated after 1517 rather than earlier, even if that cannot be certain.

This then brings Staupitz onto the scene as a possible author, as August Wilhelm Dieckhoff argued quite early.[15] Nevertheless, over the last few decades, it has been almost forgotten that reasonable observations used to promote Luther's authorship could support an identical argument for Staupitz as the author. The first of these is the emphatic use of Psalm 119:94, "Tuus sum ego, salvum me fac" (I am yours; save me) in the text.[16] Karlstadt described this verse as Staupitz's *dicterium* (a kind of motto).[17] This is supported, for example,

12 Leo X, *Intelleximus quosdam*, in *Bullarum diplomatum et privilegiorum Sanctorum Romanorum pontificium Taurinensis*, Bullarium romanum ed. (Turin: Franco et Dalmazzo, 1860), 5:710n29.

13 Johann von Staupitz, *Decisio quaestionis de audientia missae*, in *Sämtliche Schriften*, by Johann von Staupitz, ed. Lothar Graf zu Dohna and Richard Wetzel (Berlin: De Gruyter, 2001), 5:25–41.

14 S. Wolfgang Günter, "Einleitung," in Staupitz, 5:11.

15 August Wilhelm Dieckhoff, "Die neu aufgefundene Vorlesung über das Buch der Richter," *Zeitschrift für kirchliche Wissenschaft und kirchliches Leben* 5 (1884): 356–61, 359.

16 Anon., *Praelectio in librum Iudicum*, WA 4:557.19–24, 568.10f. Psalm 119 is 118 in the Vulgate.

17 Ernst Köhler, ed., *Karlstadt und Augustin. Der Kommentar des Andreas Bodenstein von Karlstadt zu Augustins Schrift De spiritu et littera* (Halle: Niemeyer, 1952), 6, 20.

by the 1517 edition of Staupitz's *Libellus de exsecutione aeternae praedestinationis*, which bears exactly this verse on the front page; it also appeared in other publications by Staupitz.[18] Another argument suggesting Staupitz as the author of the Judges lectures seems to exclude Luther completely: in his explanation of the shibboleth in Judges 12:6, the lecturer draws a comparison with the German dialects: as in ancient Israel, there was a difference between the Saxons saying *santifizetur* and "nos Misnenses" saying *sanctificetur*,[19] with the latter identifying the speaker as a person from Meißen. Even if Gustav Kawerau made some efforts to claim this as a possible Luther self-identification, there is no positive evidence that Luther referred to himself this way.[20] More honestly, Georg Buchwald states, "Here it must be admitted that Luther could not have spoken that way

---

18 Lothar Graf zu Dohna and Richard Wetzel, eds., *Johann von Staupitz, Sämtliche Schriften*, vol. 2, *Abhandlungen, Predigten, Zeugnisse* (Berlin, 1979), 70; see also Heiko Augustinus Oberman, "Tuus sum, salvum me fac. Augustinrévail zwischen Reniassance and Reformation," in *Scientia Augustiniana* (Würzburg: Augustinus, 1975), 349–94; Dieckhoff, "Vorlesung," 358.

19 Anon., *Praelectio in librum Iudicum*, WA 4:576.9f.

20 In WA 4:576n1, he refers to *Crucigers Sommerpostille*, WA 21:438.36, where Luther speaks about "unser Sachssen," thereby implying that he himself is not one of them. This is true, and Luther, identifying himself as born in Mansfeld (see the notice "de Mansfeld" in *Das Bakkalarenregister der Artistenfakultät der Universität Erfurt 1392–1521*, ed. Rainer C. Schwinges and Klaus Wriedt [Jena: Fischer, 1995], 273) with Thuringian ancestors, had reasons to do so. Nevertheless, he also refers to himself as part of "nos Saxones." WA TR 4:366.1f., nr. 4533. In no way did Luther ever have reasons to identify himself positively as a Meißen person. Another way to understand this is as a linguistic identification with the court's language, which obviously was the language of Meißen. But while that argument refers to language, the wording itself identifies persons, so the argument that Luther identifies himself as a district's vicar of Meißen and Thuringia (Hermann Hering, "Der Streit über die Echtheit eines Lutherfundes," *Theologische Studien und Kritiken* 58 [1885]: 537–60, 547; see, e.g., Luther, letter to Johannes Bercken, May 1, 1516, WA Br 1:38f., nr. 13, 27) is not convincing, since this district included monasteries in Saxony like Wittenberg and Dresden and was part of the Saxonian reform congregation of the Augustinian Hermits. Cf. Adalbero Kunzelmann, *Geschichte der deutschen Augustiner-Eremiten*, vol. 5, *Die sächsisch-thüringiche Provinz und die sächsische Reformkongregation bis zum Untergang der beiden* (Würzburg: Augustinus, 1974), 471.

and that it would not make sense to go to any pains to explain it."[21] This short remark then makes it almost impossible to identify Luther as the author of the entire text. On the other hand, as a descendant of Meißen nobility, Staupitz certainly could have used the phrase.[22]

Nevertheless, the debate between Buchwald and Dieckhoff about Staupitz's or Luther's authorship did not bring a clear result in the end, even if Heinrich Suso Denifle added more arguments against Luther as the author.[23] Denifle showed that the text was mainly a compilation of citations from Augustine. He then concluded polemically, "But Luther, then, is not the author of the Judges lectures. Or would Protestant Luther researchers rather admit that Luther was the kind of a nasty plagiarist that the author of the lectures on Judges proves himself to be?"[24] Denifle's argument was so widely accepted that he simply omitted it from the second edition of his book.[25] Later on, Carl Stange made an attempt to attribute the lecture to Karlstadt,[26] while L. M. Blankenheim pled anew for Luther. Besides some similarities in content, Blankenheim argued mainly on the basis of linguistic similarities,[27] neglecting Dieckhoff's clear argument that linguistic details in a copy of a student's report could never give a reliable basis for identifying an author because reporting and copying might have affected the language used.[28] Blankenheim's argument is therefore anything but convincing.

After long debates about Luther's theological development, one must also add that even arguments about content do not give a safe basis for identifying

---

21 Georg Buchwald, "Hat die Vorlesung über das Buch der Richter Luther oder Staupitz zum Verfasser?" *Zeitschrift für kirchliche Wissenschaft und kirchliches Leben* 5 (1884): 630–37, here 634. See also L. M. Blankenheim, "Die Richtervorlesung Luthers," *Archiv für Reformationsgeschichte* 51 (1960): 14, which somehow agrees with this.

22 Dieckhoff, "Vorlesung," 358f.

23 Heinrich Suso Denifle, *Luther und das Luthertum* (Mainz: Kirchheim, 1904), 1:46–54.

24 Denifle, 1:51.

25 Denifle, 1:X-XI.

26 Carl Stange, "Luthers angebliche Vorlesung zum Richter-Buch," *Zeitschrift für systematische Theologie* 23 (1954): 304–33.

27 Blankenheim, "Richtervorlesung," 13.

28 August Wilhelm Dieckhoff, "Antwort auf die Entgegnung des Dr. Buchwald," *Zeitschrift für kirchliche Wissenschaft und kirchliches Leben* 5 (1884): 638–49, 643.

him as the author. Some of the lecture's content might go against what we expect from Luther, but that would not necessarily contradict the possibility of its being written by him. This deliberation becomes even stronger if we take into consideration that the lectures are commonly seen as having been held in the context of the convent of the Augustinian Hermits, which might make some more traditional, seemingly not-Lutheran arguments more probable than in other contexts, even if Luther is still the author.

Bernhard Lohse was the first to examine the consequences of this complicated state of research. In his famous study on monasticism and Reformation, he discussed the question of the Judges lectures extensively, coming to the Solomonic solution that Blankenheim might have been a bit "too optimistic" ascribing the lecture completely to Luther, while Stange had gone a bit "too far" to deny it. He himself drew the conclusion that one of Luther's students might have compiled some texts relating to some of Luther's original material for his own lectures.[29] Lohse thus anticipated later insights about the Wittenberg theology as more of a group phenomenon than the work of one single person.[30] This position was widely accepted, as can be seen in the Weimar edition follow-up of 1980, which completely asserts Lohse's position.[31] Nevertheless, one has to ask if this position isn't still too focused on Luther himself. Lohse's aim was to discover Luther's early views of monasticism, which meant that he considered the question about the Judges lectures entirely under the perspective of if and how far it might give information about Luther.

However, without having Luther in mind from the very beginning, one might also revisit the Staupitz argument, together with Denifle's observation about the consistent citations of Augustine. In this way, one might slightly modify Lohse's conclusion: what we have here need not be a text based on a Luther lecture series (which would still not explain the Meißen allusion), but

29 Bernhard Lohse, *Mönchtum und Reformation. Luthers Auseinandersetzung mit dem Mönchsideal des Mittelalters* (Göttingen: Vandenhoeck & Ruprecht, 1963), 324.

30 See the dissertation of one of his students: Jens-Martin Kruse, *Universitätstheologie und Kirchenreform. Die Anfänge der Reformation in Wittenberg 1516–1522* (Mainz: Zabern, 2002). This might be the right place in a contribution to a Wengert Festschrift to mention that Philip Melanchthon was definitely a very important figure among this group, even if we cannot ascribe anything of the Judges lectures to him.

31 WA 60:327.

rather could be a compilation of pieces of different origin, some referring to Luther, but some also to Staupitz or the Church Fathers. In that case, it would not be a clear record of Luther's impact, but more a document of convictions shared in the group gathered around Staupitz in Wittenberg that increasingly came to view Luther as its leading figure. For this way of thinking, we need to leave nineteenth-century reasoning even further behind than Lohse did. This text cannot be explained by any theory of single authorship, family tree, or direct filiation. It is a compilation. That makes it less significant with respect to specific authors but more significant for an understanding of the building of a group identity in Wittenberg at the beginning of the sixteenth century.

2. Sin and Justification

The lecture does not contain a great number of references to the doctrine of justification. When it speaks about it, the phrases are neither strong nor exclusive. Again, this does not mean that they could not be Luther's. But we do not meet a strong concept of justification by faith alone here. The concentration on grace that is clearly observed throughout the lectures is not surprising against the medieval background, especially for the Wittenberg movement. However, it is interesting to see how this grace works according to the lecture: all has to be done by and be given by God.[32] What has to be touched in the human being is the heart.[33] Here, the human being has to see themselves as completely unworthy: "For God operates with his grace most in those who in their heart regard themselves truly as nothing, and who are despised by all human beings."[34] A sentence like this would clearly match what Ernst Bizer has identified as a "theology of humility" in Luther's early lectures, a kind of theology that does not prescribe any human acts for God's salvation but rather emphasizes a certain attitude.[35] If it were a Luther text, this theology of humility might support an earlier date than the reference to the *Decem praecepta* mentioned above would allow. At the same time, there is reason to view Bizer's concept

32 Anon., *Praelectio in librum Iudicum*, WA 4:530.23–26.

33 Anon., 4:566.7–9.

34 Anon., 4:557.12f.

35 Ernst Bizer, *Fides ex auditu. Eine Untersuchung über die Entdeckung der Gerechtigkeit Gottes durch Martin Luther* (Neukirchen: Buchhandlung des Erziehungsvereins, 1958).

of Luther's development as too strict.[36] Once again, this might push the traditional assumptions a little bit, but it still does not make a case—positive or negative—for authorship.

Things become even more complicated when we see what follows the grace that has entered into the hearts of believers: they will sanctify themselves and purify their hearts "through confession and penance from bad deeds."[37] Penance, good works, and confession are so completely mixed up here that we do not find that clear distinction—which Timothy Wengert has identified in Luther and the *Ninety-Five Theses*—between penance as "a change of mind or heart" and penance as a sacrament.[38] Again we might legitimately wonder if we have here an author other than Luther, an earlier Luther, or just a Luther in another mood.

The same has to be asked when we observe what is said about sin in the lectures. In an allegorical explanation of Judges 4:14, the author speaks about human weakness, saying that baptism liberates human beings, although some weakness and servitude remain. All "our earlier sin" (peccatum . . . a nobis antea), the author says, would be erased by baptism, while some weakness would remain, which could lead us to continue to serve the law of sin.[39] This sounds different from what Luther himself taught about original sin as "radical sin" in his *Lectures on Romans*, deviating even further as the argument in the Judges lectures leads to the idea that grace will reign regarding the sin of the baptized.[40] Obviously, the notion of controlling sin (peccatum regnatum) is rooted in Romans 6:12 and was not unknown to the early Luther. But the link with baptism became a major issue when Luther struggled with Latomus about the meaning of original sin.[41] Naturally, as described above, the Latomus controversy

36 See Volker Leppin, "Demutstheologie," in *Das Luther-Lexikon*, ed. Volker Leppin and Gury Schneider-Ludorff (Regensburg, 2014), 157f., Leppin, "Reformatorische Entdeckung," in *Luther-Lexikon*, 589–92.

37 Anon., *Praelectio in librum Iudicum*, WA 4:567.25f.

38 Timothy J. Wengert, *Word of Life: Introducing Lutheran Hermeneutics* (Minneapolis: Fortress, 2019), 69.

39 Anon., *Praelectio in librum Iudicum*, WA 4:550.26–36.

40 Anon., 4:550.36–551.1.

41 See Bo Kristian Holm, *Gabe und Geben bei Luther. Das Verhältnis zwischen Reziprozivität und reformatorischer Rechtfertigungslehre* (Berlin: De Gruyter, 2006), 134.

does not fit well with the Judges lectures' unsophisticated understanding of original sin.

3. Hermeneutics

A similarly confusing situation arises in the question of hermeneutics. It is certainly not new to note that the *Lectures on Romans* takes the liberty of using allegorical interpretation. Kenneth Hagen has shown that the widespread understanding of Luther as being completely against allegory is inaccurate.[42] Surprising, however, is another aspect of hermeneutics in the Judges lectures: it argues against those who interpret Scripture in an unspiritual way. The lecturer asserts that no one should try to understand Scripture according to his or her own sense ("proprio . . . ingenio").[43] This seems to fit very well with Luther's argument in the Augsburg debate with Cajetan, when he presumably referred to canon law[44] to say that no one should follow their own sense in interpreting the Scripture.[45] But while Luther here contrasted one's own sense with a pure sense of Scripture ("non afferendas, sed referendas esse ex sacris litteris intelligentias"), the author of the lectures on Judges develops the notion of a common sense of the believers in the church: "But regarding all that has been written after the Lord's ascension with canonical truth and authority: which believer and true theologian should not read this with equal sense, even if he has not yet understood it?"[46] This question directly opposes the position that Luther expressed in this period (especially after the Leipzig Disputation), increasingly stressing the difference between Scripture and tradition over against the usual attempt to harmonize them.[47] Ironically, the view of the Judges lectures

42 Cf. Kenneth Hagen, *Luther's Approach to Scripture as Seen in His "Commentaries" on Galatians, 1519–1538* (Tübingen: Mohr, 1993); see also Gerhard Ebeling, *Evangelische Evangelienauslegung. Eine Untersuchung zu Luthers Hermeneutik* (München: Kaiser, 1942).

43 Anon., *Praelectio in librum Iudicum*, WA 4:542.16f.

44 C. 24 q. 3 c. 27.

45 Luther, *Acta Augustana*, WA 2:17.8f.; cf. *Corpus iuris canonici*, ed. Emil Friedberg (Leipzig: Tauchnitz, 1879), 1:998; Reinhard Schwarz, *Martin Luther. Lehrer der christlichen Religion* (Tübingen: Mohr, 2015), 34n32.

46 Anon., *Praelectio in librum Iudicum*, WA 4:448.14–16.

47 For further arguments, see Volker Leppin, "Die Genese des reformatorischen Schriftprinzips. Beobachtungen zu Luthers Auseinandersetzung mit Johann Eck

more closely resembles the way the argument was turned against Luther in the papal bull *Exsurge Domine*, which accused him of following his own sense and neglecting the interpretation of the Scripture as given by the saints.[48] This, too, makes it rather difficult to assign the lectures to Luther himself.

4. Monastic Life

At the very least, the lecturer seems to be one of Luther's brethren in the Augustinian order. Whoever the author might be, the text makes clear that it is the work of a monk for monks, as it refers to *nobis religiosis* in a certain context.[49] The text might even have the novices specifically in mind: it contains a longer passage about those who, as the lecturer says, came to the order so as to flee to Christ and the cross and voluntarily carry the cross itself.[50] The monastic context seems to be especially clear in the notion that novices had to give up their own will and submit to their superiors:[51] "Abbot, prior, severe master, and this in behalf of the cross and the love of God."[52] In this perspective, belonging to a monastic order and being part of the monastic hierarchy enables people to fulfill the very special Christian virtue of self-abandonment.

At some point, these views about humility and carrying of the cross were taken as an indication of Luther's authorship of the lectures, because one indeed finds those values in his letters of the time.[53] Even more clearly, however, these

bis zur Leipziger Disputation," in *Transformationen. Studien zu den Wandlungsprozessen in Theologie und Frömmigkeit zwischen Spätmittelalter und Reformation* (Tübingen: Mohr, 2018), 355–97; Leppin, "Differenz oder Harmonie. Die Herausbildung der konfessionellen Unterschiede im Schriftverständnis vor spätmittelalterlichem Hintergrund," *Jahrbuch für biblische Theologie* 31 (2016): 225–44.

48 Peter Fabisch and Erwin Iserloh, eds., *Exsurge Domine*, in *Dokumente zur Causa Lutheri (1517–1521)* (Münster: Aschendorff, 1991), 2:366.

49 Anon., *Praelectio in librum Iudicum*, WA 4:535.9; cf. 4:536.30f.: "Tota vita christiani boni, presertim religiosi, sanctum desiderium est."

50 Anon., 4:546.21–23.

51 Anon., 4:546.24–26.

52 Anon., 4:546.29: "Abbatem, priorem, magistrum durum, et hoc propter crucem et dilectionem Dei."

53 Kolde, "Review," 560; Hering, "Streit," 547. Maybe the most clear indication is his letter to Spalatin, presumably December 31, 1516 (WA Br 1:81–83, nr. 31), with its criticism of the veneration of saints, neglecting the values of humility.

ideas can be found in a letter that Staupitz wrote to Luther around the time of December 1518.[54] Here Staupitz emphatically stated a common conviction about the Augustinian order, as Jordan of Saxony had identified carrying the cross as a core value of Augustinian Hermits.[55]

The lectures on Judges fit perfectly into this tradition, giving clear advice to the novices and monks on how to perform their monastic life under the sign of the cross.[56] Certainly, an important part of polemical support is the question of how to deal with doubts and even despair. The lecture here is clear: "Note that there are two kinds of despair, a good one and a bad one."[57] The good one is despair about our own means and works, while the bad one is despair about God. This sounds similar to Luther's spiritual advice. But as Richard Wetzels has shown, it is also a major issue in Staupitz's writings.[58] Here, the lecture suggests that the way to avoid the bad form of despair is immediately linked with the Staupitz motto, "Tuus sum ego,"[59] which again strengthens the track leading to Staupitz, perhaps not as the author himself but as a person in the background of the whole text.

Conclusion: A Piece of Monastic Pastoral Care in the Staupitz Circle

This overview of the lecture has confirmed its patchwork style. It might be a single person's work, combining different traditions. The date still is quite unclear. The relation to the printed version of the *Decem praecepta* makes a time after 1518 likely. If our observation regarding *peccatum regnatum* is right, we might

54 Staupitz, letter to Luther, December 1518[?], WA 1:265–67, nr. 119.1–5: "In patientia possidere animam pro salute. [. . .] Videtur mihi mundus contra veritatem exasperatus; olim in tanto odio fuisset crucifixus Christus, et quid hodie praeter crucem te maneat non video quicquam."

55 See Jordan of Saxony, *Liber Vitasfratrum* 3.11, 4.5, in *Liber Vitasfratrum*, by Jordani de Saxonia, ed. Rudolph Arbesmann and Winfrid Hümpfner (New York: 1943), 358, 402.

56 Anon., *Praelectio in librum Iudicum*, WA 4:546.20–547.15.

57 Anon., 4:557.14: "Nota igitur, quod desperatio est duplex, bona et mala."

58 Richard Wetzel, "Staupitz und Luther," in *Staupitz, theologischer Lehrer Luthers*, Lothar Graf zu Dohna and Richard Wetzel (Tübingen: Mohr, 2018), 191.

59 Anon., *Praelectio in librum Iudicum*, WA 4:557.20.

even arrive at a date after the publication of *Against Latomus* (*Antilatomus*) in September 1521.[60]

The lecture seems to have been held in the Augustinian convent of Wittenberg. This means that it must have taken place before the final closure of the monastery. The convent began imploding when it lost fifteen of its members as early as November 1521.[61] It was completely "depopulated" (entvölkert) in 1522 when no one remained besides Luther, "the former prior Eberhard Brisger and the procurator Bruno."[62] Nevertheless, we know that even in this time, beginning in February 1523,[63] Luther held lectures on Deuteronomy "for my brethren" (fratribus meis).[64] These brothers might not have been only Augustinians, as Johannes Bugenhagen reported hearing the lectures himself.[65]

This might indicate that the lectures in the monastery had continued all the time. We know that Konrad Held was a lector in the monastery starting in 1519, but it is rather unlikely that the lectures on Judges, with their somehow Lutheran sound, were given by him, since he left the monastery in 1522 in opposition to Reformation measures.[66] Therefore, one possible candidate might be his successor Eberhard Brisger, but uncertainty remains.[67] We know that in the time of Luther's exile at Wartburg Castle, others tried to replace him in delivering lectures, attempting to follow his meaning closely, as can be seen in Nikolaus von Amsdorf's university lectures on Hebrews, which he based on Luther's text.[68] The same thing might have been happening in the monastery. Thus the lectures might belong to the years 1521/22, with the awareness that

60 WA 8:40.

61 Kunzelmann, *Geschichte*, 501.

62 Kunzelmann, 502f.

63 WA 14:494.

64 Luther, *Deuteronomium cum annotationibus*, WA 14:497.6f.

65 See WA 14:744–53; see also his own lectures on Deuteronomy, to a certain degree following Luther's: *IOAN|NIS BVGENHAGII | POMERANI ANNO|tationes ab ipso iam emiss.| In Deuteronomium.| In Samuelem prophetam,| id est duos libros Regum.|* [. . .] (Basel: Adam Petri, 1524).

66 Kunzelmann, *Geschichte*, 248n1299.

67 Kunzelmann, 402n2437.

68 Ulrich Köpf, "Nikolaus von Amsdorf an der Universität Wittenberg. [mit Abdruck von Disputationsthesen Amsdorfs]," in *Nikolas von Amsdorf (1483–1565) zwischen Reformation und Politik*, ed. Irene Dingel (Leipzig: Evangelische Verlagsanstalt, 2008), 51.

this period could be prolonged a bit, as Luther might not have immediately returned as a lector in the monastery when he came back from Wartburg Castle. This then leaves time for the Judges lectures to have taken place between the Diet of Worms in 1521 and Luther's later lectures on Deuteronomy. This would be the time when Luther started translating Judges; the manuscript for his translation dates it as 1523.[69] All of this makes it quite likely that one of his brethren, possibly Eberhard Brisger, replaced him as a lecturer in the convent and worked on Judges as a help for the translation in 1522/23.[70] Brisger might then have combined quotations and fragments from Augustine, Staupitz, and Luther into a new compilation.

All of this is anything but sure. Even without an exact date and a named person, the text in itself is a compilation and combination of Augustinian reform ideas and Luther's theological novelties, showing how people involved in the process slowly adopted something that, in retrospect, we call a kind of Reformation theology. This theology did not happen all at once; rather, it evolved over time. Seen in this perspective, the lectures on Judges give insight into this process of slow transformation among the Augustinian brothers in Wittenberg, who were still influenced by Staupitz and newly inspired by Martin Luther, sometime between 1519 and 1523.

69 WA DB 1:1.

70 Unfortunately, Brisger was no Meißen native. Therefore, on this point, the most likely explanation is still a remembrance of Staupitz.

Luther, the Genitive, and the Gospel

Erik H. Herrmann

Sitting at his evening table with colleagues and students, Luther reflected back on some of his early insights into understanding the gospel. In this instance, he reminisced about how his understanding of the genitive construct, *iustitia dei*—the "righteousness of God" (e.g., Rom 1:17)—when combined with a new understanding of law and gospel, led him to what he called his "breakthrough." His colleague Johannes Bugenhagen eagerly agreed with Luther's account, relating his own similar moment of insight into another genitive phrase, *caritas dei*—"the love of God": "'I also began to change my mind when I read *caritas dei* according to what it means *passively*, namely that by which we are loved *by God*. Before I always understood the love *actively*, namely that by which *we* love God.' The Doctor [Luther] replied, 'Yes that is clear—*caritas* or *dilectione*!—it is often understood in the Scriptures in this way; namely, that by which God loves us. But the genitives of love in the Hebrew language are difficult.'"[1] Much has been written about the nature and timing of Luther's theological breakthrough; this essay will not reprise that literature or enter into that debate, which, after one hundred years, has exhausted many scholars if not every source.[2] Rather, of interest here is the pairing of evangelical insight with something as mundane and tedious as grammar and syntax. In particular, our focus is the ambiguity and versatility of the genitive construct

1 WA TR 5:210.17–22, 210.35–40, nr. 5518. See also Martin Lohrmann, "A Newly Discovered Report of Luther's Reformation Breakthrough from Johannes Bugenhagen's 1550 Jonah Commentary," *Lutheran Quarterly* 22 (2008): 324–34. Emphasis in the original.

2 See, for example, Bernard Lohse, ed., *Der Durchbruch der reformatorischen Erkenntnis bei Luther* (Darmstadt: Wissenschaftliche Buchgesellschaft, 1968); Lohse, *Der Durchbruch der reformatorischen Erkenntnis bei Luther: Neuere Untersuchungen* (Stuttgart: Steiner Verlag, 1988).

that served as catalyst for Luther's theological reflection during his early exegetical activity.

Before grammarian readers become dizzy with anticipation, a caveat needs mention: modern grammatical categories and labels for kinds and uses of the genitive are generally not part of sixteenth-century usage or consideration.[3] For example, the Luther scholar, Emanuel Hirsch, labeled Luther's evangelical reading of the "righteousness of God" as a *genitive auctoris*, but noted that any genitive construct that did not indicate possession would have been labeled "passive" by Luther (whereas a simple *Eigentumsgenitiv* would have been labeled "active").[4] Modern classifications of the genitive are legion: David Wallace identifies more than sixty uses of the genitive in koine Greek, Paul Friedrich mentions seventy-eight different subtypes of genitive in Homeric Greek, and Waltke and O'Connor list at least twenty-five "species" of the Hebrew genitive.[5] Admittedly, these are merely descriptions of various interpretations of the construct derived not from distinct grammatical forms or syntax but from contextual cues along with the interpreter's larger assumptions. Along the same lines, Luther will point to the larger contextual elements that lead him to read these constructs in a certain and very often new way.

Early on in Luther's lecturing career, he recognized the uniqueness of the biblical language and its mode of expression. In his first lectures on the psalms he followed the traditional view, one going back to Origen, that the Scriptures intentionally contain absurdities and strange expressions as signals and prompts to

---

3 E.g., the Latin grammars of Donatus and Aldus Manutius, Johannes Reuchlin's *De rudimentis hebraicis* (1506) and *Micropedia* (1478), and Melanchthon's own Greek grammar (1518).

4 Emanuel Hirsch, "Initium Theologiae Lutheri," in *Lutherstudien* (Gütersloh: C. Bertelsmann, 1954), 2:9–35. On the grammatical implications of the Hebrew "active" and "passive" for Luther's interpretation of Paul, see also Brian Cummings, *The Literary Culture of the Reformation: Grammar and Grace* (Oxford: Oxford University Press, 2002), 79–88.

5 Daniel B. Wallace, *Greek Grammar: Beyond the Basics* (Grand Rapids, MI: Zondervan, 1996), 72–136; Paul Friedrich, "Proto-Indo-European Syntax: The Order of Meaningful Elements," *Journal of Indo-European Studies* Monograph 1 (Butte: Montana College of Mineral Science and Technology, 1975), 13; Bruce K. Waltke and M. O'Conner, *An Introduction to Biblical Hebrew Syntax* (Winona Lake, IN: Eisenbrauns, 1990), 136–60.

move beyond the literal sense of the text and consider deeper, spiritual meanings.[6] But as he moved on to lecture on Romans, Luther began to see an even deeper incongruity: namely, that between the common scholastic readings shaped by Aristotelian language—*modus loquendi Aristoteli / scholastici / philosophiae*—and that manner of speaking found in Saint Paul and the rest of the Scriptures, the *modus loquendi apostoli / scripturae / theologicus.*[7] He increasingly found that the rules of language and logic in which he had been trained were ill-matched with the biblical argument. Along with the shedding of several principal frameworks by which the Scriptures had been traditionally interpreted, Luther began to reach new conclusions about the nature of theological language and the narrative context that reshaped even the simplest of phrases. In the following examples, we will illustrate this relationship between the emergence of Luther's theology and some of his "evangelical genitives."

1. *PLENITUDO TEMPORIS*: THE FULLNESS OF TIME

Luther's first lectures on the Psalms, the so-called *Dictata super psalterium* (1513–15), reveal a time of theological and hermeneutical ferment in which he tested the exegetical tradition and creatively appropriated many of its themes. While new ideas and emphases are clearly present in these lectures, in many of the most important ways, Luther is still operating firmly within the traditional framework. The most significant of these was how the relationship between the testaments was conceived, both theologically and hermeneutically.[8]

In brief, the two testaments were seen as two epochs in the divinely ordered history of salvation, unfolding in graduated continuity. The Old Testament was likened to a time of infancy and immaturity but also a time of preparation and instruction in which God's people were being formed for the coming of the Christ and his kingdom revealed in the New Testament. As such, the

6 Origen, *De Principiis* IV.1.15. See also Luther's marginal notes to Faber Stapulensis, WA 4:476.11–20.

7 E.g., WA 56:334f. (Rom 7:1f.; Sch). See also Leif Grane, "Modus Loquendi Theologicus: Luthers Kampf um die Erneuerung der Theologie (1515–1518)," in *Acta Theologica Danica*, vol. 12 (Leiden: Brill, 1975).

8 See especially Gerhard Ebeling, "Die Anfänge von Luthers Hermeneutik," in *Lutherstudien* (Tübingen: Mohr Siebeck, 1971), 1:1–68; James S. Preus, *From Shadow to Promise: Old Testament Interpretation from Augustine to the Young Luther* (Cambridge, MA: Harvard, 1969).

time of the Old Testament was necessarily imperfect in its piety, incomplete in its understanding of the truth, and inferior in its religious condition. Likewise, the deepest spiritual truths of its Scriptures were difficult to see, veiled beneath figures and types, largely inaccessible to most until its revelation with the coming of Christ and the outpouring of his grace and spirit. As the husk of a seed both hides and contains the kernel that would one day grow into a grand and magnificent tree, the Old Testament contains *in sedes* that which would come to fruition in the New, and that which was temporal, earthly, and obscure would give way to that which was eternal, spiritual, clear, and bright.

This need for spiritual insight and interpretation was also true for the Old Testament's law. On the one hand, the rites and ceremonies contained in the Law of Moses had a spiritual dimension that pointed ahead to the time of Christ. Yet without the grace and Spirit given in the New Testament, this understanding remained largely hidden from those who lived under this law. Even its moral law had a deeper spiritual meaning that required Christ's explication by the giving of his "new law" in the Sermon on the Mount. With these basic assumptions in place, the theological tradition that Luther inherited regarded the gospel as a spiritual "new law" and Christ as the new Moses, even as the entire New Testament was a perfecting and fulfilling of the Old. How this view of the Christ and the gospel affected Luther is well-known even as it rests at the heart of what he called his "breakthrough": "I lacked nothing before this except that I made no distinction between the law and the gospel. I regarded both as one thing and said that there was no difference between Christ and Moses except time and perfection. But when I discovered the proper distinction, that the law is one thing and the gospel is another, I broke through."[9]

Bearing all this in mind, we return now to the *Dictata* to look at our first example, when such a breakthrough still lay in the future.[10] The traditional salvation-historical structure of law and gospel and the two testaments holds Luther's attention throughout his various reflections on the Psalter, whether as prophetic allegories speaking with the voice of Christ or of those in Israel who faithfully waited for his coming. As he expounded these ideas, passages from

9 WA TR 5:210.6f., nr. 5518.

10 For an analysis of Luther's understanding of Galatians 3 and 4 in the *Dictata*, see Erik Herrmann, "'Why Then the Law?' Salvation History and the Law in Martin Luther's Interpretation of Galatians 1513–1522" (PhD diss., Concordia Seminary, St. Louis, 2005), 67–146.

Galatians 3 and 4 were regularly cited because of their focus on this transition from the old to the new, from the time of the law to the time of faith. Accordingly, Galatians 4 speaks of the time before Christ as a time of infancy and servitude but then, "when the fullness of time [plenitudo temporis] had come, God sent his son, born of a woman, born under the law, in order to redeem those who were under the law, so that we might receive adoption as children" (Gal 4:4). The passage seems pretty straightforward, stating that God sent the Son at the time predetermined and set for the redemption of God's people, as stated in the previous verse: "the time fixed beforehand by the Father" (usque ad praefinitum tempus a patre). But in the *Dictata*, Luther often inverts the genitive construct, "the fullness of time," to *tempus plenitudino*—the "time of fullness." Why?

Luther is simply following what he earlier learned in Peter Lombard's *Sentences* and the *Glossa ordinaria* (which was likely also derived from Lombard's glosses on the Pauline Epistles).[11] As an introduction to book 3, which was on the incarnation of Christ, Lombard begins with the words of Galatians 4:4 and then comments, "But the 'time of fullness' (*tempus plenitudinis*) is called the 'time of grace' (*tempus gratiae*), because from the advent of the Savior it took up its beginning. This is the 'time of mercy' (*tempus miserendi*, Ps. 101:14) and the 'year of kindness' (*annus benignitatis*, Ps. 64:12), in which grace and truth came through Jesus Christ (John 1:17): 'grace' because it is through love that what was commanded in the law is fulfilled; 'truth' because it is through the advent of Christ that the redemption of humanity, which was promised from ancient times, is exhibited and perfected."[12] The idea expressed here is consonant with the relation of the testaments described earlier: the New Testament distinguishes itself from the Old Testament by its spiritual plenitude. With the coming of Christ, the truth of our redemption that lay hidden in the ancient Scriptures was finally revealed. With his advent, grace is finally showered on

11 Lombard's *Sentences* was intended as an expansion and explanation of the *Gloss* compiled by Anselm of Laon. Lombard's additions to Anselm on the Psalter and Pauline Epistles, known as the *Magna Glosatura*, are represented in what later became the *Glossa ordinaria*. Furthermore, it is quite possible that Lombard envisioned his glosses on Paul as a companion text for the *Sentences*. See Beryl Smalley, *The Study of the Bible in the Middle Ages* (Notre Dame, IN: Notre Dame, 1978), 64–65; Marcia L. Colish, *Peter Lombard* (Leiden: Brill, 1994), 1:24–25.

12 Lombard, *Sentences*, III, d. 1.

his people so that by the infusion of its love, the law may be fully and spiritually fulfilled. These are precisely the same ideas that Luther continues to emphasize in his first lectures.

In Psalm 77:2,[13] the psalmist says, "I will open my mouth in a parable; I will utter dark sayings from of old." Even though this passage is cited by the gospels, Luther wonders why it does not read instead, "I will *open parables* with my mouth," given that Christ often revealed that which lay hidden. He goes on to say, "This [opening of parables] Christ did likewise and arranged for his own to do it after the sending of the Holy Spirit. For in the 'time of fullness' (*tempus plenitudinis*), he who formerly opened only the mouth of the prophets opened his own mouth. For he was not in the habit of speaking to the people with his own mouth, but he did so with the mouth of Moses and the prophets."[14] By characterizing the salvation-historical difference of the testaments as the difference between veiled, mediated speech and clear revelation, Luther follows in the footsteps of tradition. In the Old Testament, evangelical grace and the righteousness of faith were only expressed in "riddles," their meaning not yet revealed.[15] But looking ahead to the time of spiritual fullness, Christ will reveal all things: "Moses has an alien mouth, namely Aaron. But now I open my own mouth, so as not to speak through another in *umbra et figura*. . . . I will preach openly and [I will open] the revealed spirit of the letter."[16]

In the course of the lectures, Luther would invoke the same genitive construct and its inversion a handful of times, all to make the same point: the unfolding of salvation history from the Old Testament to the New was a movement from imperfect to perfect, from the incomplete to the fulfilled.[17] The problem, of course, was that this structure reinforced the idea that the gospel was merely a perfecting of the law—a new evangelical law that demanded purity in the very thoughts of the heart and not just external cleanness of the hand. It is no wonder that Luther could reflect on this period of his life as a time when the gospel seemed to him worse than the law: "As if, indeed, it is not enough, that miserable sinners, eternally lost through original sin, are crushed

13 The numbering here follows the Vulgate. According to the Hebrew psalter, this would be Psalm 78.

14 WA 55 II:534.5–535.10.

15 WA 55 II:535.20–22. Cf. WA 55 II:262.127f.

16 WA 55 I:546 (Ps 77:2), 547.

17 WA 55 II:644.409–10, 696.303–4, 871.3–6.

by every kind of calamity by the law of the Decalogue, without having God add pain to pain by the gospel and also by the gospel threatening us with his righteousness and wrath!"[18]

In the subsequent lectures, Luther began to explore a very different paradigm for interpreting the Scriptures. As he tried to understand Paul's epistle to the Romans (1515–16), he also saw that understanding the law and gospel apart from the graduated continuity of salvation history was a crucial part of the apostolic message.[19] The gospel did not complete or perfect the law; it was wholly other, distinctive in its message and effect:

> Therefore, they who interpret "gospel" other than "good news" do not understand the gospel, as they do who have turned that very thing into law rather than grace and have made for us a Moses out of Christ. . . . For the law shows nothing except sin, makes guilty, and thus distresses the conscience; but the gospel proclaims the desired remedy to those with anguish of this kind. Therefore the law is evil, the gospel good; the law announces wrath, the gospel peace. The law says (as the apostle cites in Gal. 3): "Cursed be everyone who does not abide in all things written in the book of the law that he might do them." . . . But the gospel says: "Behold the Lamb of God, who takes away the sins of the world." The law burdens the conscience with sins, but the gospel frees it and brings peace through faith in Christ. . . . Therefore there are two sets of contraries: *Law–Sin*; it shows sin and makes one guilty and sick; indeed proves him damned. *Gospel—Grace*; it offers grace and forgives sin and cures the sickness unto salvation.[20]

Because Luther no longer saw the law and the gospel primarily as attributes distinctive to each testament, he could reevaluate the nature of the traditional salvation-historical relationship. To be sure, God's work in Christ completed what lived only as a promise to Abraham and his descendants, but through that promise, God's grace and the righteousness of faith could also be found generously throughout the Old Testament. As Luther's doctrine of justification moved more completely from the healing infusion of virtue to the preeminence

---

18 LW 34:337.

19 See Herrmann, "Why Then the Law?," 147–93.

20 WA 56:338.20f., 424.8–17.

of faith, the "time of fullness" lost its intended meaning, and Luther quickly abandoned its original usage. In the next set of lectures on Galatians (1516–17), Luther glossed the "fullness of time" from Galatians 4:4 with the earlier verse (4:2), "the time fixed by the father."[21] In the published version in 1519, he notes, "*Plenitudinem temporis* refers here to what [Paul] said above as the time predetermined by the father. In this way God had predetermined the time when the promised blessing of Abraham was to be fulfilled in his seed, Christ . . . and this he calls 'the fullness of time,' that is, the fulfillment of the time previously established."[22] The interpretation of "others"—namely, those who "call the 'fullness of time' the 'time of fullness,' i.e. the 'time of grace,'"—is mentioned but with no recommendation.[23] Finally, in his published *Weihnachtspostille* (1522), where Galatians 4 appears in the lectionary for the first Sunday after Christmas, he engaged the interpretative tradition, explicitly criticizing Lombard, the "meyster von hohen Sinnen": "The 'Master of Lofty Senses' has erred when he interprets this place in St. Paul: 'the time of fullness is the time of grace that came after Christ was born.' This is exactly opposite the apostle who does not say 'the time of fullness,' but 'fullness of time,' meaning the previous time determined by the father . . . for St. Paul speaks here *according to the way of the Scriptures* [modus loquendi scripturae]."[24] While these comments are largely focused on syntax and the proper contextual interpretation of this particular genitive construct, Luther goes on to indicate why this matters theologically and is not mere wordplay:

> As this same time was fulfilled for the Jews by the bodily advent of Christ, so it is still daily fulfilled when a person is enlightened by faith, so that his slavery and the effects of the law have an end. For Christ's bodily advent would have been of no use if it had not effected such a spiritual advent of faith. For this reason he has come bodily: that he might establish such a spiritual advent. For he has come to all who, before and after [his coming], believed in his bodily advent. Hence, he had always come to the ancient fathers on account of their faith; but

21 WA 57 II:29.13–14 (Gal 4:4). See also WA 57 II:29.23–30.16 (Gal 4:4).

22 WA 2:534.15–20.

23 WA 2:534.21: "Alii plenitudinem temporis tempus plenitdunis, id est gratiae, vocant."

24 WA 10 I/1:353.1–6; WA 10 I/1:352.16f.

> down to the present he has not yet come to the Jews of today because of their unbelief. Everything, from the beginning of the world to the end, must cling to this bodily advent. Slavery ends whenever, wherever, and in whomsoever such adherence takes place. Therefore, *for each individual his time is fulfilled when he begins to believe in Christ*; formerly, as the one yet to come, and now, as the one who has come.[25]

It is remarkable to observe how the marker of time in this simple genitive construct has been transfigured so thoroughly. Before, what was merely an indicator of God's unfolding plan of salvation became a stimulus for stressing the graduated continuity of both testaments and the spiritual plenitude of the New Testament specifically. Yet as the governing framework for Luther's reading of the Scriptures shifted away from this traditional salvation-historical scheme, he not only restored the more obvious syntactical sense of the "fullness of time" but he went on to exploit the phrase toward his more existential oriented reading. The "time" of history found a home in the conscience where Christ's advent, born in our hearts through faith, brings an end to our reluctant servitude under the law's accusations and punishments. In both the tradition and in Luther, the ambiguity of the genitive becomes a window through which the larger theological assumptions of the exegete are revealed and exhibited.

2. *LEX PECCATI*: THE LAW OF SIN

This next example follows a similar trajectory with the traditional understanding of the genitive construct adopted by Luther but then revised in accordance with his new reading of the Scriptures and his theological vision. The phrase appears several times in a very difficult passage by Paul in Romans 7 and 8 featuring an interplay between the "law of God" (lex dei), a "law in my members" (lex in membris meis), the "law of my mind" (lex mentis meae), the "law of the Spirit" (lex Spiritus), and the "law of sin" (lex peccati):

> So I find it to be a law that when I want to do right, evil lies close at hand. For I delight in the law of God [legi Dei], in my inner being, but I see another law in my members [alias legem in membris meis] waging war against the law of my mind [legi mentis meae] and making

25 WA 10 I/1:353.6–354.2. Emphasis added.

> me captive to the law of sin [lege peccati] that dwells in my members. Wretched man that I am! Who will deliver me from this body of death? Thanks be to God through Jesus Christ our Lord! So then, I myself serve the law of God [legi Dei] with my mind, but with my flesh I serve the law of sin [legi peccati]. There is therefore now no condemnation for those who are in Christ Jesus. For the law of the Spirit of life [lex Spiritus vitae] has set you free in Christ Jesus from the law of sin and death [lege peccati et mortis]. (Rom 7:21–8:2)

The full scope of Paul's argument cannot be dealt with here, but the reader should be able to appreciate, even in this brief excerpt, the difficulty in keeping track of the various uses and references to *law* in this passage, all placed in a variety of genitive constructs to modify and differentiate. In the tradition, the most difficult of these genitives was the *lex peccati* because of its negative associations vis-à-vis various antinomian concerns and heresies that began as early as Marcion. Consequently, whenever Paul describes the law and its purpose in less than optimistic terms, interpreters were inclined to qualify the statement, usually by differentiating the moral law from a lesser form—for example, the ceremonial law—or by identifying another referent altogether.[26] In this particular case, we look to the interpretation of *lex peccati* in the exegetical and scholastic tradition.

The *Glossa ordinaria*, functioning as a compendium of influential and possible interpretations, rarely gives only a single meaning to a text.[27] In this instance, however, the *Glossa* is fairly consistent in identifying the *lex peccati* with the inclination of sin itself—i.e., concupiscence. Exegetically, this

---

26 For a helpful overview of some of these interpretive moves, see Maurice Wiles, *The Divine Apostle: The Interpretation of St. Paul's Epistles in the Early Church* (Cambridge: Cambridge University Press, 1967), 49–72. See also Herrmann, "Why Then the Law?," 15–66; Erik Herrmann, "A Lutheran Response to the Reformed Tradition," in *God's Two Words: Law and Gospel in the Lutheran and Reformed Traditions*, ed. Jonathan A. Linebaugh (Grand Rapids, MI: Eerdmans, 2018), 155–82.

27 On the development of the *Glossa ordinaria*, see Smalley, *Study of the Bible*, 46–66; Beryl Smalley, "Glossa ordinaria," in *Theologische Realenzyklopädie*, ed. Gerhard Müller (Berlin: De Gruyter, 1984), 13:452–57; M. T. Gibson, "The Place of the Glossa ordinaria in Medieval Exegesis," in *Ad Litteram: Authoritative Texts and Their Medieval Readers*, ed. M. D. Jordan and K. Emery (Notre Dame, IN: Notre Dame, 1992), 5–27.

identification makes sense, especially because earlier, Paul cites the commandment "do not covet," which in Latin is rendered *non concupisces*. Based on Lombard's own glosses, the *Glossa* identifies three different referents for *lex* in this passage: "This distinction is necessary: he speaks of the *lex spiritus*, this is one law. Regarding the *lex peccati et mortis*, this is another law. And following there is what is impossible for the law, this is the third law. This one is the Law of Moses given on Mt. Sinai. Two of these laws here are good—namely the law of faith which takes away sin and the Law of Moses which show and prohibits sin. But the *lex peccati* is evil, because it makes one guilty."[28]

The *lex peccati*, labeled as "evil" (mala), is distinguished sharply from the law of Moses, even though Moses reveals such sin. On the one hand, Paul defends the law, saying that it is good; on the other hand, we are dead to this same law, no longer serving the "oldness of the letter." This fluctuation of *lex* is reflected in the various readings found in the *Glossa*. When Paul speaks about being free or dead to the law, then the glosses tend toward those elements of the law in the Old Testament that have ceased in the course of salvation history—the "lex factorem" or the "lex scripta"—that is, the ceremonial laws.[29] The moral law, reflected in the *lex natura* but perfected in the *lex spiritus*, remains in force for the Christian. More difficult is the pervasive presence and ongoing power of sin indicated throughout the passage and its close affiliation with the law. Here the traditional glosses wrestle with various possibilities: (1) the command against the desires of the flesh—*non concupisces*—turns any surrender to such desires into a "transgression," thus making sin an explicit violation of the law (following the logic of Rom 4:15 and 5:13, cf. Gal 3:19); (2) the moral law, now written in the heart, comes into an inner conflict with the remaining "tinder" of sin (fomes peccati) that smolders in the soul; (3) or perhaps the stirring of sin simply comes from the outside—that is, the temptations of the devil.[30]

---

28 *Glossa*, Rom 8:2.

29 E.g., *Glossa*, Rom 7:2: "Jacob, Hoc exemplo docet christianum a lege factorum exutum, non ab omni lege, ut mulier a lege viri non a lege nature, nec ultra christianus debet esse sub lege. Si enim lex ei vivit aduter est, nec prodest ei christianum dici."

30 E.g., *Glossa* Rom 8:2, "**Lex enim Spiritus vite in Christo Iesu liberabit me a lege peccati et mortis**, lege Moysi que prevaricationis est causa et mortis a consensu et opere"; Rom 7:8, "**occasione autem accepta peccatum**, fomes initium scilicet concupiscentie vel diabolus auctor peccati, per mandatum, ecce lex bona tamen ex ea malum, quia peccatum id est fomes peccati vel diabolus."

Early on, Luther favored these same distinctions. One can see in his annotations to Lombard's *Sentences* that the notion of concupiscence and the scholastic reflections on the *fomes peccati* were significant for him.[31] Like the scholastics, the early Luther made a distinction between original sin and concupiscence. While original sin was the inherited guilt of Adam, concupiscence was its lasting effect. Baptism took away the former, but the latter remained in the life of the Christian, a tinder and *scintilla* that could be fanned into a flame of sinful desires. The struggle then for the Christian was a struggle of the will against the flesh. When the will succumbed to the desires of the flesh, then one was guilty of an actual sin (peccatum actualia). When the will resisted concupiscence, this was either due to the presence of sacramental grace or, as the later scholastics would propose, a natural inclination to the good (syntheresis) that even in its smallest gestures (facere quod in se est) was capable of moral advance in the eyes of God (quod substantiam facti—meritum de congruo). But concupiscence, the inclination itself, was regarded as morally neutral until acted upon.

But as Luther's view of the law changed during his Romans lectures, so did his view of sin.[32] The scholastics seemed too timid in their view of concupiscence and original sin. For Luther, Paul was not speaking about some dormant tendency, culpable only when acted upon, but rather a deep-seated hostility toward the things of God and the desire to twist all of creation toward oneself and one's own advantage (incurvatus in se ipsum). The concupiscence that persisted after baptism was *sin itself*, original sin, the root of all sins (peccatum radicale).[33]

Luther's rejection of the scholastic definitions of sin in Romans is well-known, yet it is a twin critique. Paired with his new, radical concept of sin, the law is presented as a ubiquitous, existential word confronting the human condition. For Luther, scholastic theology falters because it fails to recognize these concepts: "O ignorance of sin! Ignorance of God! Ignorance of the law!"[34] Both sin and law hang inextricably together—if sin is present, the law is there: "Sin

31 See Luther's comments on the *Sentences* I, d. 30–32, WA 9:73.5–76.8.

32 See Ľubomír Batka, *Peccatum radicale. Eine Studie zu Luthers Erbsündenverständnis in Psalm 51* (Frankfurt: Peter Lang, 2007); see also Batka, "Luther's Teaching on Sin and Evil," in *The Oxford Handbook of Martin Luther's Theology* (Oxford: Oxford University Press, 2014), 233–53.

33 E.g., WA 56:271.7–8, 277.12, 285.16, 290.4–5, 312.1f.

34 WA 56:279.9–10.

and the wrath of God come through the law. Therefore no one dies to the law unless he dies also to sin, and whoever dies to sin dies also to the law. And as soon as a man is free from sin, he is also free from the law. And when a person becomes a servant of sin, he also becomes a slave of the law, and while sin rules over him and dominates him, the law also rules over and dominates him."[35] *Lex enim omne peccatum tangit*: "for the law hangs on every sin."[36] Indeed, the nature of sin is so profound that perfect knowledge of it is impossible; the law must reveal only that which can be believed.[37]

For Luther, then, the ambiguity of the genitive, *lex peccati*, is a fitting vehicle to express this relationship. On the one hand, Luther can still gloss the "law of sin" with *fomes peccati* and *concupiscence*, though now as an indication of the root of all sin. On the other hand, Luther can identify the "law of sin" with the very same good law of God that exposes and exacerbates the sin in our nature: "As long as a man lives and is not taken away and changed by the renewal of grace, he can in no way do anything to prevent his being *sub peccato et lege*. . . . Therefore the law is the *lex peccati*, that is, the law of the husband [Rom 7:2f.], to which a man does not die unless he dies to sin."[38]

Likewise, when Luther lectures on Galatians in the following year, he comments on the difficult passage in 2:19: "Through the law I died to the law." Luther finds the phrase strange but characteristic of how Scripture speaks:

> But when he says, "through the law I die to the law" he shows that there is a double meaning to "law," that is, I have a law that frees from the law; just as when one says, "I know a skill against skill." Likewise, in Scripture is found "the death of death," "the captivity of captivity," the same with "night of night" and "day of day," so also there is "the law of the law," that is, that which does away with the law by fulfilling it, as in Rom. 8 "the law of the spirit of life in Christ frees me from the law of death," i.e. by faith. . . . Therefore [the latter] law is the *lex mortis et peccati*, because it neither justifies nor gives life, rather it kills and makes unrighteous by showing sin and the penalty of death.[39]

35 WA 56:334.9–13.

36 WA 56:68.10–69.21 (Rom 7:10); see also WA 56:334.9–13, 335.6, 424.8–16, 426.59.

37 Cf. WA 56:68.10–69.21 (Rom 7:10); 56:67.13–69.1, 231.5f., 235.30–38, 340.31f.

38 WA 56:335.2–7.

39 WA 57 II:73.11–24.

In the published lectures of 1519, Luther expands on this thought: "This is the law of works, the old law, the law of Moses, the law of the flesh, the law of sin, the law of wrath, the law of death. It condemns everything, makes all men guilty, increases lusts, and slays, and the more spiritual it is, the more it does so."[40] Such a bold identification of the *lex peccati* with the law itself is without precedence, but Luther is convinced that the correlation of sin with the law is thoroughly Pauline: "Thus the apostle dares to say that 'the law works wrath' [Rom 4:15], and is a 'law of sin' [Rom 7:25, 8:2], and that Moses is a servant of sin."[41] Admittedly, such an identification can be misunderstood. Luther warns his students and readers that if read as a metaphysical or moral statement, they will have missed Paul's intent: "It is evident that the apostle is not speaking of the law in a metaphysical or moral sense, but in a spiritual and theological sense. . . . The apostle's *modus loquendi* is contrary to the *modus metaphysicus* or *modus moralis*."[42] Only in this sense can the root of sin and the law of God come together in the paradoxical strife that is the *lex peccati*.

3. *Opera Legis*: The Works of the Law

One of the more controversial genitive constructs in the history of exegesis is Paul's prominent expression, "the works of the law."[43] From some of the earliest commentaries all the way to the so-called New Perspective on Paul, the phrase has been subject to intense debate, especially as to the significance of the qualifier "works."[44] Because the connotation of "works of the law" is always negative in Paul, usually set in opposition to justification or faith, the referent of the

40 WA 2:499.36f.

41 WA 57 III:196.2–3.

42 WA 56:334.1–4, 14–15.

43 For an overview of the literature among modern New Testament scholars, see Thomas Schreiner, "Works of the Law," in *Dictionary of Paul and His Letters*, ed. Gerald F. Hawthorne, Ralph P. Martin, and Daniel G. Reid (Downers Grove, IL: InterVarsity, 1993), 975–77.

44 The inception of the "new perspective" on Paul is usually identified with the publication of E. P. Sanders, *Paul and Palestinian Judaism* (Minneapolis: Fortress, 1977) and coined by James D. G. Dunn, "The New Perspective on Paul," in *Bulletin of the John Rylands University Library* 65 (1983): 95–122. For a helpful overview, see Magnus Zetterholm, *Approaches to Paul: A Student's Guide to Recent Scholarship* (Minneapolis: Fortress, 2009).

expression is particularly critical. As we mentioned earlier, the early exegetical tradition was markedly cautious about any interpretation that would impugn or malign the law. So the most common way of handling Paul's negative statements was to distinguish "works of the law" from the law itself. The "works," it was argued, were not those of the moral law expressed in nature, in the Decalogue, or in Christ's Sermon on the Mount. Instead, they were the various ceremonial laws—sacrifices, feasts, food and purity laws—that were a distinctive part of Israel's identity in the Old Testament. By stating that the "works of the law" do not justify, Paul was merely announcing that the time of Israel had been superseded by the church, which was comprised of both Jew and Gentile. But the law that Paul affirmed as "holy and good" was not the "works of the law" but the moral law perfected and fulfilled by grace, the shape and telos of justification.

As stated earlier, Luther essentially followed this interpretation until his lectures on Romans. It was then that he became much more familiar with Augustine's anti-Pelagian writings, which advanced a very different interpretation of the *opera legis*.[45] Rather than a distinction between ceremonial and moral, Augustine interpreted Paul's pessimistic statements on the law as any arrogant human effort to fulfill the law without grace (i.e., the law of faith). Likewise, this was the meaning of "the letter kills, but the Spirit gives life" (2 Cor 3:6)—the law as "letter" can only outline the demand; it offers no assistance toward fulfilling it. But the Spirit gives believers the grace to do what the law truly demands—that is, to love.[46]

Luther's adoption of Augustine's interpretation here is well-known and well-documented. Within the parameters of our question, however, after Luther was confident in the Augustinian interpretation, the *opera legis* became

45 For Luther's use of Augustine in the Romans lectures, see especially Dorothea Demmer, *Lutherus Interpres: Der theologische Neuansatz in seiner Römerbriefexegese* (Wittenberg: Luther-Verlag, 1968), 237–42; Leif Grane, "Augustins 'Expositio quarundam propositionum ex epistola ad Romanos' in Luthers Römerbriefvorlesung," *Die Zeitschrift für Theologie und Kirche* 69 (1972): 304–30; see also Grane, "Divus Paulus et S. Augustinus, interpres eius fidelissimus," in *Festschrift für Ernst Fuchs*, ed. Gerhard Ebeling, Eberhard Jüngel, and Gerd Schunack (Tübingen: Mohr Siebeck, 1973), 133–46; Grane, *Modus Loquendi Theologicus*.

46 This argument is repeated throughout Augustine's anti-Pelagian writings, but for a brief encapsulation, see *De spiritu et littera*, xiii.21–xiv.24.

a felicitous construct, with its ambiguity allowing Luther to paint a vivid image on the difference between life under the law and life under grace.

In the Romans lectures, Luther adopts not only Augustine's definition of the *opera legis* but also his notion of liberty. True liberty is not merely the freedom to choose between several possibilities, but rather it is the ability to act *freely*—that is, spontaneously, altruistically, and without coercion. The law, without the Spirit, can only coax or coerce obedience, but the desires of the heart remain untouched: "The works of the law are those, he says, that happen outside of faith and grace and come from the law which has either compelled us through fear or entices us through its promise of temporal blessings. But the works of faith, he says, are those that occur out of the spirit of liberty and solely for the love of God."[47]

Exploring this idea further in his subsequent lectures, Luther begins to play with the genitive. In the Galatians lecture (1516–17), he notes that Paul

> expressly and carefully calls it "*opera legis*" rather than the "works of the spirit" (*opera spiritus*), or "works of people" (*opera hominum*), or "our works" (*opera nostra*), because truly they are not *ours*, since they do not happen by our will or spirit. For he classifies *opera* as those things that are done by the will of the one who commands it. But the law commands by fear of punishment or promise of reward, and thus it extorts them from the external actions of the person and entices his will. Therefore they are "works of the law," not because they are according to the law, but rather because by the law they are done unwillingly by us.[48]

In other words, Luther is now pleased to read the "works of the law" as a *subjective genitive*.

It would seem that at least for several years, Luther considered this a legitimate reading of the genitive construct. He repeats and expands on the same argument in his published Galatians commentary in 1519—a commentary written for and eagerly procured by humanists, some of the most erudite linguists of the day.[49] But he also saw it fitting to dwell on this in several of his

47 WA 56:248.11–14.

48 WA 57 II:69.6–12.

49 WA 2:492f.

sermons in the *Weihnachtspostille*, published in 1522. There he elaborates on and vividly depicts the way in which an anthropomorphized law both coerces us with threats and cajoles us with its promises to bring about obedience in us. Like a stern and effective au pair (i.e., *zuchtmeister* or *pedagogus*), the law extracts external compliance, but in so doing, it exacerbates our inner resentment, exposing our natural disposition: "The more severely he is forbidden externally from evil, the more indignant he becomes in the heart toward the one who forbids him. His situation rests in the scales: as much as external sin decreases, so much does internal sin increase; one side of the scale goes up, the other down."[50] The solution, of course, is Christ, in whom one must trust instead of the works that the law extorts from him. Then Christ "will give him another spirit and will change his heart. Then he will no longer fear death and hell, no longer will seek life and heaven. To the law he will be free and will keep it freely, living by it with a clear and certain conscience in both death and life."[51]

In recent years, there have been attempts by New Testament scholars to argue for reading the "works of the law" as a subjective genitive, though this has not won broad consensus.[52] Luther, however, was not married to this interpretation and could leave it behind later when context or audience changed.[53] Even so, Luther's reading seems to be an attempt to come to terms with Scripture's *modus loquendi*, exploring the way it continually upends all of human efforts to domesticate God and the gospel.

---

50 WA 10 I/1:450.19–451.5.

51 WA 10 I/1:455.11–14.

52 See Lloyd Gaston, "Works of Law as a Subjective Genitive," in *Studies in Religion* 13, no. 1 (March 1984): 39–46; see also Gaston, *Paul and the Torah* (Vancouver: University of British Columbia, 1987), 100–106; Paul L. Owen, "The 'Works of the Law' in Romans and Galatians: A New Defense of the Subjective Genitive," *Journal of Biblical Literature* (Fall 2007): 553–77.

53 Luther's appeal to this reading of the *opera legis* was largely intended to expound and illustrate Augustine's understanding of the will and grace over against the neo-Pelagian conclusions of late-medieval scholastics, especially those of the *via moderna*. As the doctrine of justification continued to be clarified, Luther and Melanchthon would distance themselves from the Augustinian notion that even the new heart and its joyful obedience to the law were part of this doctrine. See, for example, Melanchthon's letter to Brenz from 1531 along with Luther's postscript, MBWT 5:104–13, nr. 1151.

CONCLUSION

Luther's relationship to the gospel was also a relationship with language.[54] He was informed by a culture of letters and reading even as he deeply shaped that culture.[55] That the gospel could live in syntax and be discovered in a genitive seems strange to us, but Luther inherited a long legacy of theological reflection on the relationship of language to reality. Yet the various proposals in the schools that tried to account for divine truth expressed in human language—the equivocal, univocal, analogical—did not really address the problem as Luther saw it. The transcendence of God was not the primary issue. Rather, Luther saw that it was principally the incarnation and crucifixion of God that shattered the expectations and attributions of logicians, metaphysicians, and theologians alike. Salvation through the cross—through a weak and dying God—meant that it was not the *ergo* of the syllogism but the *dennoch*—the nevertheless![56]—of evangelical irony and paradox that pulsed through the Scripture. This was the new frame of reference for the *nova lingua* of theology that led him to parse and reinterpret texts with remarkable versatility. From that standpoint, even a simple genitive could open up a whole new world for Luther, like peering through a window into heaven or passing through the gates of paradise.[57]

54 See Johannes von Lüpke, "Luther's Use of Language," in *The Oxford Handbook of Martin Luther's Theology*, ed. L'ubomír Batka, Irene Dingel, and Robert Kolb (Oxford: Oxford University Press, 2014), 143–55; Albrecht Beutel, *In dem Anfang war das Wort: Studien zu Luthers Sprachverständnis* (Tübingen: Mohr Siebeck, 1991); Jens Wolff, *Metapher und Kreuz: Studien zu Luthers Christusbild* (Tübingen: Mohr Siebeck, 2005); Joachim Ringleben, *Gott im Wort: Luthers Theologie von der Sprache her* (Tübingen: Mohr Siebeck, 2010).

55 See Cummings, *Literary Culture of the Reformation*.

56 "Faith in Jesus, like its theme, the righteousness of God, is the radical 'Nevertheless.'" Karl Barth, *Epistle to the Romans* (London: Oxford University Press, 1933), 99.

57 LW 34:337.

Foreknowledge and the Divine Counsel in Calvin's Exegesis of Acts 2:23 and 4:28

Richard A. Muller

There is an inordinate number of studies treating of Calvin's views on the general topic of the divine counsel and foreknowledge, predestination and providence, but few concerned with the way he distinguished divine foreknowledge from the eternal decree except for indicating that Calvin in no way grounded the divine decree on a notion of divine foreknowledge.[1] One study takes up the issue of the relationship between Calvin's pastoral approach in preaching of predestination and his "more didactic-polemical approach in the *Institutes*," comparing the approach in Calvin's *Insitutio* to his exposition in the *Congrégation*, which he delivered in December 1551 toward the end of the Bolsec

1 See, e.g., Paul Jacobs, *Prädestination und Verantwortlichkeit bei Calvin* (Neukirchen: Moers, 1937); Heinz Otten, *Calvins theologische Anschauung von der Prädestination* (Neukirchen: Neukirchner Verlag, 1968); Fred H. Klooster, *Calvin's Doctrine of Predestination*, 2nd ed. (Grand Rapids, MI: Baker, 1977); R. Scott Clark, "Election and Predestination: The Sovereign Expressions of God: Institutes 3.21–24," in *A Theological Guide to Calvin's Institutes: Essays and Analysis* (Phillipsburg, NJ: P&R, 2008), 90–122; Joel R. Beeke, "Calvin on Sovereignty, Providence, and Predestination," *Puritan Reformed Journal*, 2, no. 2 (2010): 77–105; Christian Link, *Prädestination und Erwählung. Calvin-Studien* (Neukirchen: Neukirchner Verlag, 2009); J. Christine Janowski, "Zu Calvins Lehre von der 'doppelten Prädestination,'" in *Johannes Calvin 1509–2009: Würdigung aus Berner Perspektive* (Zurich: Theologischer Verlag, 2012), 205–34.

controversy.[2] None, however, examines Calvin's lengthy interpretative use and referencing of Acts 2:23 and 4:28 either in detail or in relation to the development of his thought. Calvin preached on the text shortly before the Bolsec controversy and completed his commentary on the text shortly after. In the sermons and the commentary, he dealt with distinctions necessary to resolve the problem of the two causalities, divine and human, operative in the crucifixion of Christ. The text of Acts 2:23, where Christ is said to have been "delivered by the determinate counsel and foreknowledge of God" but also crucified "by the hands of godless men," was, for Calvin, one of the more significant biblical *loci* for the traditional discussion of the divine willing of all things, therefore, knowing all things eternally, and nonetheless not being the cause of evil. In addition, Calvin's development in the interpretation of the passage relates directly to the issues raised first in his response to the Council of Trent, later in the Bolsec controversy, and in his last resolutions of the problem of divine determination and the permission of human acts in debate with Sebastian Castellio and in the final edition of his *Institutio*. This use of passage, moreover, stands in some contrast to earlier Protestant commentaries by Otto Braunfels, Konrad Pellikan, and Heinrich Bullinger, who agreed as to its meaning but did not identify the text as a major *locus* for the development of a doctrinal point.

Calvin examined Acts in two extended expositions that stand in significant chronological relation to each other. The first of these is found in his sermons on Acts, preached in a series that began in August 1549,[3] roughly two

2 Wilhelm Neuser, "Calvin the Preacher: His Explanation of the Doctrine of Predestination in the Sermon of 1551 and in the Institutes of 1559," *Hervormde Teologiese Studies* 54 (1998): 60–103; Neuser identified Calvin's *Congrégation* as a "sermon," but this is technically incorrect—a *congrégation* was an instructional oration delivered in the church by one of the Genevan clergy, followed by brief determinations from the each of the other clergy. Also note Pieter L. Rouwendal, "Predestination and Preaching in Genevan Theology from Calvin to Pictet" (PhD diss., Vrije Universiteit Amsterdam, 2017).

3 Most of the series of sermons is lost. The sermon on Acts 2:22–24 was published in John Calvin, *Plusieurs sermons de Jehan Calvin touchant la divinité, humanité et nativité de nostre Seigneur Jesus Christ: item touchant sa passion, mort, resurrection, ascension, et dernier advenement: puis touchant la descente du S. Esprit sur les Apostres, et la premiere predication de S. Pierre* (Geneva: Conrad Badius, 1558), 439–59; the sermon on Acts 2:22–24 is also found in CO 48, col. 585–684, here col. 653–64. Discovery of Raguenier's transcription of the sermons on the first seven chapters of

years after he had countered the notion of divine permission of wicked acts that he found in the canons of the Council of Trent, his response to which included Acts 2:23 and 4:28 in a catena of verses.[4] In the sermons, Calvin turned to a positive use of the concept of divine permission. The second appears in his fairly lengthy exegesis of Acts 2:23, published in the first volume of his two-part commentary on Acts, followed in the commentary by a shorter reflection on the same issues at Acts 4:28.[5] While differing in style and on the particular issue of divine permission, the two expositions, sermon and commentary, complement one another, and the basic line of argument is much the same.[6] We know from Denis Raguenier's gathering of the sermon transcripts that Calvin preached on Acts 1 through 15 into late 1552.[7] The commentary on Acts 1–14 appeared in 1552. Raguenier's second gathering of sermons, running from

---

Acts led to their publication in Willem Balke and Wilhelmus H. Th. Moehn, eds., *Sermons on the Acts of the Apostles* (Neukirchen: Neukirchner Verlag, 1994), hereinafter cited as *Sermons on the Acts*, translated by Rob Roy McGregor as *Sermons on the Acts of the Apostles Chapters 1–7* (Edinburgh: Banner of Truth Trust, 2008). The sermon on Acts 2:22–24 is not included in the volume, but it does include the sermon on Acts 4:24b–31. The chronology of the sermons is given in detail in Balke and Moehn, *Sermons on the Acts*, 462–63, who argue (xv) that, for the most part, the sermons in Badius's printing of 1558 are from the series delivered 1549–51; also see T. H. L. Parker, *Calvin's Preaching* (Edinburgh: T&T Clark, 1992), 63, 150–51.

4 John Calvin, *Acta Synodi Tridentinae cum Antidoto* (Geneva: Jean Girard, 1547), 228, citing Isa 10, 17, Jer 1; Ezek 17, 37; Ps 17; Acts 2, 4; compare to CO 7, col. 475, with some alteration of chapters, supplies verse numbers, indicating Isa 7:18, 10:5; Ezek 17:20, 32:3; Ps 17:13; and Acts 2:23. Given that the *Antidotum* refers to the divine counsel and decree, CO is correct in its assignment of verses to the citations of Acts 2 and 4. Note the translation, *Canons and Decrees of the Council of Trent, with the Antidote*, in *Selected Works of John Calvin: Tracts and Letters*, ed. Henry Beveridge and Jules Bonnet, 7 vols. (Grand Rapids, MI: Baker, 1983), 3:17–188.

5 John Calvin, *Commentariorum Ioannis Calvini in Acta Apostolorum, Liber I* (Geneva: Jean Crespin, 1552), 22–23, 52 (CO 48, col. 37–40, 93), translated by Henry Beveridge as *Commentary upon the Acts of the Apostles*, 2 vols. (Edinburgh: Calvin Translation Society, 1844), 1:95–99, 187.

6 On Calvin's homiletical style, see Parker, *Calvin's Preaching*, 139–49.

7 On Raguenier's transcriptions of Calvin's sermons, see Parker, 65–68, 71, 153–57. The sermons on Acts 1–7 were not entirely transcribed by Raguenier, and given the gap in the manuscript where a sermon on Acts 2:22–24 would have appeared, it is uncertain who the actual scribe was. See Balke and Moehn, *Sermons on the Acts*, xiii–xiv.

Acts 16 through 28, began in November 1552 and extended into 1554. The second volume of the commentary, on Acts 15–28, was published in 1554. Calvin presumably began work on the commentary shortly after beginning his series of sermons and concluded his work on the commentary shortly after completing the sermon series. During this time, he was also engaged in the Bolsec controversy over the doctrine of predestination. Given the time frame of the controversy, October to December 1551,[8] Calvin had delivered his sermons on Acts 2:22–24 and 4:24b–31 well prior to encountering Bolsec's objections to his doctrine, probably in late November or early December 1549. The sermon on Acts 4:24b–31 was delivered on May 25, 1550.[9] Neither of Calvin's immediate responses to the controversy, whether the brief response made in the course of the process against Bolsec, or the *Congrégation* of December 1551, makes direct use of Acts 2:23.

By the time that the commentary appeared, following the controversy, Calvin's reading of the text differed in at least one important detail from his interpretation in the sermon, namely in his interest in divine permission. Calvin did cite the text as a proof of divine ordination of Christ's expiatory sacrifice in his *De aeterna Dei praedestinatione* published in 1552, the same year as the first part of the commentary on Acts. There also Calvin offered detailed thoughts on divine permission that are arguably different from the direction taken in the sermons of early 1551.[10] There was also a noticeable relationship between the Calvin's comment on Acts 2:23, his 1556 additions to the

8 There is a useful account of the course of the controversy in Williston Walker, *John Calvin; the Organizer of Reformed Protestantism (1509–1564)* (New York: G. P. Putnam's, 1906), 315–20. Documentation of the affair can be found in *Actes du Proces intenté par Calvin et les autres ministres de Genève a Jérome Bolsec de Paris*, CO 8, col. 144–248; and R. M. Kingdon and J.-F. Bergier, eds., *Registres de la Compagnie des Pasteurs de Genève au temps de Calvin*, 2 vols. (Geneva: Droz, 1962–64), 1:80–131, most of which is translated and edited by Philip E. Hughes as *The Register of the Company of Pastors of Geneva in the Time of Calvin* (Grand Rapids, MI: Eerdmans, 1966), 137–86.

9 See the listing in Balke and Moehn, *Sermon on the Acts*, 463, where there is a gap between the sermon on Acts 1:1–2, delivered on August 25, 1549, and the sermon on Acts 2:36–38, delivered on December 22, 1549.

10 John Calvin, *De aeterna Dei praedestinatione, qua in salutem alois ex hominibus elegit, alios suo exitio relinquit; item de providentia qua res humanas gubernat* (Geneva: Jean Crespin, 1552), 38, 187 (CO 8, col. 273, 359), translated with an introduction

commentary on Romans 8:29, and his 1558 response to Sebastian Castellio, *De occulta Dei providentia.*[11]

Calvin's homiletical and exegetical expositions were also reflected in his use of the text in the *Institutes*. The commentary on Acts was published some seven years prior to the publication of the final edition of the *Institutio*. There is no citation of Acts 2:23 or 4:28 either in the 1536 *Institutio* or in the *Catechismus* of 1537–38. Calvin did cite both texts in the 1539 *Institutio* in his new chapter on predestination and providence, together with seven other passages indicating the relationship of the divine will or decree to human wrongdoing, with little elaboration on the text—and no significant editing in subsequent editions.[12] In his 1559 *Institutio*, however, after having removed his earlier use of the passage to the chapter on providence in book 1, Calvin drew on Acts 2:23 in an entirely new paragraph, inserted into his chapters on predestination in book 3.[13] Calvin also made crucial use of Acts 4:28 in an entirely new paragraph on providence added in the 1559 *Institutio.*[14] As in the case of other editorial work leading to the 1559 *Institutio*, Calvin's added reflection on the biblical text arguably reflects the exegetical work in which he had engaged after his work

---

by J. K. S. Reid, *Concerning the Eternal Predestination of God* (London: James Clarke, 1961).

11 John Calvin, *In omnes Pauli Apostoli epistolas atque etiam in epistolam ad Hebraeos . . . commentarii* (Geneva: Stephanus, 1556); Calvin, *Calumniae nebulonis cuiusdam, quibus odio et invidia gravare conatus est doctrinam Joh. Calvini de occulta Dei providentia. Johannis Calvini ad easdem responsio* (Geneva: Conrad Badius, 1558), 70 (CO 7, col. 301); hereinafter cited as *De occulta Dei providentia.*

12 John Calvin, *Institutio christianae religionis nunc vere demum suo titulo respondens* (Strasbourg: Wendelin Rihel, 1539), viii (p. 268), citing Ezek 12, 17; Ps 17; Isa 10, 13; Jer 1; Acts 2, 4; cf Calvin, *Institutio christianae religionis, nunc ex postrema authoris recognitione, quibusdam locis auctior, infinitis vero casticatior* (Geneva: Joannes Gerardus, 1550), xiv (p. 503); Calvin, *Institutio christianae religionis, in libris quatuor nunc primum digesta, certisque distincta capitibus, ad aptissimam methodum: aucta etiam tam magna accessione ut propemodum opus novum haberi possit* (Geneva: Robertus Stephanus, 1559), I.xviii.1, where the passage has migrated to the initial discussion of providence and been edited, but not elaborated in substance.

13 Calvin, *Institutio* (1559), III.xxii.6, translated by Ford Lewis Battles as *Institutes of the Christian Religion*, ed. John T. McNeill, 2 vols. (Philadelphia: Westminster, 1960).

14 Calvin, I.xviii.3.

on the preceding (1550) edition of the *Institutio*.[15] It is also the case, here as elsewhere, that the reference to the biblical text in the *Institutio* is not simply a matter of proof-texting, but is more probably a direction to the reader to go beyond what is stated in the *Institutio* and examine a commentary on the biblical text—notably, Calvin's own commentary in which the explanation is more substantive than what is found in the *Institutio* itself.[16]

Sermons and Commentary: A Brief Comparison

Calvin's sermon on Acts 2:22–24 is fairly expansive on the topic of the divine counsel and foreknowledge, but less technically argued than the later commentary, and directed rhetorically toward a more popular audience. Both here and in the sermon on Acts 24b–31, Calvin's identification of the pericope is the same in sermon and commentary. It is also structured somewhat differently than the commentary. The sermon is primarily concerned with the identity of Christ as the promised Messiah—with the failure of the Jews to recognize Christ as ordained by God, and the failure of the papists to recognize that works and merits are excluded and salvation bestowed by Christ alone.[17] Major worry over Roman doctrine was a frequent topic in Calvin's sermons, given the precariousness of the Reformation and the perceived need to hammer at remnants of "Papist" doctrine and sentiment among the Genevan laity. The sermon then takes up the two issues that would provide the focus of Calvin's commentary, the ordination of Christ's death in the foreknowledge and counsel of God and the problem of the deeds of the wicked, this largely to exposit the identity of the Messiah following the argument of Peter's sermon to his Jewish hearers.

Calvin then turns to the issue of the divine counsel and providence, where he argues both against foolishness of those who think that God rests in heaven and leaves things on earth to chance and against the Papists who speculate on matters of foreknowledge and foreordination.[18] The reference to foolish persons who think that God is uninvolved with temporal matters is brief and

15 See my comments on this pattern of development in Richard A. Muller, *The Unaccommodated Calvin: Studies in the Formation of a Theological Tradition* (New York: Oxford University Press, 2000), 148–52.

16 See Muller, 142, 158.

17 Calvin, *Plusieurs sermons*, 443–44 (CO 8, col. 656).

18 Calvin, 452–54 (CO 8, col. 660–61).

not explicit, but it surely refers to the Epicureans against whom Calvin railed in his *Institutio*.[19] This point does not appear in the commentary on the passage, but it is present in the added paragraph in the 1559 *Institutio*, where Calvin takes Acts 2:23 as a primary *locus* illustrating divine foreknowledge.[20]

Calvin's comment on the text, as already indicated, is far more elaborate than that of earlier Protestant writers. Braunfels offered only two brief sentences of comment. Pellikan and Bullinger provided only a single paragraph. The structure of the commentary is tighter than that of the sermon and lacks the sermon's overt polemics against the "Papists," reflecting Calvin's concern to address a far broader and different audience in his commentaries than in his sermons. Calvin, in contrast to these predecessor commentaries, offered a lengthy exposition of the text that, after his preliminary remarks, was divided into in two parts dealing with the contrast between the first main subject ("by the determinate counsel of God") and the second ("by the hands of godless men").[21] Exposition of the two main points serves to explain how both of these agencies could be at work: the divine purpose is accomplished and obedience to God properly understood without falling into the errors of placing human acts purely into the hands of human beings, identifying God as the author of sin, or claiming that ungodly acts ought not to be accounted as sins because all has been willed by God. The commentary is also noteworthy from a formal perspective. Given Calvin's early declaration that *brevitas* would be a primary characteristic of his exegesis and his fairly clear indication that this *brevitas* ruled out the inclusion of theological loci in commentaries,[22] the length of his exposition of the verse marks something of a departure from his early emphasis on brevity, and his references to the passage as an important locus for the doctrine of providence may indicate a further

19 Calvin, *Institutio* (1559), I.ii.2; I.v.5, 12; I.xvi.3–4; the McNeill/Battles translation mistakenly assumes that *Sophistae* consistently references "scholastic." Cf. I.xvi.3n5.

20 Calvin, III.xxii.6.

21 Calvin, *In omnes Pauli Apostoli epistolas*, 22–23.

22 See Richard C. Gamble, "*Brevitas et facilitas*: Toward and Understanding of Calvin's Hermeneutic," in *Westminster Theological Journal* 47 (1985): 1–17; Elsie Ann McKee, "Exegesis, Theology, and Development in Calvin's *Institutio*: A Methodological Suggestion," in *Probing the Reformed Tradition: Historical Studies in Honor of Edward A. Dowey, Jr.*, ed. Elsie Ann McKee and Brian G. Armstrong, 154–72 (Louisville, KY: Westminster John Knox, 1989); Muller, *Unaccommodated Calvin*, 111–15.

shift in style or method.[23] In what follows, I use the two-part structure of the argument in the commentary to organize the analysis.

By the Determinate Counsel of God

Arguably Calvin's first substantive reference to Acts 2:23 as a text foundational to the issue of divine counsel, foreknowledge, and the problem of evil occurs in his 1547 *Acta Synodi Tridentinae cum Antidoto.* In canon six of the sixth session, Trent had declared anathema anyone who claimed that it was not within a human being's power to do evil but that God willed both good and evil, the latter not merely permissively but "properly"—as if Judas's betrayal and the Apostle Paul's calling were both "his proper work [proprium ejus opera]."[24] Calvin responded with a denial that his teaching fell under the anathema, stating his abhorrence of paradox, notably the paradox that Judas's betrayal of Christ was as much a proper divine work as the calling of the Apostle Paul. But he also went on to condemn the Council's implication that God works "only permissively in the wicked": this should convince only those "who are ignorant of whole teaching of Scripture."[25] Scripture declares that God has decreed the works of the reprobate to occur "by his hand and counsel" and, in Acts 2, that the death of Christ occurred by God's "definite counsel": to appeal to permission is to flee from the truth.[26]

Calvin also appeals to Augustine against Trent. Augustine taught that God inclines human hearts as God pleases, whether to good according to his mercy or to evil according to their just desert. Had God overtly commanded the evil, the evil act would be an obedience to be praised, but the divine inclination of some to evil acts is not by overt command, rather it is by a "secret and just judgment" on their own wickedness. The evil itself is not the work of

23 Calvin, *Commentariorum in Acta Apostolorum*, 22 (CO 48, col. 39).

24 *Canones et decreta dogmatica Concilii Tridentini*, session 6, canon 6, Philip Schaff, *The Creeds of Christendom, with a History and Critical Notes*, 3 vols., 6th ed. (New York: Harper & Brothers, 1919), 2:111.

25 Calvin, *Acta Synodi Tridentinae cum Antidoto*, 228 (CO 7, col. 474–75).

26 Calvin, 228, citing Acts 2 in the margin; n.b., CO 7, col. 475, adds the verse and cites the entire catena bracketed in the text.

God. Augustine, following Scripture, did not explain this as permission, but as a divine act of inclining, turning, hardening, inciting, and working.[27]

Calvin's point of departure both in his sermon and his commentary on Acts 2:23 is the possibility of interpreting Christ's death as something scandalous or offensive, a merely fortuitous event brought on solely by perverse human willing, unsuited either to the identity of the Messiah or to the work of salvation. In the sermon, he explains that Peter's reference to the "counsel and foreknowledge of God" served to indicate that the crucifixion occurred not fortuitously, as the Jews might well have concluded. Due consideration of the power of God dispels such fantasies. Once believers recognize that all was accomplished according to God's providence and understand the intended goal or end of his counsel, they will know that all was done for their ultimate benefit.[28]

Similarly, in the commentary, Calvin states that the apostle Peter's words concerning the crucifixion of Christ were directed toward the Jews and were intended to remove a small source of error, an *offendiculum*. The mockery and crucifixion endured by Christ might initially be seen as contradictory to the Christian proclamation of Christ as revealed by God in "powers, wonders, and signs" (Acts 2:22). To the contrary, Peter declares that the events leading to Christ's death were neither fortuitous nor due to any lack of power on Christ's part, but because these events were appointed by God ("a Deo constitutum fuerat"). By teaching that the death of Christ was "ordained by the eternal counsel of God," the Apostle obviated foolish and wicked interpretations of the cross. Inasmuch as God himself appointed the crucifixion and God does nothing that is lacking in purpose, it becomes clear that God had a reason for ordaining the death of Christ.[29]

---

27 Calvin, 229 (CO 7, col. 475), citing Augustine, *De gratia & libero arbitrio* cap. 41 [20], where Augustine also uses the examples of Judas's betrayal and the crucifixion.

28 Calvin, *Plusieurs sermons*, 448–50 (CO 8, col. 658–59).

29 Calvin, *Commentariorum in Acta Apostolorum*, 22 (CO 48, col. 38); cf. Calvin, *Plusieurs sermons*, 452–53 (CO 8, col. 660–61). See also Konrad Pellikan, *Commentarium in acta Apostolorum sermonum Lucae evangelistae*, p. 24, in *In sacrosancta quatuor Evangelia et apostolorum acta D. Chuonradi Pellicani Rubeaquensis commentarii, in quibus veluti compendio selectissima quaeque congesta habes, quae hodie in illa cum apud Priscos tum apud Neotericos Evangeliorum interpretes orthodoxos extant* (Zurich: Froschauer, 1537). Otto Braunfels, *Annotationes in quatuor Evangelia et Acta Apostolorum, ex Orthodoxis Sacrarum Literarum scriptoribus congestae*

Peter's words, moreover, provided an "eminent place," a locus, concerning divine providence and thereby the beginning point for a proper understanding of how God governs both human life and death.[30] The implication of Calvin's phrase "insignis . . . locus de providentia Dei" is that the verse is not merely the "place" or "location" under examination, but is a *locus* in the more technical sense of a focal point for developing a doctrinal argument. Calvin would use the same word, *insignis*, to describe the doctrine in his comment on Acts 4:28.[31] This usage marks out the contrast between Calvin's approach to the text and that of various predecessor exegetes. Braunfels, who understood his interpretive work to include the identification of the theological loci in each chapter of a biblical book, did not identify divine counsel, providence, or foreknowledge as one of the loci in Acts 2.[32] Bullinger, whose exegetical practice included the exposition of theological loci in commentaries, did not do so at this point and offered a very concise examination of the passage.[33] Calvin identified the passage as an important locus, offered a lengthy comment, and used the passage to introduce a series of terms and distinctions associated with the divine counsel, ordination, and foreknowledge, which evidences his assumption that this is one of the more foundational places in Scripture for understanding providence in general but also providence with specific reference to sin and salvation.

The passage is focused on Christ, but the way in which Christ is framed by Luke presents Christ's person as a mirror reflecting "the universal providence of God, that extends itself through the entire world." Calvin notes that

(Strasbourg: Georgius Ulricherus, 1535), L3v, simply notes that the text identifies the birth, temptation, crucifixion, and death of Christ as under the "providence and counsel of God," with no further elaboration. Similarly, Dionysius Carthusianus, *In epistolas omnes canonicas, in Acta apostolorum, & in Apocalypsim, piae ac eruditae enarrationed* (Cologne: Petrus Quentell, 1533), 84v, provides little elaboration on the issue of divine counsel.

30 Calvin, *Commentariorum in Acta Apostolorum*, 22 (CO 48, col. 39): "Hic autem insignis est locus de providentia Dei, ut sciamus ab ea gubernari tam vitam nostram quam mortem."

31 Calvin, 52 (CO 48, col. 93).

32 See Otto Braunfels, *Loci omnium ferme Capitum Euangelij secundum Mathaeum, Marcum, Lucam, Ioannem, Actorvm item Apostolicorum* (Strasbourg: Joannes Schotus, 1529), viii r–v; cf. Braunfels, *Annotationes*, L2v.

33 Heinrich Bullinger, *In Acta Apostolorum Heinrychi Bullingeri commentariorum libri VI* (Zurich: Froschauer, 1533), 12–27, with the comment on vv. 22–24 on p. 18.

Luke proposed two things to consider when attempting to understand providence but had reversed the usual order—the divine decree (decretum) or counsel (consilium) and the divine foreknowledge (praescientia)—for the sake of instructing believers on a particular issue. Luke identified first the divine counsel or decree and then the divine foreknowledge, "although, however, foreknowledge is prior, with the counsel or decree placed under it." Luke did this "so that we recognize God shall will or establish nothing, unless he had long before directed it towards its end." This ordering, moreover, respects Peter's point in the text that the decree is to be associated with foreknowledge: "the counsel of God is not without reason" and the divine foreknowledge is not a *nuda praescentia*.[34] Similarly, in his *De aeterna Dei praedestinatione* of the same year, Calvin remarked that Peter's words, recorded in Acts 2:23, rendered impossible any explanation of Christ's death as other than ordained by God. The text "conjoins foreknowledge with the counsel, so that we might know, that Christ was prematurely put to death neither by chance nor by the violent assault of men: but because God, the highest and most wise knower, had deliberately established it."[35]

This issue of the divine foreknowledge of those who will be saved in God as coming prior to the divine counsel also marks out a development within (or at least a difference between) the sermon and the commentary. In his sermon on Acts 2:23, Calvin simply set aside consideration of the "thousand sophistic questions" invented by "Papists" and recommended that believers simply have the humility to believe "that God not only foresees things, but [also] disposes them according to his will."[36] In the commentary, however, Calvin elaborated further on the distinction between the *praescientia* and the *consilium Dei*. The distinction must be parsed carefully, he noted, given that many people who appeal to it are misled: failing to attend to the divine counsel that governs the entire world, they "seize upon" the notion of a bare foreknowledge. This notion draws on the "common distinction, that although God foresees all things, he does not impose necessity on his creatures," given that God knows beforehand what will occur because it will indeed occur. Calvin did not dispute the point that knowledge—even divine foreknowledge, as such—is not causal. He added, however, that the divine foreknowledge of the crucifixion rests on God's eternal

34 Calvin, *Commentariorum in Acta Apostolorum*, 22 (CO 48, col. 39).

35 Calvin, *De aeterna Dei praedestinatione*, 8 (CO 8, col. 273).

36 Calvin, *Plusieurs sermons*, 454 (CO 8, col. 661).

decree. The decree, freely willed by God, establishes the work of Christ, including Christ's death: God both wills and knows with certainty the effects of the divine will. God's foreknowledge remains distinct from the will that "rules and sets the bounds of all things."[37] So also at Acts 4:28, Calvin identifies providence as the "hidden counsel" of God, which "rules all things," and chides those, presumably Roman theologians in the wake of Trent, who acknowledge only divine foreknowledge and not divine rule as well, as Luke clarifies the point by speaking not only of divine "counsel" but also of the "hand" of God at work.[38]

It is not enough, however, simply to make the distinction and leave the relation between foreknowledge and divine will undefined and liable to confusion, as if God sits "idly in heaven" and loosens the rule over creatures so that they might simply follow their own natures. Scripture however, teaches otherwise—that God exercises a "special governance" over all things, including human actions. This governance ought not, moreover, become a matter of "delirious speculations" but rather be a source of consolation and hope in the knowledge that believers are protected by God from harm by Satan and the godless. To illustrate this truth, Peter taught that in the natural order, Christ's flesh would have been subject to corruption and his bones could have been broken, but God determined that neither would occur. Peter's point serves to reassure believers by the example of Christ's suffering, ordained by God, that the providence of God extends over all things, but also to remind believers to be content with this basic knowledge and not attempt to penetrate what is hidden in God.[39]

These arguments, published shortly after the conclusion of the Bolsec controversy, prepared the way for Calvin's 1556 additions to the commentary on Romans 8:29, "those whom he foreknew he also predestined to be conformed to the image of his Son," where foreknowledge precedes predestination in the *catena* of degrees in the ordering of salvation. Calvin not only parallels what he has stated in the commentary concerning Acts 2:23; he also adds a reference to the Bolsec controversy and the adversaries indicated in the *De aeterna Dei praedestinatione*: the divine foreknowledge is not a *nuda praescientia*, a mere or bare foreknowledge, as some fools imagine. Calvin argues further, echoing

37 Calvin, *Commentariorum in Acta Apostolorum*, 22 (CO 48, col. 39): "Quare, aliud est praescientia, quam voluntas Dei, qua regit ac temperat omnia."

38 Calvin, 22 (CO 48, col. 93).

39 Calvin, 22–23 (CO 48, col. 40).

his comment on Acts 2:23, that in this "foreknowledge" God is not concerned with something "outside of himself [extra ipsum]" but a knowledge that rests on God's own good pleasure (beneplacitum) and according to which the Lord knows the elect.[40] In 1557 and 1558, Calvin drew on Acts 2:23 and 4:28 in his responses to Sebastian Castellio in order to show that the divine counsel is the ultimate rule of justice and equity, even in the crucifixion. The acts of Judas, Pilate, and the Jews accomplished what God had ordained beforehand in such a way that one thing done by both God and a human being has two causes: namely, a divine and a human, the divine righteous and the human answerable for the sin.[41] In the 1559 *Institutio*, Calvin echoes his commentaries on Acts 2:23 and Romans 8:29, remarking that this divine foreknowledge indicates that God "is the author of our salvation" who "does not pass beyond himself" to identify those who will be saved—the divine foreknowledge (praescientia) is a preunderstanding (praecognitio) of those designated by God for salvation.[42]

By the Hands of the Godless

The sermon on Acts 2:23 combined the two points and offered a further detail that would not be included in the commentary, arguably because of the events between the presentation of the sermon and the publication of the commentary—namely, the Bolsec controversy. In his sermon, as he would in the commentary, Calvin noted that divine ordination will lead some people to conclude that God must be the cause of evil and that the wicked ought to be excused. It is true "that the wicked will execute nothing, except what God has ordained."[43] But this does not mean that God is the author of sin. God "reproves" evil—and when the wicked commit evil acts, "there is a resistance to the will of God." Calvin then added an explanation that he would leave out of the

40 Calvin, *In omnes Pauli Apostoli epistolas*, 74; cf. the textual analysis in Calvin, *Commentarius in Epistolam Pauli ad Romanos*, ed. T. H. L. Parker (Geneva: Librairie Droz, 1999), 177, CO 49, col. 160.

41 See John Calvin, *Brevis responsio Io. Calvini ad diluenda nebulonis cuiusdam calumnias* (Geneva: Jean Crespin, 1557), 5 (CO 9, col. 258); Calvin, *De occulta Dei providentia*, 70 (CO 7, col. 301), citing Augustine, *Epistle 48 to Vincentium*.

42 Calvin, *Institutio* (1559), III.xxii.6.

43 Calvin, *Plusieurs sermons*, 455 (CO 8, col. 661–62).

commentary: "From which it follows that God in no way wills that they do evil: but he permits that they do it."[44]

Then, as in the commentary, Calvin indicates that God "does not commit the faults that we commit."[45] Rather God turns evil acts to divine purposes. In the sermon, however, Calvin turns to the same concept of divine permission that he had categorically rejected in his refutation of Trent. The death of Christ provides Calvin with his primary evidence that God turns evil acts to divine purposes: "Jesus Christ suffered nothing without Divine permission: even so all that happens to us, comes from God."[46] Even when the devil commits evil, with no other purpose than committing evil, God limits the act to punish those who deserve punishment. So also, when "God will permit a thief or criminal to steal something from a good person," God uses the event to test the patience of the faithful. Robbers are wicked, they act against the will of God, and they intend evil—but in all such cases (again, as Calvin would state in the commentary), one "must look much higher" and realize that the act "was not done without the providence of God."[47]

In the sermon on 2:23, as distinct from the commentary, permission enters, in juxtaposition with arguments concerning providence, as the basis for arguing two levels of causality: a human level operating within the divine willing but, as permitted, performing an act that God does not directly commit; and a divine level operating with an entirely different intention, restraining and ordering the human act in accordance with the divine counsel and God's appointed ends. Calvin also, here, employed a frequently used metaphor—the bridle—as indicating God's restraint of the wicked.[48] The contours of his argument also parallel his use of Augustine in the *Antidotum*—the wicked have not been commanded by God; they are in fact disobedient of God's commands. This explanation is not to be taken as a reversal of Calvin's position against Trent: he does not here indicate that God works "only permissively"; he also indicates the operation of an active providence, but the positive use of permission is nonetheless unexpected.

44 Calvin, 455–56 (CO 8, col. 662).

45 Calvin, 456 (CO 8, col. 662): "il ne commet pas lex vices que nous commettons."

46 Calvin, 452 (CO 8, col. 660): "que Jesus Christ n'a rien souffert sans la permission Divine: aussi tout ce qui nous adviendra, vient de Dieu."

47 Calvin, 456 (CO 8, col. 662).

48 Calvin, 451 (CO 8, col. 659–60).

In his sermon on Acts 4, with reference to verses 27–28, Calvin makes much of the failure of the evil acts of Herod and Pilate to achieve their desired end, "because they did nothing but what [God] had completed in his counsel."[49] Nothing, Calvin declared, can take place apart from the providence of God, who has cared for the church since the beginning of the world. Neither do such evil acts diminish the power of God, since they can only occur if God "has loosened the bridle on the wicked"—the disciples recognized, however, that "Christ suffered for the redemption of the world" and that this occurred because of God's "counsel and providence."[50] The bridle metaphor is repeated to the same purpose in Calvin's commentary on the text, and although here he does not mention either Herod or Pilate, Calvin does echo the sermon in his comment that the "enemies" of Christ "could do no more than God had established."[51] The sermon at verse 28 returns to the theme of the earlier sermon on Acts 2:23, that believers should not be caught up in "obscure and troublesome speculations" concerning providence but rather hold confident that "God in his strict counsel disposes nothing, except for his glory and for our salvation."[52] The commentary, which had made this point at Acts 2:23, does not repeat the warning, but only identifies the doctrine as *insignis*—eminent, remarkable, extraordinary—and notes that although the divine counsel is hidden (arcanum), we know that only what God has determined will occur.[53]

In October 1551, in his brief reply to Bolsec, Calvin denied the charge that he had ever written "that God necessitated men to sin"[54] and indicated that he "explicitly explained and declared that men are not constrained to do good or evil, but that those who do good do it of a free will which God gives them by his holy spirit. Those who do evil do it of their own natural will which is corrupted and wicked."[55] Bolsec raised the issue of foreknowledge, arguing that since God is eternal, God cannot have a greater foreknowledge of one thing than of another, and therefore distinguishes believers from unbelievers in the same

49 Calvin, *Sermons on the Acts*, 108, ll 29–30.

50 Calvin, 108, l. 39; 109, l. 4.

51 Calvin, *Commentariorum in Acta Apostolorum*, 51–52 (CO 48, col. 93).

52 Calvin, *Sermons on the Acts*, 109, ll. 11–14.

53 Calvin, *Commentariorum in Acta Apostolorum*, 52 (CO 48, col. 93).

54 John Calvin, *Résponse de Calvin*, CO 8, col. 182: "Quant est de moy il me calomne fualsement, disant que iay escrit, que Dieu necessite les hommes à peché."

55 Calvin, CO 8, col. 182.

moment.[56] Calvin made no response to this point, but the Genevan ministers writing conjointly did so: they note Bolsec's ignorance of the distinction, known even to schoolchildren, that "what is neither before nor after in time is nonetheless ordered" and that therefore God can foreknow the fall prior to establishing its remedy in Christ and of divine willing make the distinction between the elect and the reprobate.[57] Bolsec did not raise the issue of divine permission. Accordingly, Calvin did not address the issue of evil acts being done by permission, and he did not offer any further explanation of how evil occurs within the providential willing of God.

Divine permission is mentioned again, albeit almost in passing, in Calvin's closing response to Bolsec, the *Congrégation* of December 1551, with reference to the fall of Adam. Calvin asks several rhetorical questions: Didn't God foresee the fall when Adam was created? Did the fall occur according to God's will? How could God permit this to happen?[58] Calvin responds affirmatively to all of the questions but warns his hearers not to "murmur" against God, who "has ordained all things in his counsel," and whose counsels are "an abyss" too deep for human comprehension.[59] The *Congrégation* offers neither explanation nor qualification of the notion of permission. Later in the *Congrégation*, he explains that evils occur in the world according to God's will and foreknowledge as justly administered chastisements. The wicked, then, are left without excuse for violating God's revealed command, but their acts remain within the

56 Jerome Bolsec, *Les responses de Me. Iherome detenuz es mains de MM. les Sindiques*, CO 8, col. 161.

57 *Sensuyvent les repliques que font les ministres de la parolle de Dieu contre les responces escriptes par maistre Hierosme Bolsec*, CO 8, col. 169.

58 John Calvin, *Congrégation faite en l'eglise de Geneve par M. Jean Calvin. En laquelle la matiere de l'election eternelle de Dieu fut sommairement et clairement par luy deduite, et ratifiée d'un commun accord par ses freres Ministres: repoussant l'erreur d'un semeur de fausse doctrine, qui effrontement avoit desgorgé son venin* (Geneva: Vincent Brès, 1562), 43–44 (CO 8, col. 110): "Quand Dieu a creé Adam, dira-on, n'a-it pas bien preveu ce qui devoit avenir? et n'en a-it pas disposé selon sa volonté? . . . Comment a-il permis que cela ait esté ainsi fait?" Note the translation, *Calvinism by Calvin; Being the Substance of Discourses Delivered by J. Calvin and the Other Ministers of Geneva on the Doctrines of Grace*, trans. with an intro. by R. Govett (London: James Nisbet, 1840).

59 Calvin, *Congrégation*, 44–45 (CO 8, col. 110).

divine purpose and ultimately serve the divinely ordained end—a point that offers consolation to the faithful.[60]

Calvin's 1552 commentary on Acts 2:23—the first portion of the locus, where Calvin dealt with divine foreknowledge and counsel—led directly to the question, How can the fact human wickedness be reconciled with this understanding of providence? Here again, in this second part of his exposition of the verse, Calvin offered significantly more detail than his predecessors and contemporaries. Bullinger did raise the issue that whereas the divine counsel ordained the death of Christ to satisfy God's justice or righteousness, it offered no excuse to Judas and the Jews, as if they had not sinned or incurred no guilt for the crucifixion, but his argument is not as expansive as Calvin's and does draw out either the issue of the divine ordination of sin or of the requirement of obedience to the revealed will of God.[61] Calvin comments that the divine ordination of Christ's death "by the hands of the godless" can lead people to two "absurd" conclusions: namely, that God is the author of sin or that, since evil deeds are done by divine ordination, those who commit them have not sinned. In his commentary, Calvin addressed the second absurdity first by making a traditional distinction between the ultimate will of God and the revealed will that requires obedience.[62] When the "godless" bring about "what God has established for himself," they do in a sense obey God.[63] They have not, however, been truly obedient to God, "for obedience is produced by a voluntary disposition."[64] The wicked prove themselves to be ignorant of the law of God. They cannot, therefore, be seen as obedient to the will of God, given that they neither follow God's law nor make any attempt to know it. Obedience, moreover depends on a knowledge

---

60 Calvin, 61–62 (CO 8, col. 116).

61 Bullinger, *In Acta Apostolorum*, 18; note also Dionysius Carthusianus's *In epistolas omnes canonicas*, 84v–85r, commenting that Judas's act was ungodly (impie), but God, in his predetermination and foreknowledge, willed Christ's death for the sake of the human race, as the prophets foretold.

62 On this issue of distinctions concerning the divine will in Calvin's thought, see Richard A. Muller, *Calvin and the Reformed Tradition: On the Work of Christ and the Order of Salvation* (Grand Rapids, MI: Baker, 2012), 113–20.

63 Calvin, *Commentarius in Acta Apostolorum*, 2:23 (CO 48, col. 40): "quod apud se Deus statuit."

64 Calvin, *Commentarius* (CO 48, col. 40): "nam obedientiae ex voluntario affecto nascitur."

of God's revealed will as presented in the law of God. Those who truly obey the will of God, then, are those who are obedient to God's law and who "willingly subject themselves to his rule."[65]

The second issue addressed in the commentary is the implication of the divine ordination the death of Christ—namely, that God must be the "author of evil." Calvin's response denies that God is the author of evil or of sin by insisting on two distinct levels of intention and causality in the act. There is a "depraved affection" or desire underlying the acts of the wicked, whose acts are to be assessed by their intended result or end: theft and murder result from evil intentions and end in evil. The willing of God, however, in all such evil acts has a different intention and end. The divine willing or ordination of evil acts is to be placed or located on a higher level of causality, inasmuch as God uses the acts of the wicked to punish some people and to strengthen the patience of others.[66] Significantly, in neither of these two arguments does Calvin follow the pattern of his sermon and reference divine permission. He does, however, in the commentary on Acts 4:28 reiterate the metaphor of the bridle: "We know that [God's providence] is the highest & sole ruler of all that occurs in the world: that the Devil and all the godless are restrained with [God's] bridle, so that they do no harm to us."[67]

Calvin returned to the concept of divine permission in his *De aeterna Dei praedestinatione* of 1552. Here, with not only Bolsec as his adversary but also with detailed regard to the earlier polemics of Albert Pighius and Georgius of Sicily, Calvin took an explicitly negative line of argument, returning to his polemic against Trent and denying that God acts merely by permission or that "permission be substituted in place of action" in descriptions of the divine work.[68] It is foolishness to claim that things occur by divine permission apart from divine will. Although, clearly, there are evil acts, and these acts are not pleasing to God, it is a mistake to explain them as arising because of an "otiose" permission on God's part, particularly since Scripture not only describes evil events as willed by God but also identifies God as their author.[69]

65 Calvin, 23 (CO 48, col. 40).

66 Calvin, *Commentarius in Acta Apostolorum*, 23 (CO 48, col. 40).

67 Calvin, 52 (CO 48, col. 93).

68 Calvin, *De aeterna Dei praedestinatione*, 187 (CO 8, col. 359).

69 Calvin, 187 (CO 8, col. 359).

Calvin's final resolutions of the argument, still referencing either Acts 2:23 or Acts 4:28, could maintain that there is a single, simple will in God, according to which human beings like Herod and Pilate commit evil acts while God executes what has been ordained. The weakness of the human mind prevents full comprehension of the way in which God both wills and nills, or rejects.[70] Against Castellio, Calvin explicitly refers his readers to the larger exposition of the doctrine in his commentary on Acts 2.[71] It is also here, against Castellio, that Calvin poses a question: When God permits something, does it permit willing it or not willing it? The latter option is excluded by the Psalmist, who states, "God does whatsoever he wills." God, accordingly, is seen to permit willingly, not in a lazy or otiose manner.[72] Arguably, Calvin retained a notion of permission that was, in his last statements on the issue, qualified as an actively willed permission: what he originally condemned, and continued to condemn throughout his career, was a mere or bare permission unconnected with a positive divine will to bring about some end.

Some Conclusions

The broadest and most general conclusion that can be drawn from the present examination of Calvin's interpretation of Acts 2:23 is simply that his famous *Institutio* ought not to be used (as it has often been) as the sole or even the primary index to the content of his theology. Instead, the larger body of his work, in particular his interpretations of Scripture, both in sermons and in commentaries, needs to be read against the background of his ongoing work in Geneva, including the controversies in which he was involved. In addition, in this particular case, Calvin's focus on Acts 2:23 did not arise out of a reading of other commentators on the text. Rather, his developing thought on the divine, foreknowledge, the decree, or counsel, the divine will and permission, and the interpretation of Acts 2:23 belongs to a trajectory of argument that began with

70 Calvin, *Institutio* (1559), I.xviii.3, citing Acts 4:28; cf. Calvin, *De occulta Dei providentia*, 70 (CO 9, col. 300–301), citing Acts 4:28, 2:23.

71 Calvin, *De occulta Dei providentia*, 73 (CO 9, col. 302).

72 Calvin, 65 (CO 9, col. 299): "Aut si tibi tantopere arridet verbum permittendi, responde, Volensne permittat, an nolens. Huic secundo membro reclamat quod legitur in Psalmo, Deum facere quaecunque vult. Si autem volens permittit, otiosum fingere nefas erit"; quoting Ps 115:3, without citation.

Calvin's pointed negative assertions against divine permission in the 1547 *Antidotum*, and then received a more positive turn in Calvin's sermons of 1549–50. It was then modified during the Bolsec controversy, leading to a more technical version in the commentary of 1552 and a more nuanced negative accent on divine permission in the *De aeterna Dei praedestinatione* of the same year. Beyond that, exegesis of the passage, together with the Bolsec controversy, appears to have had an impact on the 1556 additions to the Romans commentary, and it served also to anchor a new paragraph in the 1559 *Institutio*.

In all of the related expositions examined concerning the issue of divine ordination even the acts of the wicked, Calvin assumes two levels of causality: the willing of the divine first cause and the willing of the human secondary causes. He also assumes a single, simple will in God that works toward a single ultimate end, while explaining its temporal execution through the use of further distinctions between the ultimate will of God that remains hidden, the preceptive will of God that is revealed in the law, and the divine willing of ends that differ from those willed by human beings in the same event.[73] This view of two levels of willing the same event, with altogether different intentions and ends, allowed Calvin to counter claims that God is the author of sin with fairly standard argumentation drawn from the scholastic tradition. When the human willing corresponds with the requirements of God's law, the divine will and the human will are in concert, and the willed good has its ultimate source in God. When the human willing is disobedient, the human and divine wills run counter to one another, although there could be no human act apart from the overarching divine causality. There is, in other words, a perverse exercise of human freedom against the revealed will of God that identifies wickedness, is rightly punished by God, is not directly caused or authored by God, but that has been ordained in God's eternal counsel and will be used for God's own purpose.

Calvin offered no explanation of the reason for his unqualified positive language of divine permission in his sermon of 1550 on Acts 2:23 or for the removal of the concept from his commentary of 1552, but the reason is fairly clear. In the sermon, he was content to make a point rather simply and without further explanation given the nature of his audience. It was not so much the term *permission* that he found obnoxious but a particular usage found or implied in Tridentine Roman theology, and he was able to argue against the

73 On which, see Muller, *Calvin and the Reformed Tradition*, 118–20.

"Papists" in his sermon without raising (or ultimately resolving) the technical issue. By the time he came to publish the commentary and the treatise, he had gone through a highly vituperative controversy in which his opponent, Jerome Bolsec, had grounded election on foreknowledge of belief and had accused Calvin of teaching that the divine will is the cause of sin. In his *De aeterna Dei praedestinatione*, Calvin provided a further development of his argument on foreknowledge and permission, returning to his anti-Tridentine position, but now clearly identifying an otiose or lazy divine permission apart from divine willing as the subject of his denial. In his final forays into the debate over the issue, still using Acts 2:23 and 4:28 as major biblical grounds of argument, he developed a distinction between mere or unwilling permission and willing permission.

In sum, Acts 2:23 and 4:28 appear consistently in Calvin's writings on the subjects of divine causality, foreknowledge, and human willing, particularly human willing of evil, as primary loci for examination and resolution of the issues. His homiletical and exegetical examinations of these texts, in the wake of his highly negative response to the Council of Trent's understanding of divine permission, were instrumental in the development of his thought both in later polemics and in the final edition of his *Institutio*. As such, his sermons and the commentary illustrate his pattern of working from biblical text to theological formulation and their argumentation, which underscores the need to look at the full corpus of his writings in order to come to an understanding of his theology.

Sam, Sham, or Satan?

Reformation Readings of 1 Samuel 28

Derek Cooper

> Art thou forlorn of God and com'st to me?
> What can I tell you then but misery?
> —Henry Purcell, "In Guilty Night"

Henry Purcell, perhaps the most famous English composer in the seventeenth century, knew a good scene when he saw it. Of all the passages in First and Second Samuel, he put to music the one that stood head and shoulders above the rest.[1] In fact, 1 Samuel 28 is a passage so daunting and dumbfounding that even modern commentators—lavishly aided by thousands of years of interpretation—still do not know what to do with it any more than the ancients did. In his commentary on First Samuel, for instance, biblical scholar Keith Bodner described this section as "the strangest episode in the entire book."[2] The challenges involved in understanding this passage so perplex many contemporary scholars that they have posited redactional changes as the most logical explanation for its strangeness.[3]

They have a point. As Francesca Aran Murphy points out, 1 Samuel 28 is "the only ghost story in the Hebrew scripture,"[4] meaning that there are

1 Henry Purcell, "In Guilty Night," in *The Beauties of Purcell: A Selection of the Favorite Songs, Duets, Trios, and Choruses from the Different Works* (Birchall, 1805), 2:8–9. Henry Purcell was perhaps the most famous English composer in the seventeenth century. He composed this song based on Saul's encounter with the woman of Endor in First Samuel 28.

2 Keith Bodner, *1 Samuel: A Narrative Commentary* (Sheffield, UK: Sheffield University Press, 2009), 290.

3 See, for instance, Kyle McCarter's *1 Samuel* commentary in the Anchor Yale Bible Commentaries (New Haven, CT: Yale University Press, 1990), 422.

4 Francesca Aran Murphy, *1 Samuel*, Brazos Theological Commentary (Grand Rapids, MI: Brazos, 2010), 254.

limited comparative clues to its interpretation. Commentators of the early church, however, agreed on at least one point: a dead prophet is better than a living king. Even though Saul was the ruler of Israel, and a king whose reign inaugurated with great promise, he was always overshadowed by his mentor Samuel, the man—or at least, his ghost—who has consistently "occupied center stage"[5] in the drama of the interpretation of this passage.

When it comes to the niceties of exegesis, however, "commentators have long struggled with this haunting episode."[6] Careful readers recognize the inherent irony of the story. Why is Saul searching for someone who practices a vocation he has outlawed? As the medieval Jewish rabbi Simeon ben Levi humorously noted, Saul's action is akin to someone who wonders why he no longer hears the crow of roosters after ordering all of their heads to be chopped off.[7] King Saul—in desperation, in disguise, in fasting, at night, in enemy territory, and at wit's end—turns to a medium for the wisdom that the Lord has hidden from him. Because of the great storytelling featured in the book of Samuel, the ultimate outcome comes as no surprise. Saul, the king who originally stood head and shoulders above his peers, now lies facedown in the mud in obeisance to a dead idol, foreshowing the death he himself will imminently encounter at the hands of the pagan Philistines.

Early and Medieval Interpretation

Before focusing on Reformation interpretations of this passage, it goes without saying that early and medieval commentators paved the road that most later interpreters have been compelled to walk. In general, these commentators erected two different exegetical paths to this difficult passage: (1) asserting that the being who materialized in front of Saul was Samuel, and (2) believing that it was a ghost or a demon. There are also, of course, subcategories that developed

5 Rowan Greer and Margaret Mitchell, *The "Belly-Myther" of Endor: Interpretations of 1 Kingdoms 28 in the Early Church* (Atlanta: Society of Biblical Literature, 2007), vii.

6 Bodner, *1 Samuel*, 290.

7 *Yalkut Shimoni: Midrash al Torah Nevim u-Khetuvim*, 2 vols. (Jerusalem: Levin-Epstein, 1966–67), 2:730; Shaul Bar, *God's First King: The Story of Saul* (Eugene, OR: Cascade Books, 2013), 110.

within these two (such as whether it was God or the witch who conjured up Samuel or a demon), but exegetes tended to follow one of these two paths.

In his dialogue with a Jewish man named Trypho in the city of Ephesus, for instance, Justin Martyr argued that the woman at Endor raised the figure of Samuel directly from hell on the basis of his prior conviction that all humans—whether living in eternal blessedness or suffering in eternal condemnation—possess immortal souls and are thus alive and able to materialize on earth upon command.[8] Origen—though ruthlessly mocking commentators who believed that Jewish saints like Samuel, Abraham, and Moses were destined to live in Hades after a lifetime of faithfulness to God—maintained that the person of Samuel truly materialized. In his sermon on 1 Samuel 28, for example, Origen stated that "the person who says these things [about Jewish saints like Samuel] does not like the struggles in admitting that Samuel is really the one who is brought up."[9] Continuing to poke fun at earlier commentators, Origen asked, "What is it that *the woman saw*?" The answer, of course, is "*Samuel*." "And why is it not said [instead]," Origen asked his exegetical antagonists, that "the woman saw a little demon that [only] pretended to be Samuel?"[10] Origen concluded that "there is nothing offensive in this passage."[11] The text means what it means: Samuel appeared from the great beyond. If anyone takes offense at a holy man of God being raised from the grave by a common witch, Augustine of Hippo would later respond that it was actually God—through the intermediary of a witch—who brought back the prophet Samuel. Either way, Augustine also pointed out, the appearance of Samuel to Saul in the Old

8 Justin Martyr, "Dialogue with Trypho 105.2–5," in *Writings of Saint Justin Martyr*, trans. Thomas Falls, The Fathers of the Church: A New Translation (Washington, DC: Catholic University of America Press, 1948), 6:312.

9 Origen, *Homilies on Jeremiah and 1 Kings 28*, trans. John Clark Smith, The Fathers of the Church: A New Translation (Washington, DC: Catholic University of America Press, 1998), 97:322. Note that First Kings 28 refers to First Samuel 28 in the Septuagint.

10 Origen, 97:323.

11 Origen, 97:332. For more on Origen's reading of this passage, see Patricia Cox, "Origen and the Witch of Endor: Toward an Iconoclastic Typology," *Anglican Theological Review*. 66 (1984): 137–47.

Testament was not any different from the appearance of Moses and Elijah to Jesus in the New Testament during Christ's transfiguration.[12]

Tertullian, by contrast, rejected the notion that Samuel himself appeared before Saul. In his ancient monograph on the soul, he asserted that while the voice of Samuel was possibly authentic, the being that appeared as Samuel was a demon and not a human.[13] "God forbid," Tertullian exclaimed, that a deceased man or woman of God could be extracted out of Hades like a common magician pulling a rabbit from a hat. The saints of old were not acts in a circus. Putting into application a passage from the New Testament, Tertullian reasoned as follows: if Satan can masquerade "as an angel of light," as the apostle Paul wrote in 2 Cor 11:14, Satan can certainly masquerade "as a human of light."[14]

Exegetes from late antiquity—such as Ambrose, Dracontius, Eustathius, Gregory of Nyssa, Jerome, and Sulpicius Severus—though differing in style and emphasizing different themes, largely agreed with Tertullian.[15] It was important for these commentators to stress that all souls remained in Hades until the general resurrection of Christ. Due to their readings of the parable of Lazarus in Luke 16, they understood the righteous to be waiting in Abraham's bosom while the unrighteous waited in a separate location filled with fiery judgment. And if the righteous and unrighteous were thus separated in Hades, how much more so are righteous figures like Samuel separate from evil demons? As a result, there is no way in hell that a human witch could bodily raise the holy and deceased Samuel from Abraham's bosom. Thomas Aquinas, though emphasizing different aspects, represents many medieval exegetes who followed in Tertullian's footsteps. In his *Summa*, Thomas wrote, "It was not the soul of Samuel, but some evil spirit personifying him" that materialized.[16] This was a common view among medieval Christian commentators.

12 Augustine of Hippo, *De diversis quaestionibus ad Simplicianum 2.3.1*-3, in *Patrologia Latina*, ed. Jacques-Paul Migne (Paris: 1865), 40:142-144.

13 Tertullian, *De Anima* 57, in *Patrologia Latina* 2:749.

14 Tertullian 57, in *Patrologia Latina* 2:749.

15 See K. A. D. Smelik, "The Witch of Endor: 1 Samuel 28 in Rabbinic and Christian Exegesis till 800 A.D.," *Vigiliae Christianae* 33 (1977): 160–79; Greer and Mitchell, *"Belly-Myther" of Endor*.

16 Thomas Aquinas, *Summa Theologica* 2da, 2dae, clxxv, 5.

Reformation Readings

Having served as co-editor of the Reformation Commentary on Scripture series' title on Samuel, Kings, and Chronicles, my research has led me to conclude that this encounter between Saul and the woman at Endor elicits more commentary from Reformation interpreters than any other passage in First or Second Samuel. Stated more directly, 1 Samuel 28 is possibly the most notorious passage in all of the historical books of the Hebrew scriptures among Reformation commentators. Indeed, as historian Charles Zika notes, there are "frequent references to this story [of Saul, the witch, and Samuel] in demonological texts of the sixteenth century, as well as its repeated depiction in woodcuts from the 1560s and 1570s."[17] It is also in this time period that commentators mostly settled on identifying the woman of Endor as a "sorcerer" or "witch" rather than merely as a woman involved in magical arts or divination. In this instance, one word makes all the difference. In the 1545 edition of Luther's Bible, the woman at Endor is called *ein Weib die hat einen Warsager geist* ("a woman who has a divining spirit"); however, in his gloss, Luther refers to her as *eine Zuberin*—that is, a "sorcerer."[18] What's more, Martin Luther's realistic readings of the Bible always assumed the actual existence of Satan and witchcraft—beliefs that were enlivened by his own personal experiences with the devil. Luther's legacy only heightened Protestant speculation about these matters in the years to come.

Due in part to the commanding exegesis of Martin Luther as well as the well-trod path of medieval commentary, virtually all Protestant Reformers who wrote commentaries on this episode argued that it was the devil who appeared to Saul. Although the ancient interpretation going all the way back to Justin Martyr and Origen that Samuel appeared as a man had not completely died, the satanic interpretation held sway over those who wrote official commentaries on First Samuel.

What is most interesting to me, however, is that most authors during this same time period who wrote demonological tracts and treatises argued that neither Samuel nor the devil appeared to Saul that fateful night. Instead, no

17 Charles Zika, "The Witch of Endor before the Witch Trials," in *Contesting Orthodoxy in Medieval and Early Modern Europe: Heresy, Magic, and Witchcraft*, ed. Louise Nyholm Kallestrup and Raisa Maria Toivo, Palgrave Historical Studies in Witchcraft and Magic (Cham, Switzerland: Palgrave Macmillan, 2017), 168.

18 Zika, 169.

doubt influenced by growing interest in scientific matters in the early modern period as well as the dramatic rise of witch trials—which were a regular occurrence throughout the seventeenth century—demonological writings largely maintained that the witch of Endor had concocted the entire ordeal of Samuel's appearance.

The Reformation Commentary Tradition: A Devil

Heinrich Bullinger, though he never wrote a commentary on this book, embodies Reformation exegetical interpretation of this encounter between the woman, Saul, and Samuel. In his book *Decades*, he wrote,

> Devils are spiritual substances. But no one, I think, is able to say exactly in what way they assume bodies or how they appear to human beings. Indeed, the story of Samuel being brought up by a witch shows clearly that devils put on bodies and shapes that are different from their own. *It was not Samuel who was brought up from the dead; rather, the chief architect of lies—the devil—deceived King Saul by pretending to be Samuel.* For Paul testifies that "Satan disguises himself as an angel of light." Other stories testify that the devil is an extraordinary deceiver who assumes various forms and shapes.[19]

Working off of the reasoning of Tertullian, Bullinger contended that it was the devil, or Satan, who appeared in the form of Samuel. The vast majority of exegetical commentators adopted this interpretation, including Thomas Adams, Lancelot Andrewes, Johannes Bugenhagen, John Calvin, Lambert Daneau, Daniel Dyke, the writers of the English Annotations, Martin Luther, Peter Martyr, Philip Melanchthon, Francois Perrault, Johannes Piscator, and Andrew Willet.[20] It is not necessary to cite all of their commentary; some examples will suffice.

---

19 Heinrich Bullinger, *Decades* 4:9, 327, citing 2 Cor 11:14.

20 Derek Cooper and Martin Lohrmann, eds., *1–2 Samuel, 1–2 Kings, 1–2 Chronicles*, Reformation Commentary on Scripture (Grand Rapids, MI: InterVarsity, 2016); J. M. Buckley, *Faith Healing, Christian Science and Kindred Phenomena* (New York: Century, 1892), 221; John Calvin, "John Calvin: Witchcraft and the Reformation,"

For instance, Lambert Daneau, a French theologian who taught in both Geneva and the Low Countries, took issue with those who denied that "Satan can appear to people in the shape of a person." After all, he reasoned, "if we should say this cannot be done, then we must deny the meeting and talking together of Christ with the devil" in the Synoptic Gospels.[21] Andrew Willet, an Anglican who wrote dozens of biblical and theological works while a parish priest, agreed. He took the view that "the devil, counterfeiting Samuel's person, said [these things]."[22] And Daniel Dyke, an English contemporary of Willet's, maintained that "the devil played with Saul" by donning the form of Samuel and assuming the mantle of deception.[23]

Likewise, the most personal of testimonies about the devil impersonating Samuel came from the pen of a French Reformed pastor named Francois Perrault, whose most prominent work was titled *Demonologie: Ou Traitte des Demons et Sorciers*, written in French in 1613, but not published for decades. Perrault wrote that "the devil . . . certainly appeared"[24] to King Saul, arguing that the devil had a long history of appearing to humans and deceiving them. In fact, Perrault knew this from personal experience. In the second part of his book *Demonologie*, Perrault detailed how a poltergeist had haunted his own Huguenot home in the tiny village of Mâcon in Burgundy, conversing with Perrault, reciting psalms, playing tricks, making predictions, throwing stones, and even pulling away bedsheets on cold Burgundian nights. The mayhem continued for months, with townspeople keeping the poltergeist company at night so the Perrault family could attempt to sleep in peace. Though surely unintended, the suffering of a Christian family—even a Protestant one in a Catholic country—at the hands of a demon was too much for the Catholic Church to abide, and so even it agreed to help, sparking perhaps the greatest act of ecumenism in that town in decades. It was not until the end of Advent that the

in *Witchcraft in Europe, 400–1700: A Documentary History*, ed. Alan Charles Kors and Edward Peters (Philadelphia: University of Pennsylvania Press, 2001), 269.

21 Lambert Daneau, *Dialogue of Witches* (London: T. East, 1575), iv.

22 Andrew Willet, *A Harmony on the First Book of Samuel* (Cambridge: Leonard Green, 1607), 315.

23 Daniel Dyke, *The Mystery of Self-Deceiving: A Discourse and Discovery of the Deceitfulness of Man's Heart* (London: William Stansby, 1633), 23–24.

24 Francois Perrault, *Demonologie: Ou Traitte des Demons et Sorciers* (Geneva: Pierre Aubert, 1653), 91–92.

poltergeist tired of terrorizing Perrault the pastor. The day after the poltergeist made it known that it was leaving the haunted Huguenot house for good, local townspeople slayed a giant serpent as it slithered away from the home, a viper unknown in those parts.

THE REFORMATION DEMONOLOGICAL TRADITION: A DECEPTION

Related to the works of Daneau and especially Perrault, one of the most interesting developments in the latter half of the sixteenth century was the rise of demonological treatises, mostly written by Catholic and Protestant authors. Though both traditions affirmed the existence of the devil, Catholic and Protestant writers differed wildly in their interpretations about the appearance, domain, and removal of the devil's power on earth. By this time, the classic text on witch-hunting, *Malleus Maleficarum*—first published in 1487—had already gone through no fewer than fourteen printed editions,[25] which is not at all surprising given that "the 'science' of demons, or demonology, [had] largely [been] a medieval creation, though it looked to the Bible to sanction its basic claims."[26]

Focusing on Protestant demonological texts touching upon 1 Samuel 28, Reginald Scot's *Discoverie of Witchcraft*, published in the year 1584, gave popularity to the view that the entire episode was a ruse. Scot, an Englishman and Member of Parliament whose demonological treatment was exceedingly influential at the time, offered a detailed treatment of this passage in his work, dutifully sifting through the entire exegetical tradition before ultimately discarding almost all of it. In the ninth chapter of his book, he wrote quite simply that "it is not likelie that God would answer Saule by dead Samuell, when he would not answer him by living Samuell."[27] Paying homage to fellow Englishman William Occam's famous logical dictum, Scot chose pure logic over the interpretive tradition he disagreed with but still respected. In short, Scot argued that "the residue of the doctors" erroneously believed that "the divell was fetcht up in

25 Gary Waite, *Eradicating the Devil's Minions: Anabaptists and Witches in Reformation Europe, 1525–1600* (Toronto: University of Toronto Press, 2007), 4.

26 Geoffrey Scarre and John Callow, *Witchcraft and Magic in Sixteenth- and Seventeenth-Century Europe*, 2nd ed. (Hampshire, UK: Palgrave Macmillion, 2001), 14.

27 Reginald Scot, *The Discoverie of Witchcraft* (1584; London: Elliot Stock, 1886), 113.

[Samuel's] likeness."[28] Continuing on, he reasoned, "For it is ridiculous . . . to leave manifest things, and such as by naturall reason may be prooved, to seeke unknowne things, which by no likelihood can be conceived, nor tried anie rule of reason . . . for what need so farre fetches, as to fetch a divell supernaturallie out of hell, when the illusion may be here by natural meanes deciphered?"[29] Instead of seeing Samuel, Scot maintained that Saul was deceived by the cunning woman at Endor, who "plaied hir part" by deceiving the king with cunning ease. So confident was Scot of his interpretation that he encouraged the reader to weigh his thoughts against the plain words of Scripture: "Read the text and see [for yourself]," he urged.[30] The case of the witch at Endor was easily solved. As he concluded, "This Pythonist being Ventriloqua; that is, Speaking as it were from the bottome of hir bellie, did cast her selfe into a transe, and so abused Saule, answering to Saule in Samuels name, in hir counterfeit hollow voice [as many other witches have done subsequently]."[31]

Witch Trials

Not surprisingly, the witch trials of the late sixteenth and seventeenth centuries ran riotously in the imaginations of men and women across the Western world, persuading many casual hearers and readers that the woman at Endor was, most assuredly and unreservedly, a witch performing dark magic and ensnared in devilish arts. As Charles Zika notes, it is in "this later period [when] the new technologies of printing and printmaking, the widespread anxiety about any practices hinting of sorcery and magic, and the increasing number of judicial trials for witchcraft" accelerated and encouraged not only commentary about this episode from First Samuel but also visual representations.[32] Things were getting scandalously out of hand. During the time of the Reformation, the reality of magic, witches, and their relationship to the devil were alive and well (at least as a figure of speech), as is evidenced through cultural artifacts.

This mindset is perfectly captured in King James's book written on this topic called *Daemonologie*. Though published in 1597, it is deeply connected

28 Scot, 114.

29 Scot, 115, 119.

30 Scot, 119.

31 Scot, 121.

32 Zika, "Witch of Endor," 169.

to a series of witch trials that the king was involved in personally in 1590—a century before America's notorious witch trials in New England. Called by historians the "North Berwick witch trials," dozens of people, including nobility, were accused of the devil's art of witchcraft. In due time, and not at all surprising given the nature of their treatment, many of the accused confessed their secret dealings with the devil under torture, revealing that they had crafted a plot to kill King James and members of his household. As the king declared in the preface to his book, "The fearefull aboundinge at this time in this countrie, of these detestable slaves of the Devil, the Witches or enchanters, hath moved me (beloved reader) to dispatch in post, this following treatise of mine . . . to resolve the doubting . . . both that such assaults of Satan are most certainly practised, and that the instrument thereof merits most severely to be punished."[33] Although King James lived during the first series of witch trials in modern England, thousands of people would be accused of witchcraft and tortured during the early modern period.[34] Indeed, notes historian Christopher Smout, "most [witch] trials took place [only] after the mid-sixteenth century," especially in North America.[35]

CONCLUSION

In their preface to patristic readings of 1 Samuel 28, Rowan Greer and Margaret Mary Mitchell make a passing comment that pertains to the phenomena of our "strange" pericope. As English speakers, the very way we are accustomed to designate the woman of Endor as a witch—"a title that perhaps evokes pointed hats and the perils of Dorothy and Toto more than necromancy, the diviner's arts, or ecstatic prophecy"[36]—demonstrates just how influential this third interpretive option, which developed most distinctly during the Reformation period, became. A whole new industry devoted to demons emerged in the sixteenth

33 King James, *Daemonologie* (1597), preface.

34 Christopher Smout, *A History of the Scottish People 1560–1830* (Fontana/Collins, 1987).

35 James Sharpe, *Instruments of Darkness: Witchcraft in Early Modern England* (Philadelphia: University of Pennsylvania Press, 1996), 5.

36 Greer and Mitchell, *"Belly-Myther" of Endor*, xii.

century, with witch-hunting becoming a favorite pastime of European towns from the latter half of that century onward.[37]

Obsession with witchcraft and wizardry was on the rise, even among the educated class of European society—whether regarded with the skepticism found in Heinrich Agrippa's *Three Books concerning Occult Philosophy* (1531, 1533), Johann Weyer's *On the Tricks of Demons* (1563), and Reginald Scot's *The Discoverie of Witchcraft* (1584) or focused on intellectual defense, as in John Calvin's *Admonition against Astrology* (1549), George Clifford's *Discourse and Dialogue*, and Lambert Daneau's *Dialogue of Witches* (1575). As P. G. Maxwell-Stuart notes, "People in sixteenth-century Europe lived amid a multiplicity of interpenetrating worlds."[38] There was the physical, the celestial, and the demonic; heaven, hell, and purgatory; humans, saints, and demons; life, death, and the in-between. Witches and warlocks roamed the earth as sneakily as they did steadfastly. And far from raising the holy Samuel out of his blessed sleep with neither nice nor nefarious features as a diviner, the "witch" at Endor either conjured up a malignant spirit through the forces of darkness or simply bamboozled the godforsaken Saul by stealth and trickery. Either way, the woman at Endor was a witch, and the being she extracted from the grave was most likely the devil—or at least, the equivalent of a rabbit from a hat.

37 Brian Levack, ed., *Gender and Witchcraft: New Perspectives on Witchcraft, Magic, and Demonology* (New York: Routledge, 2001), 9.

38 P. G. Maxwell-Stuart, *Satan's Conspiracy: Magic and Witchcraft in Sixteenth-Century Scotland* (East Linton, Scotland: Tuckwell, 2001), 1.

Chronology from World Creation up to Luther's Time

An Unknown Single-Sheet Print by Melanchthon (1521) and a Fragmentary Letter from Luther to Melanchthon (1540 or 1541)

Ulrich Bubenheimer

1. A Data Sheet of Melanchthon on Biblical Chronology in a *Biblia latina* Owned by Johannes Lang

In the Bodleian Libraries of the University of Oxford there is a copy of a Latin Bible (the so-called Vulgata) printed in Basel in 1514.[1] This unexplored copy deserves the attention of Reformation historians, as it contains new sources. The first owner of this Bible, Johannes Lang (1488–1548),[2] was Martin Luther's friend and fellow monk and later Reformer of Erfurt. Lang added extensive annotations to the Bible, providing valuable information both from his teaching and study in Wittenberg (1511–16) and from his subsequent long period of

1 *Biblia cu[m] pleno apparatu | summariorum co[n]cordantiarum et quadru|plici repertorij siue indicij numeriq[ue] folio- | rum distinctio[n]e Basilee nuper impressa.* [. . .] (Basel: Johann Froben, 1514). Lang's copy is in the Bodleian Libraries, University of Oxford, A 6.9 Th.

2 See Ulman Weiß, "Lang, Johannes," ed. Hans J. Hillerbrand, in *The Oxford Encyclopedia of the Reformation* (New York: Oxford University Press, 1996), 2:388.

activity in Erfurt (1516–48). In its present state, this volume contains Johannes Lang's *Biblia*, bound together with an unknown single-sheet print; Lang's name does not appear.[3] Older references to the provenance of the volume were deliberately removed.[4] But the paleographic comparison of the handwritten notes found in the Bible with Lang's handwriting[5] shows that Lang was the author of the numerous notes.[6] After his entry into the Erfurt Augustinian monastery (by 1506 at the latest), he was able to keep his library as private property and expand it through acquisitions. Numerous volumes from it have been preserved in various libraries, making such an observation about his ownership possible.[7]

---

3 Lang usually entered a purchase or ownership note in his books.

4 The upper margin of the title page of the *Biblia* has been cut off, but minimal remains of an earlier note can still be seen. A rubbing is found at the lower margin of the title page. In the top left corner of the upper pastedown, there is a wax seal, the seal image of which has been largely scraped off with a knife. These erasures were probably made by Samuel Leigh Sotheby, a London auctioneer and antiquarian. He claimed that he had succeeded in buying parts of Melanchthon's private library, which included the present *Biblia*. The books Sotheby had compiled stemmed from different provenances, and the notes contained in the books were written by different persons. See S[amuel] Leigh Sotheby, *Unpublished Documents, Marginal Notes and Memoranda, in the Autograph of Philip Melanchthon and of Martin Luther: With Numerous Fac-Similes. Accompanied with Observations upon the Varieties of Style in the Handwriting of These Illustrious Reformers* (London, 1841), 6. In this publication, Sotheby describes the present Bible (see plate VII, no. 5).

5 Two purchase notes written by Johannes Lang are reproduced in *Barfuss ins Himmelreich? Martin Luther und die Bettelorden in Erfurt: Textband und Katalog zur Ausstellung im Stadtmuseum Erfurt 2017*, ed. Karl Heinemeyer and Anselm Hartinger (Dresden: Sandstein, 2017), 173, 191.

6 Lang's Latin handwriting is somewhat similar to that of Luther. See Ulrich Bubenheimer, "Luthers Handschrift," in *Luther Handbuch*, ed. Albrecht Beutel, 3rd ed. (Tübingen: Mohr Siebeck, 2017), 21–27; here 26.

7 From Johannes Lang's library also comes a copy of the first printed collection of Luther's Latin writings, printed in Basel in 1518, which is in the Pitts Theology Library, Emory University, Atlanta, 1518 ADLE. See Armin Siedlecki and Ulrich Bubenheimer with Eric Moore, curs., *A Book More Precious than Gold: Reading the Printed Book Alongside Its Previous Owners and Readers: An Exhibition at Pitts Theology Library* (Atlanta: Emory, Candler School of Theology, Pitts Theology Library, 2019), 115–17.

I cannot go into detail here about the manifold contents of Lang's handwritten notes in this Bible. I am, instead, focused here on the anonymous single-sheet print, which Lang pasted into his Bible and whose author I will identify as Philip Melanchthon.

The *Biblia latina* of Lang's library begins with the title page [A1r] and an anonymous exhortation to study the Holy Scriptures on page [A1v]. On the second folio [A2], the printer Johann Froben explains to the reader the paratexts added to the biblical text and offers a scheme of the structure of the Bible and the order of the biblical scriptures. The following six pages, A3 to [A8], which are found in other copies of this printing of the Bible, are missing in Lang's copy. Lang had cut them out after the book was already bound; he glued a single page in their place, which shows a printed text on one side (see fig. 1).[8] In doing this, Lang bound the unprinted back of this broadsheet as the recto, so that the printed side became the verso in the current state of the volume.

The text of the broadsheet begins with the following heading:

> ADNOTATIO ANNORVM A CONDITO MVNDO, | Vsque Ad Annum Restitutae, | SAlutis M. D. XXI. || EX PHILONE
>
> Record of the years from the creation of the world until the 1521st year after the restoration of salvation. Taken from Philo.

The following text offers a chronological list of the history up to Christ. At its conclusion, the author adds the following computation:

> CHRISTVS IN ANNO 30 Herodis natus est. | ANNO MVNDI. 3947. | HOC ANNO M. D. XXI. agitur. | ANNVS A mundo condito, | 5 4 6 S.[9]
>
> In the current year 1521, we live in the 5468th year after the creation of the world.

---

8 The first two folios of the Bible, which I call [A1] and [A2], do not bear any signatures. In the copy kept in the Bayerische Staatsbibliothek München (2 B. lat. 20), one finds the six pages missing in Lang's copy, three of them with the signatures—A3, A4, A5—and three without signatures. Folio [A8] is followed by folio B1. In Lang's copy, the folios A3 to [A8] are missing, since here after [A1] and [A2], the glued-in single-leaf folio B1 of the Bible print follows (B1r with header "Tabula alphabetica historiarum").

9 Printing error instead of "5 4 6 8."

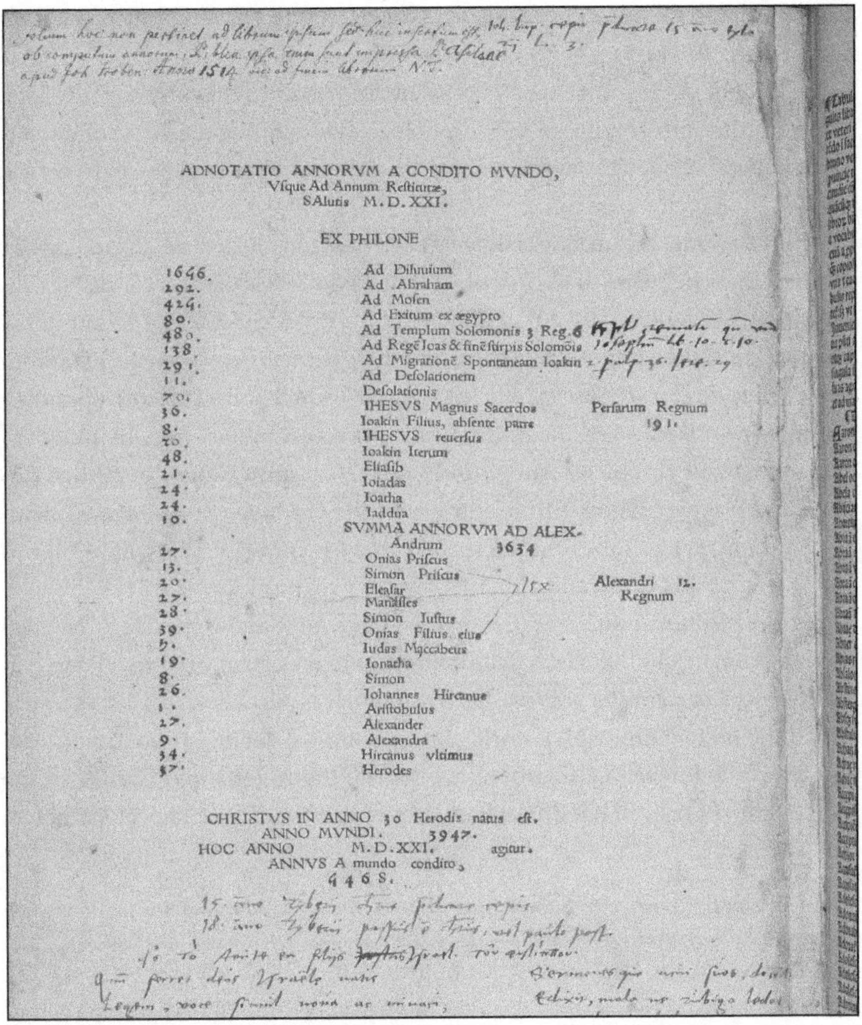

ADNOTATIO ANNORVM A CONDITO MVNDO,
Vsque Ad Annum Restitutae,
SAlutis M.D.XXI.

EX PHILONE

1646.	Ad Diluuium
292.	Ad Abraham
424.	Ad Mosen
80.	Ad Exitum ex aegypto
480.	Ad Templum Solomonis 3 Reg. 6
138.	Ad Regē Ioas & finē stirpis Solomōis
291.	Ad Migrationē Spontaneam Ioakin
11.	Ad Desolationem
70.	Desolationis
36.	IHESVS Magnus Sacerdos
8.	Ioakin Filius, absente patre
70.	IHESVS reuersus
48.	Ioakin Iterum
21.	Eliasib
24.	Ioiadas
24.	Ioatha
10.	Iaddua

Persarum Regnum 191.

SVMMA ANNORVM AD ALEXAndrum 3634

27.	Onias Priscus
13.	Simon Priscus
20.	Eleasar
27.	Manasses
28.	Simon Iustus
39.	Onias Filius eius
5.	Iudas Maccabeus
19.	Ionatha
8.	Simon
26.	Iohannes Hircanus
1.	Aristobulus
27.	Alexander
9.	Alexandra
34.	Hircanus vltimus
37.	Herodes

Alexandri 12. Regnum

CHRISTVS IN ANNO 30 Herodis natus est.
ANNO MVNDI. 3947.
HOC ANNO M.D.XXI. agitur.
ANNVS A mundo condito,
4468.

FIG. 1. Single-sheet print on biblical chronology (Wittenberg, 1521). Bodleian Libraries, University of Oxford: A 6.9 Th., between A2 and B1.

From these data, it is clear that this text was published in its present form in 1521.[10] A typographical comparison with the printed matter of that year showed that the single-sheet print was produced in the office of the Wittenberg

10 A later scribe, probably in the eighteenth century, noted at the top of the sheet that it could not have been part of the Bible printed in 1514.

printer Johann Rhau-Grunenberg, who, from 1508 to 1527, mainly printed for university teachers, especially Luther and Melanchthon.[11]

In light of the location of its printing, it is obvious that one ought to look for the author or compiler of the chronological list among the circle of university teachers who taught in Wittenberg in 1521 and were engaged in historical studies.

In the title, the author claims to have taken his historical chronology *ex Philone*. Thus he refers to the Jewish author Philo of Alexandria (d. ca. 50 CE). However, a chronology like that offered by the broadsheet is not found in the writings of Philo. The author of the Wittenberg list has excerpted his data from the pseudo-Philonic *Breviarium temporum*,[12] which offers a corresponding chronology not as a list but in the format of a continuous text. In 1498, the Italian forger of chronicles Annius of Viterbo (Giovanni Nanni) published this *Breviarium* under Philo's name, along with the chronicle of a so-called *Berosus Babylonicus* and other chronicles invented by Annius.[13] This collection was reprinted in Paris (1510 and 1512),[14] as well as in Strasbourg in 1511.[15]

The identification of the pseudo-Philonic source as the model for the present list points to Philip Melanchthon as its compiler, who used that source in other places in a similar way for his chronological purposes. In 1558, he published the first volume of his world chronicle under the title *Chronicon Carionis*, which he himself had written, not his late friend Johannes Carion, as the title might suggest.[16] Here Melanchthon inserted the chronological list before

11 Christoph Reske, *Die Buchdrucker des 16. und 17. Jahrhunderts im deutschen Sprachgebiet: Auf der Grundlage des gleichnamigen Werkes von Josef Benzing*, 2nd ed. (Wiesbaden: Harrassowitz, 2015), 1077–79.

12 Also called *Breviarium de temporibus*. The reference to this source I owe to Dr. Harald Bollbuck in Göttingen.

13 Mark A. Lotito, *The Reformation of Historical Thought* (Leiden: Brill, 2019), 118–20.

14 For the Paris prints compare James S. Hirstein, *Tacitus'* Germania *and Beatus Rhenanus (1485–1547): A Study of the Editorial and Exegetical Contribution of a Sixteenth Century Scholar* (Frankfurt: Peter Lang, 1995), 95n38, 183n11.

15 Giovanni Nanni, *BEROSVS BABYLONICVS DE HIS | Quae praecesseru[n]t inundatione[m] terraru[m]. | Item | [. . .] Philo in breuiario temporum [. . .]* (Strasbourg: [Johann Grüninger], 1511). The *Breviarium temporum* on XXIIr–XXIVr. The *Breviarium* is quoted in WA 53:19–21.

16 Lotito, *Reformation of Historical Thought*, 112–91. See also Heinz Scheible, *Melanchthon: Vermittler der Reformation. Eine Biographie* (München: C. H. Beck, 2016), 311.

the beginning of the *Liber primus* of his *Chronicon* with the title *Annorum series ex Philone*.[17] The list here runs from creation to Herod, as in the broadsheet, and offers some explanatory additions. In the Latin *Chronicon* of 1558, Melanchthon states that he is publishing it so that students of history could have the list before their eyes.[18] The 1521 broadsheet also serves this purpose. The print of 1521 shows that Melanchthon was already engaged in historical studies with his circle of students at that time. The single-sheet print was a perishable medium, meant only as a teaching manual, which explains why, according to current knowledge, only the Oxford copy survived because Johannes Lang had made it a permanent part of his Latin Bible.[19] On the sheet, below the last line of the print, there are notes in Lang's hand. A two-line chronological note on the activity of Christ at the time of the Roman Emperor Tiberius[20] is followed by the heading to a twelve-line Latin poem on the revelation of God on Mount Sinai, which—from another handwritten tradition—is already known as a poem by Melanchthon.[21] At the end of the heading, Lang identified the author in Greek: του φιλίππου (by Philip). Since the Greek scholar Lang was in correspondence with his fellow Greek scholar Melanchthon, he could have received the broadsheet directly from Melanchthon.

A letter from Melanchthon to Georg Spalatin dated March 2, 1521, provides the background for the former's preoccupation with historical chronology at that time. He asked Spalatin, who was in Worms because of the imperial diet, to search for records of ancient history in a Worms library. For many years, Melanchthon wrote, he had been planning to carefully research the history of

---

17 Philip Melanchthon, *CHRONICON | CARIONIS LATI=|NE EXPOSITUM ET AV=|CTVM [. . .] | A PHILIPPO MELAN=|THONE* (Wittenberg: Georg Rhau, 1558), B2r–B3r.

18 Melanchthon, *Chronicon*, B3r.

19 I could not find any reference to this single-sheet print in bibliographies or in research literature.

20 "15. Anno Tyberii christus praedicare cepit | 18. Anno Tyberii passus est christus, vel paulo post."

21 The poem was edited from a sixteenth-century copy by Otto Grotefend, "Beiträge zum Briefwechsel Melanchthons," in *Zeitschrift für Kirchengeschichte* 28 (1907): 69–70 (here the heading that Lang used to prefix the poem is missing). Listed by Wilhelm Hammer, *Die Melanchthonforschung im Wandel der Jahrhunderte: Ein beschreibendes Verzeichnis*, vol. 2 (Gütersloh: Gütersloher Verlagshaus, 1968), nr. 3016.

the church.[22] The single-sheet print shows that Melanchthon started to carry out this plan in the same year.

Between Melanchthon's Latin versions of the chronological list of 1521 and 1558, a German-language version appeared in the *Chronica* of Johannes Carions, first published in 1532[23]—the one that Melanchthon had corrected, reworked, and expanded before it went to print. Melanchthon's contribution to this *Chronica*, in which he is not mentioned, cannot be defined in detail. However, in a letter to Anton Corvinus, presumably in May 1532, he expressly stated that he himself added the table found in the concluding section of the *Chronica*: "At the end I have added a useful and accurate table of the years of the world, which I hope will be appreciated by you and other scholars."[24] Here, the list is entitled "Tabula annorum mundi / nach der Bibel vnd nach Philo" (Table of the years of the world, according to the Bible and Philo).[25] Compared to the 1521 version, the list is shorter. In the *Chronica*, Melanchthon does not mention the names and reigns of the Jewish high priests and kings who came after the Babylonian Exile in detail but rather summarizes them in two groups: "146 [Jahre] Der Grecken Reich bis auff Judam Machabeum" and "127 [Jahre] Der Machabeer Reich bis auf Heroden den ersten" (146 years of Greek rule until Judas Maccabeas; 127 years of the Maccabean kingdom until Herod the First).[26] Finally, the year after creation is calculated for the year of publication of the book: "Inn gegenwertigem 1532 jar / sind nach anfang der welt.

22 MBWT 1:263, 15–21, nr. 128.

23 Johannes Carion, *Chronica | durch Magi=|strum Johan Carion / | vleissig zusamen ge=|zogen / menig=|lich nu(e)tzlich | zu lesen* [. . .] (Wittenberg: Georg Rhau, 1532). Universitäts- und Landesbibliothek Halle: Pon Vg 4104 a.

24 "In fine adieci tabellam annorum mundi utilem et veram, quam spero tibi et aliis doctis placituram esse." MBWT 5:568, no. 1250. Melanchthon's epistolary statements about Carion's *Chronica* are compiled by Harald Bollbuck, "Universalgeschichte, Kirchengeschichte und die Ordnung der Schöpfung: Philipp Melanchthon und die Anfänge der protestantischen Geschichtsschreibung," in *Humanismus und Europäische Identität*, ed. Günter Frank, Fragmenta Melanchthoniana 4 (Ubstadt-Weiher: Verlag Regionalkultur, 2009), 129–52; here 131–33.

25 Carion, *Chronica* g4r, fully cited in WA 60:172nA. Cf. Martin Schneider, "Geschichte," in *Philipp Melanchthon: Der Reformator zwischen Glauben und Wissen: Ein Handbuch*, ed. Günter Frank (Berlin: De Gruyter, 2017), 577–90; here 584–85.

26 Carion, *Chronica* g4r.

5476. Jar" (The present year is 1532, the 5476th year since the beginning of the world). Thus Melanchthon shortened his 1521 computation of the time elapsed since creation by three years in 1532.

2. Chronological Debates: A Fragmentary Letter from Luther to Melanchthon

A Luther autograph preserved in the Pitts Theology Library at Atlanta (see fig. 2) contains fragmentary Latin notes on biblical chronology.[27] The text of this fragment was first edited by Hans Volz in volume 60 of the Weimar edition of Luther's works (1980) but without any description of the manuscript.[28] According to Volz, the manuscript was in private hands at the time. In 1988 it was acquired by the Pitts Theology Library and integrated into the Richard C. Kessler Collection.[29]

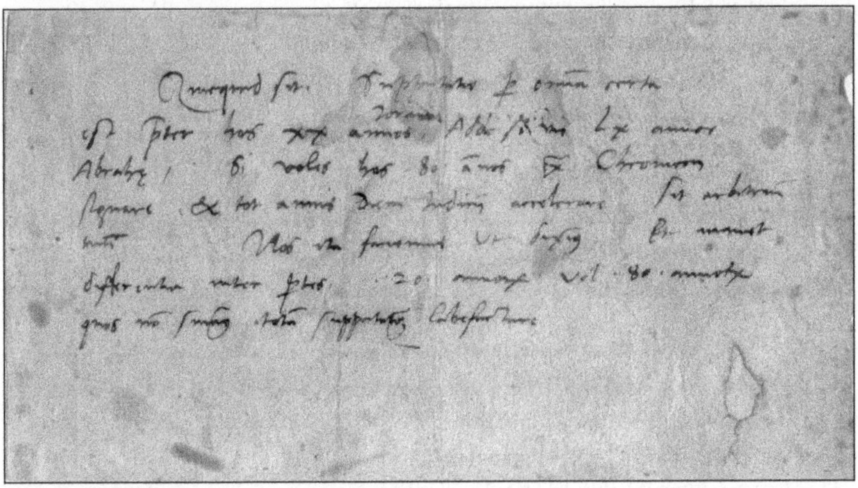

FIG. 2. Letter fragment, written by Martin Luther. Pitts Theology Library, Emory University, Atlanta: MSS 090. Image provided courtesy of the Richard C. Kessler Reformation Collection, Pitts Theology Library, Emory University.

27 See also Siedlecki and Bubenheimer with Moore, *Book More Precious Than Gold*, 20n520.

28 WA 60:163.

29 Dr. Armin Siedlecki, personal communication with author, Pitts Theology Library, May 18, 2020.

I have transcribed the seven lines of Latin text located on the front of the fragment:[30]

> Quicquid sit, Supputatio per omnia certa | est praeter hos xx annos Joram,[31] Adde si vis lx annos | Abrahae, Si voles[32] hos .80. annos extra Chronicon | signare et tot annis Diem Judicij accelerare sit arbitrium | tuum[.] Nos ita faciemus vt diximus[.] Et manet | differentia inter partes, .20. annorum vel .80. annorum | quos non sinamus totam supputationem labefactare.
>
> Be it as it may. The *Supputatio* [Computation] is safe in all points except those 20 years of Joram. If you want, add the 60 years of Abraham. If you are going to indicate these 80 years outside the *Chronicon* and bring the Day of Judgment closer by that amount of years, that's your decision. We will do it as we have said. And so the difference between the parties will remain 20 years or 80 years. We don't want to concede that these will shake the whole *Supputatio*.

In this text, the word *Supputatio* is used twice to refer to the title of one of Luther's writings first printed in 1541, the *Supputatio annorum mundi*[33] (Computation of the years of the world). The Reformer worked on this chronology of world history from creation to his present day for a long time before he put it into print in April 1541.[34] The printing was completed on August 31, 1541.[35] Luther's working process is reflected in two preserved manuscripts.[36] On the

30 Unlike the edition in WA 60, I transcribe without changing the character set.

31 "Joram" added by Luther above the line.

32 Volz deciphered *velis* (WA 60:163).

33 Martin Luther, *SVPPVTATIO ANNORVM MVNDI* [. . .] (Wittenberg: Georg Rhau, 1541), Pitts Theology Library, Atlanta: 1560 ASPH: 2. A second, revised edition with an introduction appeared in 1545, both by Ferdinand Cohrs (WA 53:1–182). See also Volker Leppin, "*Supputatio annorum mundi*," in *Das Luther-Lexikon*, ed. Volker Leppin and Gury Schneider-Ludorff (Regensburg: Bückle & Böhm, 2014), 667–68.

34 Georg Selcorv, "*Luthers* supputatio annorum mundi," in *Welt-Zeit. Christliche Weltchronistik aus zwei Jahrtausenden in Beständen der Thüringer Universitäts- und Landesbibliothek Jena*, ed. Martin Wallraff (Berlin: De Gruyter, 2005), 126–31.

35 WA 53:8.

36 Incomplete description of the manuscripts by Ferdinand Cohrs in WA 53:2–8.

one hand, there is Luther's handwritten working copy,[37] which contains many additions and changes.[38] On the other hand, there is an elaborate redaction of the text,[39] probably written in 1540 in Luther's environment, which represents a further developed version of the text. Neither of the two manuscripts served as a direct printing template. The first print of 1541 again shows changes compared to both manuscripts.

Hans Volz, in connection with his edition of the small Luther autograph cited above, had attempted to establish a literary connection between the text of the autograph and the origin of the *Supputatio*. He recognized that the surviving text is a fragment in which there are formulations that refer back to previous statements that have not been preserved. The first sentence of the text begins with the transitional words "Quicquid sit" (Be it as it may). Shortly after this, Luther speaks of "hos xx annos Joram" (those twenty years of Joram). These formulations presuppose that Luther had already said something about the topic under discussion. Volz suspected that our text was originally a part of an earlier version of Luther's *Supputatio*, though it was not included in the printed version.[40] However, in this reconstruction, Volz had not taken into account that Luther spoke to a second person in our text to whom he addressed in the document: "si voles" (if you want) and "sit arbitrium tuum" (that's your decision). This issue can be explained by considering the back of this manuscript, which Volz probably did not see. First, the reverse side confirms that the small piece of paper was a fragment of a more extensive manuscript, because, at the upper edge of the verso, a small remainder of cutoff text is still recognizable.[41] A corresponding note had already been written by a previous Italian owner:

37 Sächsische Landes- und Universitätsbibliothek Dresden: Mscr.Dresd.F.66.b. https://digital.slub-dresden.de/werkansicht/dlf/156627/1/0/. In the autograph, Luther's chronology has no title.

38 Reproductions of four pages in WA 53, following p. 6, and one in Martin Treu, "Luthers Kalender der Weltgeschichte," in *Manu propria—Mit eigener Hand: 95 Autographe der Reformationszeit. Aus den Sammlungen der Sächsischen Landesbibliothek—Staats- und Universitätsbibliothek Dresden (SLUB)*, ed. Hans-Peter Hasse et al. (Markkleeberg: Sax Verlag, 2017), 43–44.

39 Sächsische Landes- und Universitätsbibliothek Dresden: Mscr.Dresd.F.35. I could not consult this manuscript before finishing this article and therefore refer to the information provided by Cohrs.

40 WA 60:163.

41 The fragment is the lower part of an originally larger sheet of paper.

"Frammento autografo di M Lutero."[42] In addition, a small remnant of red sealing wax and sealing paper can still be identified on the back. From this finding, it is clear that the present manuscript is a fragment of a former letter.

The question of the addressee of the letter that Luther was referring to in this fragment can be answered from its content. Luther deals with two controversial questions of biblical chronology. The first problem addressed in the letter fragment is the computation of the reign of the Judean king Joram, who, according to biblical tradition, became king at the age of thirty-two and reigned for eight years (2 Kgs 8:17; 2 Chr 21:20). The data handed down about his youngest son and successor, Ahazia, are contradictory: According to Second Kings 8:26, Ahazia became king at the age of twenty-two and reigned for one year; however, according to Second Chronicles 22:2, he was forty-two years old when he began his reign. In order to resolve this ambiguity, some exegetes assumed a much longer reign for Joram, twenty-eight years in total—that is, that Joram reigned eight years alone and twenty years together with the crown prince, Ahazia. For this assumption, Luther referred to the Church Father Jerome and to Nicholas of Lyra in a marginal note of his *Supputatio* autograph,[43] where he had already recorded Joram as having an eight-year reign. The second problem concerns different computations of the lifetime of Abraham with a difference of sixty years.[44] Together, the two differences add up to eighty years.

In the letter fragment, Luther spoke of two parties that differed in their chronological computations by an amount of twenty or sixty years. He favored the shorter chronological calculation, and to his addressee, he said: "If you are going to indicate these 80 years outside the *Chronicon* and bring the Day of Judgment closer by that amount of years, that's your decision." According to Luther, the addressee could, if he wished, indicate the additional eighty years outside the *Chronicon*. By *Chronicon*, Luther was referring to Carion's

---

42 There are also notes from a previous German owner, "EJC" and "S. 9," as well as a French note, "Question de chronologie biblique."

43 The relevant page from Luther's autograph (Mscr.Dresd.F.66.b, 23v) is shown in WA 53, following p. 6. Luther added to *Ioram* on the inner margin: "Huic Ioram dant Hiero:[nymus] et Lyra .28. annos."

44 According to Genesis 12:4, Abraham was 75 years old when he left Haran; according to a combination of Acts 7:4 with Genesis 11:26 and 11:32, his calculated age was 135 years. Consequently, in the second case, Abraham's lifetime would be 60 years longer than in the first case.

and Melanchthon's *Chronica* from 1532. While Luther called his chronological work a *Supputatio*, not a chronicle,[45] he introduced the 1532 work of Carion and Melanchthon as *Chronicon Carionis Philippicum* in the preface to the printed version of the *Supputatio*: "Of course Philip's *Chronicle of Carion* is the first and best example of a computation, in which the whole course of the years is very nicely divided into six millennia, so that I also followed this example."[46] In the 1532 *Chronica Carionis*, the two chronological points of disagreement mentioned by Luther, concerning Abraham and Joram, were not addressed,[47] so that Luther left it to Melanchthon's discretion how to deal with the calculation of whether to add twenty or eighty years.

Luther's fragmentary letter belongs to the time before the *Supputatio*'s publication was completed in August 1541. Luther assumed that the addressee already knew the chronology presented in the *Supputatio*. In the autograph, Luther concluded his chronological table, which was provided with a continuous timescale, with the year 1540 by designating it as the current year: "Annus .1540. hodiernus" (The present 1540th year).[48] At the beginning of March 1540, Luther's Wittenberg colleagues Caspar Cruciger and Justus Jonas already had handwritten copies of the text.[49] It is obvious that Melanchthon also knew the *Supputatio* in a handwritten version, and it is even likely that he looked through it before it went to print. He was the most competent historian in Luther's circle and had been working on chronology since 1521. Luther had built on Melanchthon's research, as he said in the preface of the *Supputatio*. In view of this,

45 Hans Volz said that Luther had used the term *Chronicon* in the letter fragment to refer to his own *Supputatio* (WA 60:163n3). Volz supported this interpretation with a passage in the *Supputatio* where Luther referred to a *Chronicon* for his computation of the so-called *Siebzig Jahrwochen* (Dan 9:24): "Hac sententia stante, quam libens sequor, fiet, ut ultimus annus ultimae hebdomadae sit ipse quater millesimus annus mundi, ut vides in *Chronico*" (WA 53:180.10–11). Here, Luther refers to Melanchthon's comments on the computation of the *Siebzig Jahrwochen* in the *Chronica* of 1532. In the *Supputatio* (WA 53:125), Luther took over Melanchthon's "Rechnung der LXX. wochen Danielis" (Carion, *Chronica*, H7r–I1v) without naming the source. Cf. WA 53:153–54.

46 WA 53:23.

47 Cf. Carion, *Chronica* C2v–C4r (Abraham), D2r (Joram).

48 Mscr.Dresd.F.66.b, 42r.

49 The data are compiled by Ferdinand Cohrs in WA 53:5–8.

I would like to date the letter fragment to the period between 1540 and August 1541 at the latest.

Apparently, the handwritten circulation of Luther's computation, in which he named the year 1540 AD as the year in which he had reached the end of his chronological timescale in the first pass, had triggered discussions in Wittenberg about the reliability of this calculation. Since Luther continued to work on his text until it went to print, changes made by Luther after his letter was sealed seem to have fueled the discussion. In the autograph, Luther synchronized the year 1540 with the year 5483 after creation, with the result that he was only one year below the calculation that Melanchthon had presented in Carion's *Chronica* in 1532. Thus Luther initially followed Melanchthon to a large extent.

With the following changes, it was important that the autograph version recognizably had the character of a private work,[50] while, in view of publication, Luther was beginning to elaborate the motive of placing his own person and work in the depicted order of salvation history. While in the autograph for the year 1517, Luther only briefly notes, "Lutherus contra indulgentias" (Luther against the indulgences), this line takes on a dimension of salvation history in the print of 1541: "The Papal indulgences were fought by Luther in the 102nd year since the death of Jan Hus. This year is approximately the 1000th year since Phokas confirmed the papacy."[51] By using numbers that are as round as possible, Luther constructs a God-willed order of history—for example, by seeing a prophecy of Hus fulfilled in his person. Even more far-reaching is Luther's new computation for the year 1540 in the 1541 print of the *Supputatio*: "In this year 1540 the number of years of the world is exactly 5500. Therefore, there is hope for the end of the world. For the sixth millennium will not come to an end, just as Christ was not dead three complete days . . . , but rose again in the morning, in the middle of the third day."[52] Luther thus places himself in line with Abraham (around 2,000 years *post creationem*) and Christ (4,000 *post creationem*) by

50 An example: For the year 1484, Luther notes, "Nascor" (I am born). Mscr. Dresd.F.66.b, 41v.

51 "Indulgentias Papales impugnatae per Lutherum, post mortem Joh. Hus anno 102., qui est annus fere 1000. confirmati Papatus per Focam." WA 53:170.

52 "Hoc anno 1540 numerus annorum Mundi precise est .5500. Quare sperandus est finis mundi, Nam sextus Millenarius non complebitur, Sicut tres dies mortui Christi non sunt completi. . . . Sed mane surrexit in medio diei tertiae." WA 53:171.

claiming a prominent place in God's history with the date 4500. Abraham and Christ are the main witnesses of his spiritual genealogy.[53]

It is understandable that Luther's synchronization of the year 1540 AD with the year 4500 *post creationem*[54] encouraged discussions in his circle about the validity of such computations. The uncertainties regarding the dates of Abraham and Joram were suitable examples of this. The letter fragment shows that no common position had been reached at the time it was written. Luther expressly emphasizes that he did not want to change his computation: "We will do it as we have said. And so the difference between the parties will remain 20 years or 80 years. We don't want to concede that these will shake the whole *Supputatio*." However, for the published version of 1545, Luther deleted the quoted claim that the year 1540 was exactly the year 5500 *post creationem*.[55]

According to Luther, two parties (partes) had formed in the discussion about the chronological problems. This could be an indication that a disputation about the open questions had taken place at the university. This is also suggested by the fact that Luther offered a text titled *Scheda* (meaning "paper sheet" or "placard") in an appendix to the 1541 print edition, in which the chronological issues surrounding Joram are formulated in the format of three theses.[56] Melanchthon's 1521 broadsheet is an early witness to the gradual institutionalization of religiously motivated historical research at the university.

53 See Bollbuck, "Universalgeschichte," 128.

54 This synchronization is first found in the Mscr.Dresd.F.35.

55 For more, see the information in WA 53:171.

56 WA 53:180.12–181.6; Luther, *Supputatio*, penultimate folio. The last two folios of the *Supputatio* are recognizably a supplement. The print of the *Supputatio* at first ended with Bb3; Bb4 is unprinted. Then follow two folios, signed with a cloverleaf. On 1r is the *Scheda*, on 1v–2r Luther's commentary, and on 2v the imprint.

MELANCHTHON'S *HISTORIAE*

THEMES AND SOURCES

Stefan Rhein

1. MELANCHTHON'S NARRATIVE TEACHING STYLE (DIDACTICS)

Amid the forest of praise for the *Praeceptor Germaniae*, the view of what Melanchthon the Teacher signifies can easily get lost.[1] For just as the title *Praeceptor Germaniae* was hardly contemporary (as Theodor Mahlmann has proven),[2] so can the success of Melanchthon's teaching be counted merely by the number of subjects he taught, textbooks he wrote, or students he educated. These numbers are still impressive today, demonstrating how the Wittenberg professor left an encyclopedic imprint on scholars and generations of students in Germany and Europe. But what was the *charisma*, the gift, of this teacher's personality?

1 Timothy J. Wengert, to whom this essay is dedicated with sincere affection, began his study of Melanchthon's thoughts about time and history with an anecdote, which also appears in the following detailed presentation of the *Historiae*. For the Wengert article, see *Consensus* 30 (2005): 24; see also CR 20:549–50, nr. 122. With it, he showed how instructive and stimulating the engagement with one of the most undervalued genres of Melanchthon's work—his *Historiae* (histories), *Dicta* (sayings), and anecdotes—can be. The author also wishes to thank Alexander Bartmuß (Leipzig), Matthias Dall'Asta (Heidelberg), Christian Heitzmann (Wolfenbüttel), Johannes Klaus Kipf (Munich), and Antonia Landois (Nuremberg) for their support and assistance.

2 Theodor Mahlmann, "Die Bezeichnung Philipp Melanchthon als Praeceptor Germaniae auf ihre Herkunft geprüft," *Melanchthonbild und Melanchthonrezeption in der lutherischen Orthodoxie und im Pietismus*, ed. Udo Sträter (Wittenberg: Drei Kastanien, 1999), 135–222.

Or, more pragmatically asked, what was Melanchthon's didactics—that is, his teaching style?

Melanchthon did not write a methodology for successful instruction or a pedagogical textbook, which means that his didactic method can only be extracted from his schoolbooks and from lectures that were passed along. Fortunately, one of Melanchthon's students—who later became an influential university professor himself—described the successful pedagogic strategies of his teacher. That student and professor was David Chytraeus, who not only studied in Wittenberg with Melanchthon from 1544 to 1547 but even lived in his house and thereby experienced daily lessons in the close relationship of the *schola domestica* (school of the household). Beginning in 1548, Chytraeus held lectures on his teacher's *Loci communes*, giving him an intensive knowledge of Melanchthon's lessons and publications.

Two years after Melanchthon's death, in an introduction to *De ratione discendi et ordine studiorum in singulis artibus recte instituendo* (Methods of learning and the right way to study the individual sciences), Chytraeus characterized Melanchthon's books—which "rightly earned the admiration and love of all students" for their author—with the following honors. First, Melanchthon's textbooks focus on the most important and useful matters, omitting sophistries, using clear and understandable words, and describing applications for life. Second, the books illustrate the teachings and rules with examples from the past and the present, thereby revealing the real-world relevance of the individual subjects. Third, they also make complex topics attractive through a great variety of stories, proverbs, aphorisms, analogies, and other allusions and "thus fill the spirit of the learners with a singular joy."[3] The honors bestowed upon the textbooks are also reflected in the lectures that follow, for here too one sees Melanchthon's own goal of shaping lessons that are multifaceted and lively. Complex themes are simplified through clear language, made understandable

3 On Chytraeus as a student of Melanchthon, see Rudolf Keller, "David Chytraeus (1530–1600). Melanchthons Geist im Luthertum," in *Melanchthon in seinen Schülern*, ed. Heinz Scheible (Wiesbaden: Harrassowitz, 1997), 361–71. On his introductory text *De ratione discendi* and on the passage cited above, see Walther Ludwig, "Art und Zweck der Lehrmethode Melanchthons—Beobachtungen anläßlich der ersten Übersetzung seiner Initia doctrinae physicae," in *Opuscula historico-philologica. Ausgewählte Aufsätze 2008–2013*, ed. Astrid Steiner-Weber (Hildesheim: Olms, 2014), 135–60, esp. 138–40.

through practical comparisons with daily life, and explained with examples from antiquity to the present in a wide variety of narrative forms.[4]

The function of these examples can best be seen in the lectures that Melanchthon regularly held on Sundays and festivals, beginning in 1522. They took place at six o'clock in the morning before the worship service so that the foreign students, some of whom had little mastery of German and would thus be left out of worship in the vernacular, could participate in Reformation interpretations of the Bible. The themes of the hour-long Sunday lectures, therefore, always came from a biblical pericope, which Melanchthon explicated through his loci hermeneutic and his wide general knowledge. These were not sermons but rather lectures given in a university context. They therefore focused not on pastoral care but on guidance in philology and theology, albeit with a consistent sense of the unity shared between *pietas* and *eruditio* (piety and learning). The Sunday lectures were edited in 1594 by Christoph Pezel as *Postilla Melanthoniana*. Pezel condensed many of the different lectures according to their themes into a single text. But even in such a *mixtum compositum*, one sees

4 There is as yet no comprehensive study of Melanchthon as a lecturer or on his teaching methods and strategies. Most of the attention goes to his educational-political contributions (his praise of education, organization of schools, university reforms, etc.) or praise him emphatically, mostly without textual basis (e.g., Wilhelm Dilthey's study, "Melanchthons didaktische Genialität"). Several directions toward a didactic praxis appear in Wilhelm Schwendemann, "Melanchthons reformatorische Pädagogik. Programm und Wirklichkeit," in *Philipp Melanchthon 1497–1997. Die bunte Seite der Reformation*, ed. Wilhelm Schwendemann (Münster: LIT, 1997), 70–94; e.g., "Melanchthon himself was enamored by narrative didactics, such that there are a great many fables, little stories, and tales from world history that have a didactic—even action-oriented—function" (89). Schwendemann, among other things a professor of religious instruction in schools, presents Melanchthon as "the first progressive educator [*Reformpädagoge*] of the modern era," summarizing in his concluding sentence, "One element, which has again become important for teaching in primary schools today, should be mentioned again: namely, Melanchthon's affection for stories, fables, and anecdotes; he intuitively did the right thing, telling children the stories that he knew they needed to hear" (94). See also the instructive insights of Jürgen Leonhardt, "Melanchthon als Verfasser von Lehrbüchern," in *Melanchthon und das Lehrbuch des 16. Jahrhunderts*, ed. Jürgen Leonhardt (Rostock: Universität, 1997), 13–32; e.g., on the praxis-oriented choice of teaching materials in the Latin and Greek grammars, see 26–28, or on the clever choice of specific examples in the textbook on dialectics, see 29.

the persuasive placement and the didactic function of the stories Melanchthon quoted. They explain and illustrate the main points, which become easier to grasp and remember through the exempla (examples). They also break up complex streams of thought and invite new attention from the listeners.

2. MELANCHTHON'S THEORY AND PRAXIS OF EXEMPLA

Melanchthon provided fundamental reflections on the use of exempla in his *Elementa Rhetorices* (Elements of rhetoric), as he discussed the *genus deliberativum* (the deliberative style of rhetoric). This form of speech wants to advise and warn, encourage and admonish, and has as its goal a course of action based on reason. Above all, in such a context, examples can affect the emotions and inspire motivation:

> After the students have understood these methods, one must provide them with examples. These show far more clearly the suitable uses of this form of speech than the rules do. One need only raise these examples in order to show these methods to those who previously had no experience with them. In this way, they will understand the examples, as well as recognize the economy of words and how the parts of speech are arranged. They will also be able to mentally grasp the form of the entire speech. A depth and breadth of examples can be found in literature, history, and letters. In any case, to me it is most preferred when the teacher selects examples from Livius.[5] These work so well because they convey the meaning of things, and because they vividly and concretely express the tone of the language, providing a great fullness of words and thoughts.[6]

Melanchthon further elaborated on the literary sources of exempla in his Dialectics: "The example [exemplum], which the Greeks call the *paradigma*, rests upon the relationship between similarities and differences.... Attentive readers will perceive from the poets, rhetors, and historians how far their argument might apply. Especially outstanding is the use of examples in giving advice,

5 Titus Livius, a Roman historian of the third century BCE.

6 CR 13:447–48.

where we can extrapolate the result of our case from what other people with a similar purpose did. . . . A systemic view of examples would include fables, allegorical stories, proverbs, and parables from literature."[7] Here Melanchthon added weight to the persuasive and affective value of examples—more than of rules—and revealed a wide field of literary subgenres as reservoirs for examples.

At the same time, it is important to emphasize that not only do the exempla serve to illustrate abstract principles or enliven a lesson but that they also possess an intrinsic persuasive value in themselves. Aristotle had explained this in his *Rhetoric*: there are two kinds of examples, the historical and the literary. An example is in effect a shorthand means of providing rhetorical proof, in which one specific instance is directly applied to another in such a way that the conclusion of one case can be implicitly attached to the other—that is, an individual case provides evidence. Aristotle's own example is this: the war of the Athenians against neighboring Thebes is bad; therefore, the Thebians' war against their neighbors in Phokaia is also bad. The conclusion that wars against neighbors are fundamentally bad is implied. This marshaling of evidence is therefore rhetorical because it uses the familiar outcome of a story (whether historical or fictitious) as an invitation to concrete application in a specific moment. For Melanchthon, too, the example not only provides understanding but should also produce actions, whether through the inspiring stories of historical authority figures or through cautionary examples.[8]

For an examination of Melanchthon's didactics at the university, the Sunday lectures provide a way to understand his general lecture style, because

7 CR 20:746–47 (*De exemplo*). Melanchthon's model—as he himself admits—are the statements of Quintilian (*Institutio oratoria* 5, 11).

8 See William Lyon Benoit, "Aristotle's Example: The Rhetorical Induction," *Quarterly Journal of Speech* 66 (1980): 182–92. For further details (for instance, for the Aristotelian foundation of the example) see Gert Ueding, ed., *Historisches Wörterbuch der Rhetorik* (Tübingen: Niemeyer, 1996), 3:60–70, which provides only a short and by no means exhaustive reference to Melanchthon. The definitions contained there—of examples used persuasively as evidence, expanded upon for the sake of explanation, providing aesthetical elaboration, and giving orientation for real-life praxis that come with the endorsement of historical authorities—also describe the use of examples in Melanchthon. In his reflections on examples, Melanchthon drew primarily from Quintilian's *Institutio oratoria*, in which the ῥητορικὴ ἐπαγωγὴ (rhetorical induction) is explained with many examples in chapter 5.11.

they demonstrate the encyclopedic knowledge of the humanist and Reformer through a single text that gathers together philological, historical, and theological explanations and excurses. It is evident not only in the Sunday lectures but also in topical lectures on specific authors, texts, and themes that Melanchthon's lessons were characterized by a narrative didactic that made exemplary use of history. A philological commentary like the *Explicatio sententiarum Theognidis*—which appeared in 1560, edited by Melanchthon's student Johannes Major—consisted primarily of the 1551/52 lecture notes of the esteemed teacher.[9] With its detailed explanations of vocabulary, the expositions of the text and its many maxims (which often only had a tangential relationship to the text they are connected to), and the inclusion of historical as well as contemporary examples, the commentary introduces illuminating insights into Melanchthon's lecture style, which pursued the goal of making the thought-world of the early Greek poets useful for the ethical-religious instruction of the present.[10] A surviving handwritten transcript of lectures on Cicero's *De Officiis* held from 1555 to 1557 similarly conveys a lively impression of Melanchthon's lecture style. Here, too, the great abundance of examples is striking, as they describe everyday occurrences surrounding Wittenberg and stories concerning craftsmen and scholars, emperors and princes.[11]

3. MELANCHTHON'S *HISTORIAE*: THE ULRICH VENDENHAIMER COLLECTION

Remarkably, the *Historiae*, *Dicta*, and *Sententiae* were compiled outside their original teaching context and were transmitted in specifically designed

9 Theognis of Megara, a Greek poet of the sixth century BCE.

10 See the preface by Johannes Major: "Doctissimas enarrationes in morales sententias Theognidis, quas cum multis aliis ex ore Reverendi praeceptoris nostri in Academia Witebergensi bona fide excepi." CR 19:53–54. The commentary itself follows in CR 19:57–178. See also Dieter Kaufmann-Bühler, "Eine Vorlesung Ph. Melanchthons über das Theogniscorpus: Ein Beitrag zur Geschichte der Philologie des Humanismus," *Philologus* 100 (1956): 113–31.

11 See Wilhelm Meyer, "Melanchthons Vorlesung über Cicero's Officia," in *Nachrichten der K. Gesellschaft der Wissenschaften zu Göttingen* (Göttingen: Dieterichsche Verlagsbuchhandlung, 1894), 146–81. In his overview of the thought process and rhetorical development of the lecture, Meyer only selects the contemporary examples and entirely left out the examples from antiquity.

collections. These mostly handwritten collections seem to have primarily existed for private use—for instance, as historical ammunition for speakers and writers—coming with the authorial weight of the teacher and paragon Melanchthon. In his *Imagines elegantissimae* (published from 1558–67), Johannes Cogeler integrates many such histories, which he describes already on the title page as the fruits of his years of study in Wittenberg with Melanchthon: "Partially collected from the lectures of Master Philip Melanthon, and partially from the writings of the fathers."[12]

Only one collection was published in the sixteenth century—the *Locorum communium collectanea* of 1562 by Johannes Manlius—containing texts almost exclusively from Melanchthon's lectures. It appeared in a German version in 1566. This enormously successful publication—as well as a 1565 edition of Melanchthon's letters that Manlius published—was greatly attacked by the curators of Melanchthon's memory, especially by Caspar Peucer (Melanchthon's son-in-law) and Joachim Camerarius (Melanchthon's closest friend), who both accused Manlius of insulting Melanchthon's image through his unacademic and amateur approach.[13]

12 "Collectae partim ex praelectionibus Domini Philippi Melanthonis, partim ex scriptis Patrum." See Stefan Rhein, "Johannes Cogelerus, Verbi Divini Minister Stettini (1525–1605). Zu Leben und Werk eines pommerschen Theologen," in *Pommern in der Frühen Neuzeit*, ed. Wilhelm Kühlmann and Horst Langer (Tübingen: Niemeyer, 1994), 153–170, especially 164–67. "Melanthon" is an alternate form of Melanchthon, which Philip himself used in his lifetime.

13 For more about Manlius, see Armin Kohnle, "Der Drucker und Buchhändler Johannes Manlius als Förderer der Reformation in Krain und Ungarn," in *Primus Truber 1508–1586. Der slowenische Reformator und Württemberg*, ed. Sönke Lorenz, Anton Schindling, and Wilfried Setzler (Stuttgart: Kohlhammer, 2011), 217–26. For his edition of Melanchthon's historical examples, see Alexander Bartmuß, "Die Loci communes Manlii. Ein Beitrag zur Überlieferungsgeschichte und Rezeption der Exempla Melanchthons," in *Philipp Melanchthon. Lehrer Deutschlands, Reformator Europas*, ed. Irene Dingel and Armin Kohnle (Leipzig: Evangelische Verlagsanstalt, 2011), 163–75. Camerarius and Peucer were especially provoked by the great success of Manlius's *Collectanea*, which existed in fourteen Latin editions and two German editions before 1600; see Wilhelm Hammer, *Die Melanchthonforschung im Wandel der Jahrhunderte*, bks. 1–4 (Gütersloh: Gerd Mohn, 1967–96), nos. 300, 327, 342, 349, 350, 351, 362, 386, 401, 428, 441, 590, 639, 704; and nos. 352 and 363. The critique against Manlius specifically was presented by Georg Theodor Strobel, *Neue Bibliothek von seltenen Büchern* ed. Bernhard Friedrich Hummel

Such collections were not without precedent and belonged to a literary genre that already came with a distinguished exemplar—namely, the *Dicta et facta* of Valerius Maximus, a colorful mixture of sayings and acts of famous people from the past and present, which was later used as a book of examples for teaching. Among Renaissance humanists, Erasmus took up this form with his *Apophthegmata* (Maxims) of 1532, in which he gathered almost three thousand witty and trenchant sayings of famous, mostly classical, personalities in eight books, complete with moral implications. Protestants also developed numerous collections of examples, the main purpose of which was to provide ready illustrations for preachers. Sharing Luther's authoritative words for the sake of building up faith was the goal of publishing his *Table Talk*, making it also very similar to these compilations of sayings and the *Apophthegmata*.[14]

Melanchthon was personally unfamiliar with most acts of self-fashioning or self-canonization, working to hinder the publication of both his poems and his Sunday lectures.[15] He would never himself have collected or edited the *dicta* or *historiae* that he used in his teaching. Some of the students who heard

---

(Nuremberg: Bauer, 1777), 2:302–13. According to Peucer, Manlius only published these stories for the sake of profit and without proofing or ordering them correctly, thereby making Melanchthon appear to be a substandard writer of anecdotes, like Heinrich Bebel. In his biography of Melanchthon, Camerarius polemicized against the collectors of the confidential or conversational sayings of his hero because they might drag his reputation through the mud.

14 For the history of these literary compilations, see Bärbel Schwitzgebel, *Noch nicht genug der Vorrede. Zur Vorrede volkssprachiger Sammlungen von Exempeln, Fabeln, Sprichwörtern und Schwänken des 16. Jahrhunderts* (Tübingen: Niemeyer, 1996); Wolfgang Brückner, "Historien und Historie. Erzählliteratur des 16. und 17. Jahrhunderts als Forschungsaufgabe," in *Volkserzählung und Reformation. Ein Handbuch zur Tradierung und Funktion von Erzählstoffen und Erzählliteratur im Protestantismus*, ed. Brückner (Berlin: Schmidt, 1974), 82–110.

15 In the first edition of the Sunday lectures, he wrote in the foreword (dated April 1544), "Among a small circle of people, I have lectured on many themes, which I have already made known in earlier works. I have not been of the opinion that these house sermons (which I myself have not written down) should be published by anyone." MBW 3546. Apparently, Melanchthon was not the editor of *Annotationes in evangelia, quae usitato more diebus dominicis et festis proponuntur* (Wittenberg: Peter Seitz, 1544). In the foreword of the first edition of his *Epigrammata*, published through Hildebrand Grathusius, Melanchthon called his poetic pieces *ineptiae* (ineptitudes), refused to give himself the honorable name of *poeta*, and

Melanchthon's lectures, however, did just that. One of them was Ulrich Vendenhaimer, whose collection exists in handwritten form in the Herzog August Bibliothek in Wolfenbüttel and was published in volume 20 of the *Corpus Reformatorum*. The manuscript is titled *Historiae quaedam / recitatae a Praeceptore / Ph[illipo] M[elanthone] inter publicas lectiones* (Histories which were told by Praeceptor Philip Melanchthon during public lectures) and labeled as the work of *Ulricus Vendenheimer / Noribergensis / Anno 1557.*[16] It is very likely that this student, a native of Nuremberg who heard lectures from Melanchthon in 1557, can be identified as the "Ulricus Fendenhaimer Noricus" who appears in the matriculation records of December 12, 1559.[17] Regardless, Vendenhaimer also attended Melanchthon's lectures in 1559, for he cited one of Melanchthon's stories as coming from precisely that year.[18] The author's hometown certainly

---

recommended "real poets" like Eobanus Hessus, Johannes Stigel, or Georg Sabinus. MBW 9120.

16 Herzog August Bibliothek Wolfenbüttel Cod. Guelf. 21 Aug. 4°; see Otto von Heinemann, *Die Augusteischen Handschriften. Codex Guelferbytanus 77.4 Aug. 2° bis 34 Augusteus 4°* (Frankfurt am Main: Vittorio Klostermann, 1966), 307, nr. 3252; the collection is presented in CR 20:519–608. The individual histories, translated into the German with commentary, appear in Stefan Rhein, Gottfried Naumann, and Matthias Dall'Asta, eds., *Melanchthon deutsch*, vol. 6 (Leipzig: Evangelische Verlagsanstalt, 2020).

17 Karl Eduard Förstemann, ed., *Album Academiae Vitebergensis* (Leipzig: Tauchnitz, 1841), 1:369. On Vendenhaimer and his collections, see also Bartmuß, "Loci communes Manlii," 171–72. Viewing this particular collection as an example, Volker Honemann appreciated the variety among Melanchthon's stories; see Honemann, "Melanchthon als Erzähler," in *Literaturlandschaften. Schriften zur deutschsprachigen Literatur im Osten des Reiches*, ed. Rudolf Suntrup, Maryvonne Hagby, Franziska Künzlen, Nine Miedema, and Friedel Helga Roolfs (Frankfurt: Peter Lang, 2008), 33–45. In Nuremberg, there was a town clerk named Ulrich Vendenheimer from Westhofen in the Alsace (now Westhoffen) who was a student in Freiburg im Breisgau and was a council clerk from November 6, 1534, in Nuremberg and worked there as a town clerk beginning in 1537. He was married to Elisabeth, who died in 1546 or 1547; thereafter, he married Helene (née Wagner). He died between December 17, 1550, and February 2, 1551, so the Ulrich Vendenhaimer (or Vendenheimer) who listened to Melanchthon's lectures was probably a son from the first marriage. On the town clerk Vendenheimer, see the biography in Manfred J. Schmied, *Die Ratsschreiber der Reichsstadt Nürnberg* (Nuremberg: Stadtarchiv, 1979), 231.

18 CR 20:589.

played a part in his text, because it preserves a good deal of Nuremberg history: it describes one Nuremberg wholesaler who complained about Luther's writings against usury and tells of a Nuremberg cannon manufacturer who treated his mother poorly and then died; it tells Dürer's stories of the physical strength of Emperor Maximilian I and of Emperor Charles V's stay in Antwerp. The Nuremberg preacher Veit Dietrich is presented in two stories. It also describes how the personal motto of Emperor Frederick III was inscribed on the Nuremberg castle, and it shares sayings from Nuremberg mayors Hieronymus Ebner and Anton Tucher.[19]

The collection was unmistakably later created by Vendenhaimer, as the individual stories are numbered and partially given headings. While Manlius organized his collection systematically by loci (individual topics), no strict thematic or chronological order is visible with Vendenhaimer. The arrangement of individual histories appears to be more associative, as, for instance, when *Historiae* numbers 5 through 8 concern themselves with Emperor Charles V. Similarly, both anecdotes about French King Louis XI are next to each other as well (numbers 79 and 80), two Wittenberg experiences—which each feature the exclamation "It's burning!"—appear as numbers 120 and 121, numbers 161 and 162 are about predestination, and numbers 171 and 172 about divorce. Furthermore, the subtitle "On the Same Topic" appears over sections that build on each other (as in numbers 251–52 and 255–56), three poems are told in one group (numbers 254–56), and three more are included in the same collection at the very end.

Melanchthon himself almost never named the sources of his *Historiae*, leaving their places of origin unknown. In the following, the history of only a few stories can be presented. Nevertheless, it is very stimulating (in the sense of suggesting further avenues of study) to get to know a Melanchthon who went beyond the realms of high literature and was not afraid, for instance, of being concerned with the stories about the devil told by the common people.[20]

19 For these references, see, respectively, CR: 20:589, 525, 537, 553, 537, 567, 588, 606.

20 The precise title of Melanchthon's lecture stories varies in the handwritten and printed editions, but *Historiae* seems to dominate, as the genre was connected more to factuality and reliability of content more than a genre like *fabulae* (fables or tales). *Historiae* was used this way by Vendenhaimer and by others like Johannes Reckemann (*Historiae collectae Wittebergae ex lectionibus D. Praeceptoris Philippi Melanthonis*) and Apollo Speiser (*[. . .] judicia [. . .] etymologiae pleraeque*

4. THE *HISTORIAE* AND THEIR SOURCES

A. PERSONAL EXPERIENCES

Readers today are most interested in Melanchthon's *Historiae* because they provide previously unknown biographical details about their author or other people in his surroundings. They also expand our knowledge of everyday life in Wittenberg at the time of the Reformation. These stories, which Melanchthon reported as an eyewitness, are included not as a form of self-expression that might implicitly help us reconstruct something biographical; rather, they always remain faithful to their function as rhetorical examples. As they do this, of course, they also convey a personal memory: for instance, something of the wisdom of Melanchthon's mother about frugality and sustainable life on a farm, or the experience of a public execution of a criminal in Tübingen, who supposedly had succumbed to the devil's temptation. If Melanchthon describes a dream, then he does so primarily to raise awareness among his listeners about the prophetic power of dreams and to show how to evaluate their truth. For instance, one day before the death of the Luthers' eldest daughter, Magdalena, her mother saw in a dream that young men—angels—were leading the girl with them.[21] He frequently reports on the political figures of his time whom he encountered in imperial settings. The Salzburg bishop and cardinal Matthäus Lang especially impressed him, as they spoke together in a six-hour-long, intense conversation in Augsburg in 1530. In this way, he presented a Catholic dignitary who was vigorously opposed to the Reformation showing understanding about the efforts of the Wittenbergers on topics like communion in both kinds and priestly marriage. Even though Lang rejected these reforms, he was fully aware of the power of inertia over the clerical system, maintaining his intention not to disturb the public peace, as it seemed unimaginable to him

---

dictatae a Philippo. Ultimo historiae et facetiae scitu dignissimae; see Bartmuß, "Loci communes Manlii," 172n52). While Manlius used subtitles to describe the form of the stories (e.g., *Exempla, Similitudines, Sententiae, Consilia, Bellici apparatus, Stratagemata, Historiae, Apologi, Allegoriae, Sales*) underneath his main title of *Locorum communium collectanea*, Johann Ulrich Ragor summarized all of these genres as *Historien* in his German translation, *Loci communes Manlii, das ist: Herrliche schöne Historien allerley selten und neuen Exempel, Gleichnis, Sprüche, Rathschläge, Kriegsrüstung* [. . .].

21 For the examples above, see CR 20:549, 542, 527.

that a little nest like Wittenberg might try to carry out a reform of the entire Christendom.[22]

Vendenhaimer either wrote the personal experiences of his teacher as first-person stories or as secondhand accounts with Melanchthon as a character in them. Melanchthon would have originally told these experiences in the first person during his lectures. That is the way Vendenhaimer described a story about Melanchthon's aunt: her deceased husband once appeared to her and gave her his hand after a half-hour-long leave-taking conversation; at this, her hand was scorched and became black as coal. Melanchthon also told this story in his Sunday lectures, emphasizing its truthfulness, because he had seen her blackened hand himself.[23] Vendenhaimer also presented Melanchthon in the first person in the recollection of a conversation with Henning Goede about the Aristotelian definition of the soul, in which the lawyer (who was almost fifty years older) could not remotely begin to grasp the complex philosophical rationale of his younger colleague.[24]

B. Stories of Contemporaries

Without a doubt, Johannes Reuchlin belonged among the most influential people in Melanchthon's life. For Melanchthon, the distantly related humanist from Pforzheim was the model for his choice to become a Greek scholar and to pursue peace and tolerance. The lifelong memories of Reuchlin stayed with Melanchthon to the last stage of his life, as he followed Reuchlin's advice when he was deathly ill, covering himself with three white shirts and using a linen head cover to protect himself from chills.[25] It is therefore no wonder that the stories of Reuchlin remained prominent in Melanchthon's memory and were repeatedly

22 CR 20:592. See also Justus Jonas's letter to Luther concerning the same, WA Br 5:427–28.

23 CR 20:535, 24:498.

24 CR 20:552. Further stories from Melanchthon's biography can be found at 20:526, 533, 534, 543, 549–50, 553, 558, 584, 597, 606.

25 See Nikolaus Müller, *Philipp Melanchthons letzte Lebenstage, Heimgang und Bestattung nach den gleichzeitigen Berichten der Wittenberger Professoren* (Leipzig: Heinsius, 1910), 76. On Reuchlin's influence upon Melanchthon, see Heinz Scheible, "Reuchins Einfluß auf Melanchthon," in *Melanchthon und die Reformation. Forschungsbeiträge*, ed. Gerhard May and Rolf Deot (Mainz: Philipp von Zabern, 1996), 71–97.

told so that Württemberg remained astonishingly present in Wittenberg. Students at the Leucorea regularly heard laudatory stories about Reuchlin's longtime patron, Duke Eberhard of Württemberg. These reached a highpoint on May 31, 1552, when a Melanchthon-penned oration was given, entitled *De Eberhardo Duce Wirtebergensi.*[26] Vendenhaimer's book featured Eberhard's experiences of criminal behavior in Rome: a cardinal was murdered, signifying a pre-Reformation "Roman sewer" described by the Wittenberg Reformers. It also described how the wealth of Eberhard differed from the wealth of the Saxon electors, which came from the mining and silver industries, as the Württemberg duke could lay his head in the lap of any of his subjects without fear. Even Eberhard's anger about the torn clothing of a cleric was valued as a story about true worth.[27]

Another contemporary was Albrecht Dürer, whom Melanchthon met in Nuremberg in November 1525, as he was planning the new high school, and then again in May 1526, when the school was opened. From him, Melanchthon learned about the powerful arm and throwing ability of Emperor Maximilian I, whom the artist met and painted at the imperial diet held in Augsburg in 1518. Dürer also had stories to share of Maximilian's successor, Emperor Charles V. For instance, when both were residing in Antwerp near the end of September 1520, Dürer observed that the emperor did not avert his eyes at the sight of scantily dressed women.[28]

Melanchthon repeatedly shared stories that he learned from friends and colleagues in his lectures of contemporary events, as when he received a letter from someone named Hermann (probably former student Hermann Wilcken) and three days later told his audience its story of a magical werewolf in Latvia. Another time, he recalled the story of a religious official who made a dumb mistake in a formal exam and yet was "saved" by a kind participant.[29]

c. The Historical Writings of Antiquity

Antiquity provided an inexhaustible reservoir for histories, which the renowned Greek scholar Melanchthon drew upon frequently as an exemplary epoch. He

26 CR 11:1021–30.

27 CR 20:554, 540, 528.

28 CR 20:553, 537.

29 CR 20:552, 581.

especially made use of historical writings, whose rich experiences and destinies Melanchthon viewed not as a distant other but rather as current examples for teaching. He occupied himself especially intensely with writers like Herodotus, Thucydides, and Tacitus and the comprehensive church histories of writers like Eusebius of Caesarea or Theophylact Simocatta while he worked on his world history, *Chronicon Carionis*. He could therefore draw from a wide array of knowledge from secular and Christian resources.

In Vendenhaimer's *Historiae*, Herodotus, Eusebius, and Nikephoros Kallistos Xanthopoulus serve as models. From Herodotus, Melanchthon shared stories like the marriage of Cambyses with his sister, the burial of Semiramis, and the wife of Intaphrenes; from Eusebius, Melanchthon frequently mentioned the martyrdom of Saint Polycarp.[30] The speed with which Melanchthon incorporated ideas he learned from new books is visible in his remarks about the life of Saint Mary, who was supposedly about twenty when she became the mother of Jesus, lived for another eight years after the ascension of her son, and died at the age of fifty-nine. He learned these things from the eighteen-volume church history of Nikephoros, which first appeared in a Latin translation in 1553 and whose sections on Mary were cited by Melanchthon already in September of that same year.[31]

D. Humanist Sources

Among Melanchthon's favorite personalities of recent history was King Alfonso V of Aragon and Naples, whom he viewed to be the epitome of a wise ruler. The *Historiae* presents this king as a successful yet moderate military commander who spared the citizens of Gaeta and whose wisdom appeared in sayings about ingratitude and the meaning of science.[32] Erasmus, too, dedicated eighteen *apophthegmata* (maxims) to this ruler and his cleverness. The basis for such a rich historical legacy came from the humanist Antonio Beccadelli Panormita, who praised his patron in 229 anecdotes that present the king as an ideal ruler. The collection also became known in Germany, especially through Jakob

30 CR 20:531, 533, 604, 587.

31 CR 20:588; see also MBW 6962–67, 6977. Further stories from antiquity can be found at CR 20:520–21, 532, 533, 534, 535, 557, 579, 580–81, 583, 585, 588, 592, 603.

32 CR 20:556, 539, 554.

Spiegel's *De dictis et factis Alphonsi Regis Aragonum libri quatuor*, published in Basel in 1545. Melanchthon knew at least the German translation, *Die hohen reden und thaten Alfonsi weyland konigs zu Aragonien*, published in Frankfurt am Main in 1545, as he sent a copy of this new book to King Christian III of Denmark on October 16, 1545.[33]

Erasmus himself is the source of the story of a tragic case of vain jealousy, which Melanchthon also told in his lectures. In Basel, a prominent citizen named Christoph Baumgartner suspected his young wife of infidelity, killing her and their four-year-old daughter in August 1532, when she was pregnant, and then took his own life by throwing himself off the roof of their house. Erasmus recorded this story and sent it to numerous friends so that it could be published, which is how Melanchthon came to know it in such great detail.[34] In a different place, two poems of Petrarch provided Melanchthon with literary examples of a shepherd who first discovers a mirror when he is at court, providing him with a way to critique the vanity of courtly life.[35]

Melanchthon also borrowed from the satirical writings of the humanists—for instance, the story of a lying miller: "A knight with golden spurs caught his miller stealing and wanted to hang him. When the miller climbed the gallows, the knight urged him to name a miller who was a reliable and upright man. The miller, however, swore under oath that he could not mention anyone, saying that all millers were just as much thieves as himself. 'If that is so,' said the knight with the golden spurs, 'then step down, because I would rather suffer from you than from another thief, who is maybe even worse.'"[36] This story of the deception of all millers—the proverbial "greatest thieves in the land" because they gave back less than they were given—was shared in the critiques

33 MBW 4034. Melanchthon identified the translator as a young Rheinlander named Eberhard. The popularity of stories about King Alfonso among Melanchthon's colleagues and students can be seen in the 1585 Wittenberg publication of *De dictis et factis Alphonsi regis* by David Chytraeus. On Beccadelli's collection and its reception in Germany, see Johannes Klaus Kipf, *Gewitzte Herrscher in Handschrift, Druck, Kommentar und Übersetzung. Antonio Beccadellis "Dicta et facta Alphonsi regis Aragonum" in Deutschland* (forthcoming).

34 CR 20:601–2. See also *The Correspondence of Erasmus. Letters 2635 to 2802* (Toronto: University of Toronto Press, 2019), 127–29; Peter G. Beitenholz, ed., *Contemporaries of Erasmus* (Toronto: University of Toronto Press, 2003), 1:101.

35 CR 20:596.

36 CR 20:541.

of church and society of Heinrich Bebel's *Facetiae*, which was first published in 1508 and which Melanchthon very likely already knew from his student days in Tübingen.[37]

E. Stories about the Devil, Farces, and Legends

Melanchthon mentioned the devil willingly and frequently in order to give personal examples of the dangers of temptation into evil. Common motifs of devil stories included mothers and fathers who were impelled by the devil to murder their own children. Melanchthon also reported one such case: a *furor diabolicus* (diabolical fury) seized a mother so that she killed her two children right after their birth and was therefore executed; she was not afraid of dying, however, because in her terrible pain, she no longer wanted to live.[38] The devastating work of the devil as the author of death (auctor mortis) gained Melanchthon's attention in a particularly gruesome story that—following Manlius's edition—appeared in numerous Protestant collections. In the region of Berlin, two female magicians killed a small boy, in order to cook him and generate a terrible storm. According to Melanchthon, the lesson for his audience is clear: "These are no human deeds, but rather devilish ones. Thus, after he was expelled by the Holy Spirit, the devil transforms creatures into living devils. Therefore, one must diligently pray that God guides us through His Holy Spirit, because people are either a temple of God or an abode of Satan."[39] Such stories were transmitted through medieval collections, farces of the sixteenth century, or oral traditions. In any case, the path of their reception is quite unclear. For

37 See Heinrich Bebel, *Fazetien*, ed. Gustav Bebermeyer (Leipzig: Hiersemann, 1931), 6.

38 CR 20:540. On the motifs of sixteenth-century devil stories, see Wolfgang Brückner and Rainer Alsheimer, "Das Wirken des Teufels. Theologie und Sage im 16. Jahrhundert," in *Volkserzählung und Reformation*, 394–519. Although the theme of the devil has been the subject of research in works like Heiko A. Oberman's *Luther: Man between God and the Devil* and Volker Leppin's essay "'Der alt böse Feind. Der Teufel in Martin Luthers Leben und Denken," in *Jahrbuch für biblische Theologie* 26 (2011), 291–321, there has been no work on Melanchthon and the devil, even though fifty-five stories about the devil appear in Manlius's collection (see Brückner and Alsheimer, 448–52).

39 CR 20:579–80. Further stories about the devil: CR 20:523, 523–24, 529–30, 540–41, 587.

instance, an anonymous story from the second half of the thirteenth century was known by the title *Das Gänslein* (The little goose). It receives the following treatment from Melanchthon: "A farmer had a son, who did not often go among other people. One time it happened that he headed off to the city with his father. When he got there, he saw a pretty girl and said to his father, 'Oh, Father, what is that?' The father said, 'It's a goose.' The boy then replied to his father, 'Oh, Father, if only we had such geese!' Such were the stirrings of love for this young man."[40]

The *Historiae* also tells the story of a woman who called her husband "knicklaus," because he was full of lice. She would not stop her teasing, even though he beat her and finally threw her into a fountain; when she was almost entirely underwater, she stretched her hand out of the water and made the same motion with her fingers that her husband made when he crushed the lice. In a letter of November 27, 1537, to the city captain of Nordhausen, Jonas von Stockhausen, Luther also mentioned "the example of the lice crusher" as a way to drive away depressing thoughts with funny stories. The story of the lice crusher first appeared in a 1522 book of jests called *Schimpf und Ernst* (Insults and earnestness) by the Franciscan Johannes Pauli. It found a wide audience, including the Wittenberg Reformers.[41]

Two other stories that Vendenhaimer shared from Melanchthon's lectures belong to the popular tales of the time. In the late middle ages, a farce called "The Bacon Thief" was well known. In it, a thief breaks into a farmer's kitchen by going naked through the chimney at night. Seeing his blackened face, the farmer believes him to be the devil and lets him leave with the stolen ham. Melanchthon located that story in Zwickau and gave it a new ending: after many other thefts using the same devilish trick, the thief is caught and executed.[42] In the German collection of sayings called *Bescheidenheit* (Humility; dated 1215 and 1230), the medieval poet Freidank described peacocks as a symbol of pride, hypocrisy, and idleness: "The peacock sneaks like a thief through the

40 CR 20:579–80. See Klaus Grubmüller, ed., *Novellistik des Mittelalters* (Frankfurt am Main: Deutscher Klassiker Verlag, 1996), 648–64.

41 CR 20:598; WA Br 6:387. See also, Johannes Bolte, ed., *Johannes Pauli, Schimpf und Ernst* (Berlin: Stubenrauch, 1924), 595.

42 CR 20:594f. See also, *Enzyklopädie des Märchens* 12 (2007): 959-961.

land, with the devil's voice and an angel's clothes."[43] A 1508 published edition by Sebastian Brant first gained this work great popularity in the sixteenth century, so that this view of peacocks is referenced in both Luther's *Table Talk* and Melanchthon's lectures.[44]

In order to make his lectures vivid and lively, Melanchthon also used historical legends. Three such legends—still known today—appear in Vendenhaimer's collection: the legend of the Mouse Tower of Bingen, the legend of the Count of Gleichen and his two wives, and the legend of the Wives of Weinsberg, in which the women of the town were allowed to escape the siege of their city, taking with them whatever precious items they could carry on their backs; in the end, they carried their husbands on their shoulders, saving them from the besieged castle. Melanchthon especially treasured this story and referred to it frequently, probably also because the original castle ruins—the "Weibertreu"—were not far away from his hometown of Bretten.[45]

F. *DICTA LUTHERI*

The *Historiae* preserves many of Luther's sayings, which have almost without exception been kept in the *Table Talk* too. By contrast, Melanchthon mentioned Luther in his Sunday lectures relatively rarely and in passing.[46] Only on the topic of the veneration of saints (appearing only once in the entire *Postilla Melanthoniana*) was a longer citation from Luther used as an authoritative source. Melanchthon gave the citation from memory—"I remember Luther saying . . ."—and emphasized Christ as the sole mediator in contrast to the invocation of saints. He did so in a way that is different from what is found in the *Table Talk*.[47] This presence of Luther in the collections of Melanchthon's *Historiae* is remarkable for how it is much more extensive than in the preserved lectures. Vendenhaimer counts four sayings in his headings as "Sayings of Luther" ("Dicta Lutheri"). Of these four, three appear almost word-for-word in the

43 German: "Der Pfau schleicht wie ein Diebs durchs Land, hat Teufels Stimm und Engels G'wand."

44 WA TR 4:572; CR 20:569.

45 CR 20:544–45, 591, 603.

46 Luther is mentioned by name in the following places, among others, CR 24:745, 749, 758, 876; 25:21, 24, 81, 134, 175, 504, 630, 797, 804, 811, 835, 916. Stories about Luther appear in CR 25:89, 173, 184, 355, 534, 707, 738, 777, 781.

47 CR 20:860.

Table Talk. In another twenty sections, Luther appears mostly as a character; these, too, closely correspond to texts in the *Table Talk* or are quite similar.[48]

The extended citations from Luther and their agreements between the *Historiae* and the *Table Talk* convinced Ernst Kroker that Melanchthon had likely made his own compilation of Luther citations from which he drew individual passages as the occasion arose.[49] In contrast, Alexander Bartmuß has suggested that oral traditions and Melanchthon's great memory are the source of these sayings.[50] Melanchthon's own lecture habits contradict both ideas, however, as Melanchthon improvised his Sunday lectures and spoke without a manuscript.[51] Similarly, his citations of classical authors came from his memory and were not derived from a prepared written list. Therefore, they rarely follow the exact original syntax but rather convey the sense of whatever point belongs to the overarching relevant context. The sense of meaning—not the literal syntax—was the hermeneutical importance of the citations that Melanchthon used.

The listening students, however, held a different perspective. For them, the words of their teachers possessed a canonical character so that they labored to offer a precise rendering of the authentic texts. In my view, therefore, the Luther texts in Melanchthon's *Historiae* do not represent Melanchthon's words but were instead blended in by the collectors. Their goal was to emphasize the unity between both Reformers and to prove Melanchthon's agreement with Luther,

48 *Luther* in the headings: CR 20:562, 563, 575, 592; Luther as character: CR 20:523, 525, 526, 527, 531, 548–49, 549, 561, 563, 573–74, 574, 589–90, 590, 605; similarities between the texts of the *Historiae* and the *Table Talk*: CR 20:519, 523, 524, 525, 527, 533, 536, 537, 540, 542, 543, 543–44, 544, 544–45, 545, 547, 548, 558–59, 560, 561, 562, 562–63, 565–66, 566, 567, 567–68, 569, 570, 571–72, 572, 573, 574, 574, 574–75, 575, 575–76, 576, 576–77, 577, 577–78, 578, 578–79, 580, 587, 588, 592, 593, 594–95, 595, 600, 601. See the references to the individual sections in *Melanchthon deutsch*, vol. 6.

49 WA TR 4:XL.

50 Alexander Bartmuß, "Martin Luthers Tischreden und die Wittenberger Gruppenidentität. Philipp Melanchthons Exempla," in *Martin Luthers Tischreden. Neuansätze der Forschung*, ed. Katharina Bärenfänger, Volker Leppin, and Stefan Michel (Tübingen: Mohr Siebeck, 2013), 82.

51 Melanchthon made known in the foreword to the first edition of the Sunday lectures (1544) that he had not written the text of these "Hauspredigten" himself and was therefore against their publication.

which could best be achieved if Melanchthon himself referred to Luther and cited him in his public lectures. This reason shaped the collections of Melanchthon's *Dicta* and *Historiae* of the 1550s.[52] Current research of Luther's *Table Talk* connects the view of Luther's speech (vox ipsissima Lutheri) with the literary construction of collections by editors. This change in perspective is also important with respect to the Melanchthon collections because, in my view, it is the only explanation for such a consistent and literal presence of Luther in the transmission of Melanchthon.[53]

5. MELANCHTHON'S *HISTORIAE* AND LUTHER'S *TABLE TALK*

Luther's *Table Talk* receives attention especially for its usefulness as biographical source material. In popular biographies, it provides presumably reliable, first-hand dates. Current research increasingly views the *Table Talk*, however, as testimonies to the monumentalizing of the Reformer and correspondingly as a more dubious autobiographical source. The table as the site of these events appears to have given a great advantage to the trustworthiness of these exchanges and their participants. It stands in contrast to the formal, non-private setting of public lectures for Melanchthon's *Historiae*. But the conversations at Luther's table were also public, as the notes make clear. Numerous stories of Melanchthon are in both collections. The contrast between private (*Table Talk*) and public (lectures) does not sufficiently describe the difference between both forms of texts.[54]

---

52 On the accusation that Melanchthon turned from the Lutheran doctrinal consensus, see Beate Kobler, *Die Entstehung des negativen Melanchthonbildes. Protestantische Melanchthonkritik bis 1560* (Tübingen: Mohr Siebeck, 2014), e.g., 481–84.

53 For recent research on the *Table Talk*, see the instructive overview of Ingo Klitzsch, *Redaktion und Memoria. Die Lutherbilder der 'Tischreden'* (Tübingen: Mohr Siebeck, 2020), 1–16. The German text in the *Historiae* (CR 20:564, nr. 164) can only be explained as a direct import of a written account and is quite clearly not from a Melanchthon lecture. It revolves much more around a faculty opinion that Luther, Bugenhagen, Cruciger, and Melanchthon wrote on February 7, 1544, concerning a divorce and potential remarriage. MBW 3449. Vendenhaimer took this text but left out the names of the parties involved.

54 Klitzsch, 47; differently accented in Bartmuß, "Wittenberger Gruppenidentität," 81.

All the same, the lecture context is clearly part of the *Historiae*'s character, playing an important role in the dramatization of the lectures and making it clear that these are not only relevant sayings (*Dicta*) but rather examples (*Exempla*). While current research on the *Table Talk* views its subject in the tradition of *Apophthegmata*, Melanchthon's stories seem to belong to the deep literary tradition of collections of *Exempla*.[55] The *Historiae*'s rich use of examples is based on an understanding of history as "moral exemplar," in which history is seen as a reservoir of edifying stories that have immediate moral and didactical application for the present, even as the applications remain connected to their origins in the past.[56]

The listeners who collected Melanchthon's *Historiae* used them as examples in their own sermons, lectures, and publications, as Cogeler's *Imagines* showed. It was only infrequently the case with the *Table Talk* that these individual pieces were received into Protestant collections of examples.[57] Melanchthon, however, expanded his examples into little stories and through them became a teacher of great narrative and rhetorical range. To the list of honorary titles given to Melanchthon—humanist, Reformer, *Praeceptor Germaniae*, father of ecumenism, and so on—another one should be added, which his students clearly perceived as the charism of his fascinating and efficacious teaching style: Philip Melanchthon, a great storyteller!

Translated by Martin J. Lohrmann

55 Klitzsch, 69–70; Alexander Bartmuß, "Melanchthon erzählt. Ein Beitrag zu den 'Dicta und Exempla Melanchthons,'" *Luther: Zeitschrift der Luther-Gesellschaft* 79 (2008): 26–40, esp. 39.

56 See Matthias Pohlig, *Zwischen Gelehrsamkeit und konfessioneller Identitätsstiftung. Lutherische Kirchen- und Universalgeschichtsschreibung 1546–1617* (Tübingen: Mohr Siebeck, 2007), 69–70, 175–76. On Melanchthon's view of history not as a collective abstraction but as a summary of many individual histories, see Joachim Knape, "Melanchthon und die Historien," *Archiv für Reformationsgeschichte* 91 (2000): 111–26.

57 Klitzsch, 48–49.

Part 3

Forming the Faith

Ever at Rest

Martin Luther's Sabbatarianism

Mickey L. Mattox

In my present life situation, retirement still seems a distant mystery. What does one do? Professor Timothy J. Wengert's case sheds little light on this mystery, for *in Ruhestand* he seems to have become busier and more productive than ever! How does an object seemingly at rest continue to work? Attempting to make sense of this Lutheran paradox, I consider below Martin Luther's remarks on the God who not only instituted the Sabbath but is *simul requiescens et operans*. Perhaps the Reformer can shed some light on the matter?

My subject in what follows is Martin Luther's understanding of God's Sabbath rest. If I were writing as systematic theologians have typically written about Luther for perhaps the last one hundred years, then I would be determined to discover in his work the new and different. Not atypically, this search for the new and different would be carried out on the supposition that Luther broke free of the constraints of traditional metaphysical thought, shattering the medieval Aristotelian framework and so opening the way to a new, post- or even anti-metaphysical theology, one that puts front and center the divine/human relationship. As a relational theologian, I might say, Luther had only a relational ontology, one that enabled him to limit the speculative scope of Christian theology, as seen, for example, in his oft-quoted statement that the proper subject of theology is "man the sinner, guilty and lost, and the justifying God his savior."[1] If our topic is God's Sabbath rest, then we would soon discover that rest itself is not properly a theological concept—a description, that is, of something God does in God's self—but is instead relative to the divine act of creation. Hence the concept could even be called anthropological. Luther, it would turn out, had already made the decisive modern turn to the subject.

1 WA 40 II/2:328.17–18; LW 12:311.

But I will not say any of that. Intellectual fireworks like that are not my forte. More importantly, such a reading of Luther gets him wrong historically. Therefore, in what follows I will do my best to read Luther historically and contextually and will thus presume that he can be best understood as a later medieval catholic whose understanding of God, including the divine Sabbath, rests comfortably within the bounds of the antecedent Christian tradition. Space does not allow that this exercise be extended to include the voices of Luther's "predecessors and contemporaries,"[2] so I will have to content myself here with a down payment on a task that remains to be completed. This brief foray into Luther's writings will suffice, however, to highlight something of Luther's distinctive understanding of God the Creator. Perhaps, too, it will bring us a step or two closer to answering the question of the *simul requiescens et operans*.

In what follows, I rely on two texts, drawn from two very different times in Luther's life. The first is a sermon on Exodus delivered in the mid-1520s and the second a lecture on Genesis 2 delivered in the summer of 1535. Both these texts address the problem of the Sabbath rest, with the sermon emphasizing its subjective and soteriological implications and the lectures bringing to the fore the mystery of God at work in time and eternity. My conclusion will attempt to assess the internal consistency and coherence of Luther's soteriological claims with his properly theological ones. To be sure, scholars have long and rightly noted the ad hoc character of Luther's work, and "a foolish consistency" may be, as Emerson once remarked, "the hobgoblin of little minds."[3] As will become clear, however, Luther is as convinced as anyone that the truths of revelation, which tell of both the God who saves and the God who is, are not self-contradictory. Indeed, they agree and reinforce one another.

2 In a volume that might be read as a footnote—admittedly, a very long one—to the question, What do they know who only Luther know? where the author emphasizes the necessity of reading the exegesis of the Reformers in the context of the antecedent exegetical tradition, see Timothy J. Wengert, *Philip Melanchthon's "Annotationes in Johannem" of 1523 in Relation to Its Predecessors and Contemporaries* (Geneva: Librairie Droz, 1987).

3 As quoted by David C. Steinmetz during the CH 14 Lectures on Martin Luther at the Divinity School, Duke University, ca. 1992. Spoken in response to a student's question about Luther's seeming inconsistencies.

"Remember the Sabbath Day, So That You Make It Holy!"

To that end, we begin with an imaginary journey back to Wittenberg, where we find the forty-one-year-old Martin Luther hard at work, almost halfway through a three-year sermon series on Exodus.[4] It continues to surprise people that the man whose history is so inextricably linked to a struggle over the gospel spent most of his career as a professor lecturing and/or preaching on the Old Testament. Today he is preaching his third sermon on Exodus 20, this one on the Third Commandment, which enjoins Sabbath observance.[5] The date is October 22, 1525. It's a Sunday afternoon, and we are in the City Church, the townspeople's church, rather than the famous Castle Church where Luther will later be said to have posted the *Ninety-Five Theses*.[6] It is only twelve months now since our preacher stopped wearing his monk's habit. Oh, and he is a newlywed, having married the former nun Katharina von Bora four short months ago, on June 27. Just about nine months from right now their first child, Johannes, will be born. So the preacher standing before us today is in a strikingly different *Sitz im Leben* than the one who began this sermon series back in 1523. He is dressed in the simple black gown worn by doctors of theology. If Luther looks a bit haggard, perhaps that's because he stayed up late last night working on a new book, *The Bondage of the Will*, which will offer a forceful rejoinder to Erasmus's "Diatribe on Free Will."[7] Surely too he is aware that the "Sacramentarian" controversy, not unrelated to Erasmian spiritualism,[8] is also heating up. Oecolampadius has just published a treatise on the Lord's Supper, *De genuina verborum Domini*, in which it is made clear that he is following the Zwinglian path.[9]

---

4 "Predigten über das zweite Buch Mose," WA 16:477–85; here, at 477.27.

5 The date of the sermon is given in the WA. For dating Luther's other activities here and in what follows, I rely on Andrea van Dülmen, *Luther-Chronik: Daten zu Leben und Werk* (Munich: Deutsche Taschenbuch Verlag, 1983).

6 For the current state of this vexed question, see Volker Leppin and Timothy J. Wengert, "Sources for and against the Posting of the Ninety-Five Theses," *Lutheran Quarterly* 29 (2015): 373–98.

7 WA 18:600–787.

8 For the definitive word on spiritualist Sacramentarianism, see Amy Nelson Burnett, *Debating the Sacraments: Print and Authority in the Early Reformation* (Oxford: Oxford University Press, 2019).

9 *Luther-Chronik*, 126.

Tending to a new wife, starting a family, preparing to take on the Sacramentarians, and rebutting the prince of the humanists, all while holding down his day job as preacher and professor? It's just another day's work for Martin Luther.

As he rises to the pulpit, he is determined in spite of all the distractions to preach with clarity the gospel of Jesus Christ. These sermons on the Ten Commandments are therefore much more than moral exhortations aimed at moving the Wittenbergers to behave. To be sure, he does mean to persuade, and as soon becomes clear, he also wants his people to follow the path of faith and holiness. But more importantly, he wants them to know that this path begins with a readiness to rest one's weary soul in the saving God and, indeed, that the soul's rest in God is both this path's beginning and its final end.

Today's sermon is the last of three he preached on the "first table" of the law, which specifies our duties toward God: have no gods before me; take not God's name in vain; keep the Sabbath. Luther believes that if one understands these three commandments aright, then one will see that they encompass the whole Christian life, especially when we remind ourselves that all the commandments are informed by the wondrous annunciation with which they begin: "I am the Lord, your God." The Sabbath, it seems, has to do with remembering that Lord is *my God*. In this sermon, Sabbath observance is beginning to take on a new and interesting shape, one that underscores the faith that believes and so receives God's word. It is this faith that saves, Luther insists, and not one's works or ritual observances, for God wants true obedience to flow from hearts transformed.

We wince when we hear him remark that the New Testament has dispensed with the "Jewish Sabbath,"[10] and he worries some of us a bit more when he says that the same thing applies to the Sabbath of the papists, as well as their holy days of obligation.[11] His understanding of Sabbath rest is thus defined at the outset by contrast. The true Sabbath, Luther wants to say, is neither Jewish nor papist. Moreover, "the son of man is the Lord of the Sabbath."[12] For that matter, the commandment of love may require that one break one's Sabbath

10 WA 16:477.29–32. The literature on the problem of Luther and the Jews is now quite extensive. For a brief introduction to the problem, see Thomas Kaufmann, "Luther and the Jews," in *Jews, Judaism, and the Reformation in Sixteenth-Century Germany*, ed. Dean Philip Bell and Stephen G. Burnett (Leiden: Brill, 2006), 69–104.

11 WA 16:479.16–24.

12 WA 16:478.11–12.

rest in order to help a neighbor.[13] Luther's more fundamental concern, however, is that neither Jewish ritual observances nor papist days of obligation succeed in orienting one toward the soul's true rest. The conscience has been set free from all such required observances, he says, through faith in Christ.[14] Mandatory holy days—whether Jewish or papist—provide only an "exterior Sabbath," which is not at all the "interior Sabbath" one really needs.[15] Nevertheless, Luther allows that this interior rest requires exterior observance, a particular day one makes holy. Embracing the traditional practice, he concludes that Christians have been right to set apart Sunday, the day of Jesus's resurrection, as their day of rest. In this sense, the Jewish Sabbath is transformed to become a festival or holiday and so the Hebrew term is rightly *verdeuedscht* as a *feyertag*.[16]

But how does one make a day holy? The interior stillness of the Christian faithful on Sundays, Luther answers, fulfills what was foreshadowed in the Sabbath of Israel.[17] The reality foreshadowed by the Jewish Sabbath is Christ's own sacrificial death, so one needs to die with Christ in order properly to keep the Sabbath. The allusion of course is to Christian baptism, which Luther construes as the rite in which the putting to death of the old Adam is begun. That's something one will never get quite right in this life: "The Sabbath will finally be properly kept for the first time when we are dead."[18] The death of Christ and our own one-day-soon death meet in the daily practices of the faith. Sabbath-keeping is thus a form of mimesis, an *imitatio Christi* in which Christians enter spiritually into the power of Christ's death and resurrection.

Stepping away from the broom or the plow (or the keyboard!), one ceases to busy oneself with this-worldly duties and so finds time to be still and listen as "God speaks to us." "Keep still," God says, "consecrate the Sabbath to me, and let me do the work.'"[19] God only works, Luther says, when we cease to work and instead rest in him. Holiness and great works of faith follow when one keeps this Sabbath. As one rests and God works, eternity enters time. The ever-active God speaks his word and so makes his grace effective, just as he did in the

13 WA 16:479.27–29.

14 WA 16:479.18.

15 WA 16:478.8–10.

16 WA 16:480.14–16.

17 WA 16:481.31–32.

18 WA 16:481.14–15.

19 WA 16:482.19–20.

apostle Paul.[20] God is the worker who effects the believer's inner peace, which Luther just a few years ago famously described as Christian freedom.[21] Seek out, he exhorts us, not a day of mere external obedience but a spiritual Sabbath, a "proper Sabbath," where the heart rests in God.[22]

He echoes the treatise on Christian freedom again when he insists that God produces willing servanthood. Just so, the Christian's internal Sabbath rest becomes the foundation for deeds of active love. Living in the power of the Sabbath all week long, so to speak, believers return to their respective places—butcher or housemaid, prince or shepherd—and offer their daily work as a gift consecrated to God.[23] The orders of everyday life here take on a new and fundamentally religious significance. The Christian at work in family, home, church, and society honors God and so consecrates all of life to him.[24] The weekdays, it turns out, are the true and proper days for fastings and disciplines of all sorts, offered in service to the neighbor in need.

So it is that the third commandment brings to completion the duties given in the first and second. The first commandment teaches one to believe in God alone and to give God thanks, the second teaches one to honor and praise God with mouth and mind, and the third teaches one to rest before God without works. Thus in the lived experience of faith, the one who rests in God returns to the works of the first and second commands, renewing faith in God anew and honoring him in word and deed. The first table of the law thus presents the man or woman of faith with "a lovely golden ring,"[25] which encompasses the whole life of faith and service.

The irony we might note here is that when the Christian enters by faith into the stillness of God's Sabbath rest, they discover that the God who once "rested from all his works" is, as Jesus said in John 5, still very much at work by making grace present and effective in the believer themselves. For a closer look

---

20 WA 16:482.27f.

21 Luther explicitly notes here his "von der Christlichen freiheit und von den guten wercken," both published in 1520. WA 16:484.25–26. For a fresh translation and commentary with an extensive introduction to Luther's treatise on Christian freedom, see *The Freedom of a Christian* (1520), TAL 1:467–538.

22 WA 16:480.24–26.

23 WA 16:483.21–484.4.

24 WA 16:483–84.

25 WA 16:484.32.

at Luther's understanding of the God who rests even as they continue to work, we jump now some ten years into the future to listen in on Luther's lectures on Genesis.

The Genesis Lectures

The year is 1535, and it is a warm summer day in late June when we return to Wittenberg. Just a couple of weeks from now, the university will close and move to Jena temporarily on account of the plague. Classes won't resume here for almost a year. We are in luck today, however, as we are seated in a crowded classroom in the Leucorea, where Luther just a few weeks ago began a lecture series on Genesis. Again, he is dressed in the doctor's gown. The room is crowded with students, and a few of them seem to be trying to take down everything the professor says. Luther is now the most (in)famous man in Europe, a friend and patron to his friends and a fearsome foe to his enemies. He and Frau Katharina have also become the parents of six children, five of whom are still living. Their youngest, Margareta, is still in diapers, just a year old. Immersed in the toil and trials of both the churchman and the *Hausvater*, our fifty-one-year-old Martin Luther still has a lot going on.[26]

Lecturing today on the first few verses of Genesis 2, Luther offers the intriguing suggestion that this text seems already to anticipate what was to come of God's good creation—that is, that it would be the site of struggle and, indeed, of armed warfare. The Vulgate text, he says, has wrongly translated the Hebrew *Zebaam* as if it referred to the ornate furnishings of the heavens—that is, the stars and planets.[27] Instead, it means that the created heavens included a

26 The most vivid English-language study of the elder Luther is surely H. G. Haile, *Luther: An Experiment in Biography* (New York: Doubleday, 1978).

27 In both the *Wittenberger Sonderausgabe des Pentateuchs* (1523) and the final edition of the *Deutsche Bibel* (1545), Luther translates the first clause of Genesis 2:1 as "Also ward volendet himel und Erden mit irem gantzen heer" (Thus was heaven and earth completed with their whole army or hosts) WA DB 8:40–41. In his remarks on Genesis 2:1 Luther observes, "Our text [i.e., the Latin] has 'and all their furnishings', but in the Hebrew it is 'assembly' or 'their military' [Zebaam]. And the prophets continued this manner of speaking so that the stars and the planets were called the army of the heavens." The original published version of the text offers a marginal note to alert the reader to this important amendment to the translation of the text. The Wittenbergers' *Vulgata Revision* of 1529 translates this phrase with "et

vast host or army. "Are these perhaps angels or spirits?" you may be wondering. Yes, the professor indicates, but the term should probably be understood much more broadly to include the "whole creation," which stands ever at the ready to fight and keep the good creation, well, good. How so?

Speculating as to the answer, Luther tries to peer beyond the horizons. In the beginning, it seems, God, per Genesis 2:1, foresaw the fall of humankind. But the created things other than humankind did not for that same reason "fall." Thus he figures, from the very beginning until the last day, the stars and all the luminaries stand at the ready, as do the first created human beings, the beasts, and even the trees. Satan rages against this creation, particularly living things. If he could, he would rob the seas of their fish, the skies of their birds, and the earth of every fruit and, indeed, destroy all things. "But God creates all those creatures," Luther insists, "that they should stand as an army and fight for us without end against the devil and [wicked] men and in this way serve and benefit us."[28] The God of Genesis 2:1 is the Lord of this vast host, and so the text gestures forward and back, both to the battle that would soon come to the creation and to its origins in Satan's own cosmic fall. As the apostle affirms in Romans 8, the whole creation groans in anticipation of the revelation of the sons of God. So also here, Luther sees creation as having been enlisted from the very beginning in the fight against wickedness. Eschatology brackets history, so to speak, both forward and back. God is the Lord, then, now, and always.

While Luther is sure that Satan is a fallen angel, and that his fall predates his upcoming conversation with the first-created woman, he does not think one can know much more. In the lectures on Genesis 1, he has warned his students not to worry too much about insoluble questions related to the origins of the angels or the heavenly conflict that led to Satan's demise. Consistent with that warning, he has also rejected Augustine's reading of the "days" of Genesis 1 as a pre-temporal event in the minds of the angels. Likewise for Dionysius's list

omnis *exercitus* eorum" (with the italicized text indicating an emendation), as does the first published volume of the Genesis lectures. See WA DB 5:14; *In Primum Librum Mose Enarrationes* (Wittenberg: Seitz, 1544). Luther's remarks here suggest that he used the traditional Latin text in the classroom, while his editors updated the published version to refer instead to the Wittenberg *Revision*.

28 On the active role of the creation in resisting the devil, see Steven Tyra, "All Creatures Are Martyrs: Martin Luther's Cruciform Exegesis of Romans 8:19–22," *Westminster Theological Journal* 76 (2014): 27–53.

of the ranks and choirs of angels. Instead of teaching us about the times before or after history, Genesis has to do with *our time*. And indeed, for Luther, God's deeds are to be understood as taking place within time. God's word of creation, moreover, abides within it. The creation itself does not simply exist. It is not, so to speak, ontologically neutral. On the contrary, as God's good creation, it is already inclined to God and just so engaged in the fight against Satan.

How is it, then, that the God whom the whole militant host of heaven and earth stand ready to serve remains at rest? Part of the answer to that question is readily at hand in the form of the traditional response that God rested from the work of making new things but works still in governing and conserving the creation. Jesus himself says, "My father works until now, and I work."[29] Luther's own ideas about God's preservation of the creation tend to collapse the traditional logical distinction between *creatio* and *conservatio*.[30] Why? Because the divine words of creation are God's word, which accomplishes what it says. The ten repetitions of "and God said" in Genesis 1 exist today not as a distant echo or as a dead letter on the page of recorded history. On the contrary, these words still ring out in all their original power and effect. There is in a certain sense no difference between the creation of Adam and that of, say, Timothy J. Wengert. As Luther writes in the *Small Catechism*, "I believe that God has created <u>me</u> and all things that exist."[31] Attempting to bring home for us the meaning of the present and active word of God, Luther resorts to a financial metaphor. The word of God always brings an increase, "to express myself so, through the power of the original endowment."[32]

A further part of the answer is to be found in correlation with the soteriological concerns mentioned in the Exodus sermons. God rested from the work of creating new things precisely because the faithful and merciful-hearted God was committed to what he had made. God did not abandon or destroy the creation, nor turn his attention from it in order to create something else altogether new. The word of God abides, both in the sense of being ever present and active, as well as in demonstrating God's continuing love and concern for the creation. Luther believes, in short, that the God who has begun a good work

29 LW 1:74.

30 On this issue, see David Löfgren, *Die Theologie der Schöpfung bei Luther* (Göttingen: Vandenhoeck & Ruprecht, 1960).

31 BC 354.

32 LW 1:75; WA 42:57.12–14.

in the creation will also bring it through to its fulfillment. God's abiding love promises that.

The Sabbath rest of the Christian, per the Exodus sermon examined previously, calls for a cessation of personal striving to achieve a kind of surrender in which God does the work, creating a heart that reaches out to the neighbor in love. Luther's remarks at Genesis 2 show that for him, personal salvation is included alongside a divinely foreseen cosmic destiny, which was given already in the divine decision to create. The vast and diverse creation has somehow become God's own army, joining itself to God in echoing the still-reverberating words by means of which God created all things. God, therefore, is surely at work in our world, in God's own inimitable way as well as in the Lord's creatures. The rest of God means that God has in God's freedom decided to do this, and not something else. God's freedom as Luther understands it is a form of the Augustinian "freedom for," in this case "for us and for our salvation." The rest of God, in short, is the rest of a free commitment to a good end. Perhaps with that, we begin to glimpse the answer to the Lutheran paradox with which I began? The *simul* at the heart of the mystery of being retired and working at the same time, it would seem, is a heart full of love for a task not yet brought to completion. Which sounds just like the Tim Wengert I know.

Diluting Luther

Baptism in Sixteenth-Century Catechisms

Mark D. Tranvik

Timothy Wengert has long been an eager and able teacher of Lutheran doctrine and practice to American audiences. In many ways, he has single-handedly revived the reputation of Philip Melanchthon, who has been seen as suspect in some Lutheran quarters for straying from the key teachings of Martin Luther. But Wengert's interests and contributions go far beyond that. He has also done much to translate and teach the key insights of the tradition as contained in the catechisms of Martin Luther.[1] And he has done so with the mind of an academic and the heart of a pastor. Unlike some professors of theology, Wengert strives to be understood. He wants the truths of the gospel to ring in the ears of the people in the pews, and he knows that in order to do that he must first reach the pastors and teachers who will deliver the good news.

In this essay, I would like to honor Wengert's love of the catechism by looking at how Martin Luther's teaching on baptism was transmitted to the second and third generation of sixteenth-century Lutherans. As Wengert recognized, Luther made a radical break with the catechetical tradition he inherited. Based in a view of the self and the world that sees one moving from vice to virtue, these catechisms were heavy on the law, or the "musts," as Wengert put it.[2] Luther's theological revolution turned this way of thinking on its head. Instead of stressing the movement from humanity to God, the new way of thinking underlines how God moves in on us, the wholly unworthy recipients of his love. And the best way to illustrate this is the sacrament of baptism, which

1 In addition to his articles and essays, see Timothy J. Wengert, *Martin Luther's Catechisms: Forming the Faith* (Minneapolis: Fortress, 2009).

2 Wengert, 6.

Wengert says provides the framework for a gospel message that entails death and resurrection.[3]

I will proceed by providing a brief review of Luther's teaching on baptism. That will be followed by an examination of baptism in the catechisms of four well-known sixteenth-century Lutherans. I will conclude with some thoughts about how baptism is uniquely suited to house Luther's radical teaching on justification by faith.

Martin Luther saw baptism as central to his theological revolution. However, on all sides, he saw the sacrament being diminished by legal schemes of various sorts, all designed to rein in the freedom bestowed by Christ in the waters of baptism. Luther's earliest battles were with the late-medieval church. While Rome praised baptism as necessary for salvation, its significance was eclipsed by the sacrament of penance. By Luther's time, penance had been encumbered by rules and laws that seemed designed more to trouble the consciences of the faithful than to offer a word of forgiveness. Furthermore, penance was entangled with the indulgence controversy. Making satisfaction for sin was possible by means of a monetary payment. The end result was that the living Christ bestowed in baptism was submerged by a church determined to control the faithful by a web of laws and rules. This situation was exacerbated by the greed of the church as the indulgence trade became a key source of income for a hierarchy that appeared largely oblivious to the poverty of most of the people.

Luther's early writings on baptism make it the center of the Christian life. It is no longer the sacrament of infancy (nor is it merely a rite of initiation) that is superseded by penance at the age of seven. Rather, we are adopted by the living Christ in the waters of baptism and our relationship with him does not cease until death. In an ingenious move, Luther folds penance into baptism by saying the entire Christian life is a daily, even hourly, dying and rising with Christ. Baptism is never left behind. Because Christ is risen and alive and present in our lives, our baptism has real power and vitality.[4]

It must be stressed that this evangelical understanding of baptism ("full and complete justification") becomes the fulcrum by which Luther tackles the

---

3 Wengert, 6.

4 See Mark D. Tranvik, "Luther on Baptism," in *Harvesting Martin Luther's Reflections on Theology, Ethics, and the Church*, ed. Timothy Wengert (Minneapolis: Fortress, 2017), 23–37.

indulgence trade as well as the whole monastic system.[5] With regard to the former, the living Christ bestowed in baptism gives us status before God as God's beloved and forgiven children. There is no need to cooperate with grace performing works of satisfaction, whether those be acts of piety or financial contributions. With regard to the latter, Luther notes that monastic vows add nothing to the vow God has made to us in our baptism. The underlying rationale for the entire monastic system was the notion that so-called works of supererogation were deserving of special merit from God. Luther responds with a vigorous no. In baptism, all Christians are given vocations. In effect, the monastery is turned inside out and now encompasses the home, workplace, and community—the very places where our good works are needed.[6]

Later in his life, Luther would be attacked by another form of legalism. The battleground was centered on the sacrament of baptism. Two key presuppositions undergirded the movement of opposition known generally as "enthusiasm."[7] One was a metaphysical assumption that spirit and matter were completely separate. The second was the belief that a person's activity in the world in some way reflected a person's status before God. Both of these presuppositions led to a significant divergence from Luther's understanding of baptism.

With regard to the first point, the enthusiasts had a difficult time believing that something actually happened in baptism. In some of its cruder expressions, the element of water was denigrated as a "dog's bath."[8] All that matters is faith (and therefore infant baptism was denied). Others recognized the importance of water but denied the presence of the living Christ in and with the water. Rather they said baptism *pointed* to Christ but in no way contained Christ. The underlying fear was a return to the "superstitious" practices of the late-medieval church. On the second point, some were nervous about Luther's emphasis on our freedom in Christ. They felt there was a need to pump the

5 Martin Luther, *The Babylonian Captivity of the Church*, TAL 3:70.

6 Wengert, *Martin Luther's Catechisms*, 104.

7 The difficulty with translating the word *Schwärmer* has been widely noted. I will use the word *enthusiasm* to describe the broad movement that was suspicious of external things and focused on what was inward or "spiritual." In most of Luther's writings on baptism, he is using the word to describe the Anabaptist movement and their rejection of infant baptism.

8 Martin Luther, "Concerning Rebaptism," TAL 3:312.

brakes and continually qualify freedom by making sure faith was "genuine" by acts of discipleship. Luther, of course, thought the most genuine faith of all was totally focused on the neighbor and not concerned with whether or not one's works counted in heaven.

For Luther, the centrality of baptism is not diminished by the concerns of the enthusiasts. In fact, he emphasizes even more clearly in the later part of his life that something *actually happens* in baptism.[9] The incarnation has rendered invalid any final separation of spirit and matter. For him, it is the place in time and space where the almighty Trinity itself enters our experience and reverses our earthly path from one headed toward death to one headed toward life. Baptism doesn't simply point to a Christ abstract and remote. Rather, it is an astonishing *rupture* in our life whereby Christ himself in word and water drowns us and raises us up. This event forms the entire horizon of the Christian life. It does not need to be supplemented by good works. In our daily callings, we have nothing but good works, albeit works done solely for the sake of the neighbor and creation. Furthermore, because God is the one acting in baptism, it makes perfect sense to include infants in the sacrament. After all, if God can make John the Baptist leap in Elizabeth's womb at the greeting of Mary (Luke 1:41), can the Lord not create faith in infants?[10]

Since we will be reviewing catechetical material in this essay, we should remember Luther's own small and large catechisms are filled with these insights. Written in the late 1520s, they bear the fruit of his struggles with Rome and the enthusiasts. Luther is explicit about the benefits bestowed in baptism: it forgives sin, delivers from death and the devil, and gives salvation to all who believe in the promise. This remarkable trinity of goods is given to the one being baptized when the word and the water combine (so that it becomes a "life-giving" water) to make this event the most important thing that can happen to a person.[11] Equally important, this event is not momentary but encompasses all of life, as the living Christ kills and makes alive the one baptized in the callings of daily existence. Gone is the notion that baptism is a sacrament of infancy, once done and soon forgotten. Also now missing is the idea that baptism is a mere sign pointing to an abstract Christ who is only "real" when comprehended by an

9 See the fine study by Jonathan D. Trigg, *Baptism in the Theology of Martin Luther* (Boston: Brill, 2001).

10 See Luther's defense of infant faith in "Concerning Rebaptism," TAL 3:293–97.

11 BC 458.

adult faith.[12] Finally, there is no mention of works needed beyond baptism to somehow make it genuine.

Having outlined Luther's profound theology of baptism, let us look at how four catechisms by theologians in Luther's wider circle assimilated and understood his teaching. While we should not expect Luther to be simply parroted by his associates and followers, there is little doubt they sought to be faithful transmitters of his insights. Of course, the medium of the catechism becomes a key way to pass along the tradition. To what degree did that happen? This is the question to which we now turn.

The first work we will examine is that of Johannes Brenz, the Lutheran Reformer of Württemberg in southern Germany. Luther's presentation at the Heidelberg Disputation in 1518 included a youthful Brenz in the audience. The Wittenberg Reformer's words would change the course of the young man's life. Committed to reform, Brenz wrote a small catechism in 1535 to help implement evangelical changes in the church in southern Germany. It was held in high esteem for generations. Brenz's work went through many editions and was even used well into the twentieth century. In 1551, Brenz wrote a large catechism that is basically a commentary on the shorter one.[13] Most of our comments on Brenz will be based on this longer text. Because of the popularity of this work, we will give it close attention.

The first thing to strike the eye is the unusual order of the catechism. Luther's is arranged to reflect his law-gospel dialectic: the commandments, creed, Lord's Prayer, and sacraments. Brenz's work, however, has a completely different structure. He begins with baptism and then proceeds to the creed, Lord's Prayer, commandments, and Lord's Supper. This does not so much reflect baptism's importance in evangelical teaching as it does pedagogical concerns. The catechism is a chronological replication of the Christian life, beginning

12 While Luther will use "sign" (Zeichen) on occasion, it is fairly rare in his writings on the sacraments.

13 Christoph Weismann's *Eine kleine Biblia. Die Katechismen von Luther und Brenz. Einführung und Texte* (Stuttgart: Calwer Verlag, 1985), 74–77. Some material in this section is taken from Mark D. Tranvik, "A Water Gracious, Heavenly and Divine: Baptism in the Lutheran Reformation," *Currents in Theology and Mission* 19, nr. 4 (August 1992): 250–58.

with baptism and moving through the chief articles of the faith to the goal of the instruction, preparation for the Lord's Supper.[14]

Of course, this arrangement is not only suited to the didactic needs of its users. There are also theological presuppositions present here, particularly in the understanding of the law. Luther does not speak of Christ until he reaches the second article of the creed. For him, the law must do its work because it comes first experientially and because of the need to call a rebellious humanity to repentance. Thus it makes sense to place the commandments first. Brenz, though, begins with baptism. This suggests that humanity stands in the light of the gospel and the law has primarily a directing or guiding function.[15]

Another of Brenz's concerns was to confront the question that was asked of Reformers: If faith alone justifies, what need is there of the sacraments? For Brenz, the answer lay in the command and example of Christ and in the need for a public witness to God's prior election. This latter point, unusual in Lutheran thinkers, is given an elaborate defense by Brenz in his large catechism.

First, he likens baptism to the anointing of a king. He notes in the Old Testament the anointing of David did not confer royal status on him. He had already been chosen for kingship. The anointing by Samuel was a public recognition of a prior reality: "This anointing does not make David a king. For had he not been chosen and called to be a king, this anointing would not make him a king. However, the anointing was a public ceremony . . . [showing] that he was called and chosen to be a king."[16] The meaning of this for baptism is clear: the bestowal of the sacrament is not the event of salvation but rather the ratification of God's prior calling.

Brenz also draws a similar analogy from marriage. The core of marriage, says Brenz, is the free agreement of husband and wife to enter into a relationship. But beyond this is the need for a public consecration of the previous accord. He likens baptism to a wedding: "When one is baptized one should regard it as a public confirmation of a heavenly marriage."[17] As in the anointing of a king, baptism for Brenz is not the place of salvation but rather the confirmation of what God has already decided in the heavenly counsels.

14 Weismann, 56.

15 Weismann, 55.

16 Johannes Brenz, *Catechismus* (Leipzig: Hartman Beyer, 1551), D5r–D6v.

17 Brenz, D6v–D7v.

Continuing his interpretation of the smaller catechism, Brenz focuses next on the definition of baptism. He urges his readers not to give undue attention to the externals of the rite (godparents, font, water, etc.) but to remember that the Holy Trinity itself with all its gifts is present at baptism. Recalling God's promise allows the baptized to withstand the doubts and anxieties that plague the conscience.[18]

Finally, Brenz takes up the difficult issue that all the figures in the magisterial Reformation had to confront: infant baptism. Due to the challenges posed by the Anabaptists, it was necessary in most catechisms to treat this topic. Brenz roots his defense of this teaching in a *fides infantium*, something that was also defended by Luther. His warrants for infant faith were traditional (circumcision of infants in the Old Testament). But Brenz also gave some ingenious arguments to support his position, grounded in the creative power of God's word. To cite one example, he notes that if God can speak to a whale (as in the story of Jonah) in such a way that the fish is able to understand, why could not God tailor divine speech to the capabilities of an infant?[19]

In the final analysis, the reader is struck by how Brenz repeatedly refers to the sacraments as *Wahrzeichen* (emblems). He certainly affirms the physical element in baptism but the power belongs with God's word. In the final analysis, he separates baptism from faith and warns that only the latter is truly necessary: "Indeed, baptism is useful. . . . However, it receives its usefulness from faith . . . thereby, whoever does not believe in Christ, even if he has all the sacraments, all the treasures and earthly and spiritual gifts, all wisdom and all power of the world, nevertheless he will be condemned."[20] No Lutheran would deny this. But the way Brenz states it appears to undermine the material element. For example, Luther said baptism exists for the sake of faith!

Luther's friend and colleague, Philip Melanchthon, also wrote a catechism that went through a number of editions in the Reformation era. It was written in Latin and probably intended for use in the upper levels of the school system. Because of Melanchthon's fundamental role in the transmission of Lutheran theology and his influence on future German education, this work deserves our attention. The text we will look at is from 1558 with editions traced as far back as 1532.

18 Brenz, E1r–E4r.

19 Brenz, D1r.

20 Brenz, G2r.

The section on baptism is fairly short, with well over half the material devoted to the question of infant baptism. Indeed, the 1559 *Loci communes* (the last edition of his famous theological work) displays an even higher percentage of material in the segment on baptism devoted to this issue. Perhaps Melanchthon's discussion of the sacrament is overwhelmed by the polemics of the age. As we move to his definition, baptism is identified as immersion in water with the concurrent proclamation of the promise. Moreover, the sacrament is not only a ceremony by which we are received into God's grace, but it is also a means by which the church is distinguished from unbelievers.[21]

In his discussion of baptism's effects, Melanchthon is concerned with distinguishing his view from those who see baptism as a human act of commitment to God. Rather, he argues that in baptism God is coming to the sinner with blessings and benefits. Unless this fundamental point be understood, baptism will simply degenerate into a human work. Once this is grasped, however, the baptized one receives the favor of God: salvation, sanctification, and a future secure against all evil.[22] He clearly favors the words *testimonia* and *signa* to his understanding of baptism, suggesting a reticence to link the sacrament too closely with the earthly element. And what does baptism signify? Our immersion in water means first that sin is drowned and we are given new life in Christ. But baptism has a secondary meaning as well. It also refers to the daily afflictions by which sin is destroyed. Therefore, we would do well to remember our baptism so that we keep God's love before us and that our troubles be seen, not as evidence of abandonment, but as the fruit of our obedience.[23]

As previously discussed, Melanchthon devotes a significant part of the catechism to a defense of infant baptism. There is little that is new in his arguments, though he seems to favor syllogistic logic (four of his five reasons for infant baptism have syllogisms) to underline his point of view. Perhaps the relative silence of the Bible on infant baptism (it is implied—the baptism of households, etc.—but never explicitly stated) made Melanchthon resort to more philosophical method of argumentation.[24]

Next, we move to the Lutheran Reformer, Erasmus Sarcerius. Sarcerius was born in ducal Saxony and educated at Leipzig and Wittenberg. After serving

21 Philip Melanchthon, "Catechesis Puerilis," CR 23:183.

22 CR 23:184.

23 CR 23:186.

24 CR 23:184–85.

in various places as a parish pastor, he became a superintendent in Mansfeld, Luther's home region. He authored numerous theological books and commentaries, including a popular set of postils for use in preaching. He also wrote a catechism to which we now turn to examine his understanding of baptism.

Sarcerius's work exhibits familiar Lutheran themes. Baptism is established by Christ and the effect of the sacrament is the forgiveness of sins, whereby we are moved from the kingdom of Satan to the kingdom of God.[25] There is but a brief reference to the daily meaning of baptism. However, the link with repentance is key for Sarcerius, and he wants to stress how our remorse for sin is preparation for our participation in the Lord's Supper.[26] He concludes his main section with forty-nine questions that have arisen with regard to baptism. His answers are brief and usually limited to one or two sentences. Among the issues he covers are the meaning of the water in baptism, the correct baptismal formula, the choice of godparents, the validity of baptism by heretics, how baptism is a defense against temptation, and so on.[27] The section on the sacrament is rounded out by a twenty-five-page discourse on the errors of the Anabaptists, again employing a question-and-answer format. Most of this segment involves the typical arguments used by Lutherans in their defense of infant baptism.[28]

Perhaps most noteworthy for the subject of this essay is the way Sarcerius continually refers to baptism as a "sign" (zeichen) and even in one case as a "naked sign" (blosse zeichen). In one fairly short paragraph on the use and effect of baptism, he calls it a "sign" seven times.[29] He has relatively few references to *wasser*, though, of course, as a good Lutheran he certainly is not denying or even undermining the objective command of Jesus to baptize using water. But the paucity of references to the material element is suggestive—something we will explore further in our conclusion.

Finally, we examine the catechism of Cyriakus Spangenberg. A Lutheran pastor who served in a number of different posts, he was involved in many of the difficult controversies that convulsed the generation of theologians following Luther's death. In particular, Spangenberg found himself in the middle of the debate on original sin and became a staunch defender of the views of

25 Erasmus Sarcerius, *Catechismus* (Leipzig, 1550), T5r.

26 Sarcerius, T7v.

27 Sarcerius, T8v–U8v.

28 Sarcerius, X8r–X8v.

29 Sarcerius, T5r–T6v.

his friend, Matthias Flacius Illyricus. He was also a popular interpreter of the Bible and authored numerous commentaries, sermons, and historical works.[30] Our attention will be to his catechism and the edition we will be using dates from 1564.

Spangenberg's catechetical teaching on baptism brings us into a world that is considerably different from those of the works of Brenz, Melanchthon, and Sarcerius. He begins by stressing that baptism belongs in the center of the Christian life. Spangenberg says we have a powerful tendency to get caught up in earthly pleasures, especially the chase after money and material goods. Baptism is the best antidote for this disease, for it is there that we are reminded that we are created in God's image and therefore destined for something more than the satisfaction of earthly desires and bodily needs. In fact, says Spangenberg, nothing is more important than knowing we are baptized.[31] It is not enough, he says, to be born of Christian parents. Our core identity comes from our belief in Jesus Christ as our savior and that we are baptized in his name.[32]

Spangenberg is also not hesitant to talk about how God's word charges the water of baptism with power. He says the word is "in and next" (im und neben) to the water so that it literally becomes a "holy bath" (heiliges Bad). Further on in the catechism, he will echo this reference when he calls God's act in baptism a "grace-sign" (Gnadezeichen). God's dynamic presence in baptism means the water becomes a "holy bath for the soul" (ein heilsam Seelbad) and a "sin-flood" (Sündeflut).[33] The latter, of course, recalls Luther's flood prayer that he incorporated into his rite for baptism. Accordingly, Christians are to regard their baptism as the place where the entire power of the Trinity is present. It is an event in our lives that is equivalent to the way God appeared to Moses in the burning bush. Those called by God in baptism are joined to Christ in a royal marriage.[34] As has been the case in the other catechisms we have reviewed, Spangenberg also has a section on the importance of baptizing infants as well as

30 Robert Kolb, "Cyriacus Spangenberg," in *The Encyclopedia of the Reformation*, 4 vols., ed. Hans J. Hillerbrand (New York: Oxford University Press, 1996), 4:99–100.

31 Cyriacus Spangenberg, *Catechismus* (Erfurt: Konrad Dreher, 1568), H4r–H5v.

32 Spangenberg, H6v–H6r.

33 Spangenberg, I3v.

34 Spangenberg, I1v.

moving pastoral guidance for how to handle cases where the baby dies before being baptized.[35]

What conclusions might be drawn from this brief survey of the catechetical material? We must be careful not to claim too much, as our sample is fairly small. Nor should we expect those in Luther's circle to equal or exceed his considerable rhetorical skills. He had a unique ability to make words come alive in person and on the page. But it is also clear there are some differences in the understanding of baptism, especially when it comes to seeing the sacrament as the significant *event* in the life of a Christian. As Luther put it, "No greater jewel can adorn body and soul."[36]

Brenz, Melanchthon, and Sarcerius all affirm the necessity of baptism, of course. In the united front against enthusiasm, they make the case that the material element, when joined to the word, is not irrelevant or unimportant. As we have seen, their catechisms also echo other themes of the Lutheran Reformation in precise and formal ways. However, there also appears to be a reticence to invest baptism with the importance accorded to it by Luther himself. In particular, they are concerned the water in the sacrament not be understood in a "magical" or "superstitious" fashion. Thus the emphasis in all of them on baptism as a "sign" (zeichen/signa) that points to something else.

Luther's idea that God is actually doing something in word and water is stressed only by Spangenberg. He seems to best capture the dynamics of the sacrament and, as we have shown, sees baptism as an ongoing event that empowers the entire life of the believer. The Christian journey actually begins in baptism and then—in lifelong engagement with the world—becomes a daily dying and rising with Christ.

The case being made here is that many in Luther's circle unwittingly diluted baptism and turned it into a mere "sign" that provides information about our status before God. As Timothy Wengert has noted, the framework for the gospel is death and resurrection. When this is dislodged, the door is opened for a legal scheme to enter into the way we think about our relationship with God. Instead of seeing the life of faith as an ongoing "actual death and resurrection," as Luther put it, we tend to go back to some type of legal structure where we cooperate with God on the front end (free will) as Rome taught or we

35 Spangenberg, L6r–M4r.

36 BC 462.

look to our life of discipleship as some sort of confirmation of the genuineness of our faith (the Reformed temptation). If that happens, then we are back in the realm of the law and the language of the "musts," as Wengert has put it, reigns supreme. A robust proclamation of the gospel has never been needed more in the church and in the world. This would necessarily include a dynamic view of baptism that keeps the sacrament front and center in the preaching, worship, and daily life of the Christian community.

Henry Melchior Mühlenberg's Catechetical Efforts in Colonial America, 1742–52

Mary Jane Haemig

Timothy Wengert's scholarly work has been marked by a strong interest in Luther's catechisms and in catechesis generally. As the Ministerium of Pennsylvania's professor of church history, he is also well aware of the ministry of Henry Melchior Mühlenberg (1711–87), the first leader of that ministerium, and of Mühlenberg's significance for colonial Lutheran history.

Born in Einbeck, Hannover, in 1711, Henry Melchior Mühlenberg was the son of a shoemaker. After studying at the University of Göttingen and being influenced by pietism there, he went to Halle to study at its mission institute. Ordained in Leipzig in 1739, he served as assistant pastor in the village of Groβhennersdorf, near Leipzig. In September 1741, Mühlenberg met with Gotthilf August Francke (1696–1769), the influential director of the Francke institutions in Halle, who discussed with him a call to serve Lutherans in Pennsylvania. Those Lutherans, having frequently experienced spotty and shoddy pastoral work, had written to Francke requesting his assistance. Mühlenberg accepted a term call to serve three German Lutheran congregations in Pennsylvania. Arriving in Philadelphia in November 1742, Mühlenberg never returned to Europe. He found Lutheran congregations disorganized, pastoral care virtually non-existent, and many German Lutherans with little or no contact with the church. He commented frequently on the spiritual poverty he encountered in the wilderness of colonial Pennsylvania. He journeyed energetically through Pennsylvania and other states, preaching, teaching, and offering pastoral care. He planted some congregations and nurtured many. He is known as the organizer of the first Lutheran synod in North America, the Ministerium of Pennsylvania. He also aided the ministries of Lutheran congregations by helping provide a liturgy, congregational constitution, and a hymnal. Though his ministry was centered in Pennsylvania, he also traveled to neighboring states to minister to congregations. He is also known for nurturing relationships with other Christian groups.[1] His extensive correspondence and his journals provide a picture of his work.

One of the outstanding figures of colonial America, Mühlenberg's accomplishments in both church and civil society have been valued by many. Less well considered is his pastoral work in catechizing both youth and adults. This essay contributes to understanding that aspect of Mühlenberg's work and examines Mühlenberg's correspondence to see what he reports about catechisms and catechesis in colonial America during the first ten years (1742–52) of his ministry there.[2] The letters give insight not only into Mühlenberg's activities but also into the importance assigned to catechesis and the state of catechesis generally among colonial Lutherans in the mid-Atlantic states.[3]

Needs for and Contexts of Catechesis

Not long after his arrival in Philadelphia in November 1742, Mühlenberg discovered the great need for catechesis among both youth and adults.[4] Writing in

1 Karl Krueger, "Mühlenberg, Heinrich (Henry) Melchior," in *Dictionary of Luther and the Lutheran Traditions*, ed. Timothy J. Wengert (Grand Rapids, MI: Baker, 2017), 520–22.

2 *Die Korrespondenz Heinrich Melchior Mühlenbergs: Aus der Anfangszeit des Deutschen Luthertums In Nordamerika*, vol.1, *1740–1752*, ed. Kurt Aland (Berlin: De Gruyter, 1986). All correspondence cited is from this volume. Translated by Mary Jane Haemig.

3 Arthur C. Repp has a brief discussion of Mühlenberg's catechetical activities in his *Luther's Catechism Comes to America: Theological Effects on the Issues of the Small Catechism Prepared in or for America Prior to 1850*, Atla Monograph Series 18 (Methuchen, NJ: Scarecrow / American Theological Library Association, 1982), esp. 32–35. Repp used Mühlenberg's journals as his source. Theodore G. Tappert and John W. Doberstein, eds. and trans., *The Journals of Henry Melchior Mühlenberg*, 3 vols. (Philadelphia: Muhlenberg, 1942).

4 Wokeck sees "the long-term neglect of proper teaching and order among the German Lutherans" as one of the fundamental observations that Mühlenberg made in

March 1743, Mühlenberg complained of lack of knowledge of the faith among young and old. He reported that he had met a woman "who already had three children and is not yet herself confirmed." He also noted her deep desire to be instructed and grounded in the teaching of the faith.[5] A few months later Mühlenberg sounded even more pessimistic, writing, "There are such miserable conditions and deterioration among our poor Lutheran people. . . . The youth grow up, the parents allow their children to grow up, in part without baptism, without information and knowledge, and depart into heathenism."[6]

Not only was the need great, but Mühlenberg soon understood that catechetical instruction must and could take place in many different contexts. His letters noted his efforts to use diverse opportunities for instruction. (His use of sermons will be discussed below.) One such letter mentioned several opportunities, both during and after worship services. He noted that, after the sermon, he listened to confession and explained the teaching on the Lord's Supper and claimed that "the people were very moved."[7] He also recorded that after the Lord's Supper, a baptism took place: "The Anabaptists come diligently to this and listen to what is explained at the infants' baptism."[8] This comment also gives insight into the larger, multi-religious context, a context that made

---

his early letters. Her essay focuses not on catechesis but rather on issues of obtaining properly educated pastors. Marianne S. Wokeck, "The Desert Is Vast and the Sheep Are Dispersed: Muhlenberg's Views of the Immigrant Church," in *Henry Melchior Muhlenberg: The Roots of 250 Years of Organized Lutheranism in North America: Essays in Memory of Helmut T. Lehmann*, ed. John W. Kleiner (Lewiston, NY: Edwin Mellen, 1998), 85–106.

5 To G. A. Francke and [F. M. Ziegenhagen], "Es meldete sich auch eine Frau, welche schon 3 Kinder hat und ist noch nicht confirmiret worden. Sie hat ein hertzlich Verlangen in den Glaubens Lehren und Lebens Pflichten unterrichtet und gegründet zu warden." March 17, 1743.

6 To J. Oporin: "Es ist ein solcher erbärmlicher Zustand und Verfall unter unsern armen Lutherischen Leuten . . . die Jugend wächset heran, die Eltern lassen ihre Kinder zum Theil ohne Taufe, ohne Information und Erkäntniβ aufwachsen, und ins Heidenthum gehen." 101/23/August 12, 1743.

7 To G. A. Francke and [F. M. Ziegenhagen]: "Sontags den 16. Jan. . . . Nach der Predigt hielt Beicht Examen und erklärte auch die Lehre vom heil. Abendmahl. Die Leute waren sehr bewegt." 71–72/17/March 17, 1743.

8 To G. A. Francke and [F. M. Ziegenhagen]: "Nach dem heiligen Abendmahl hatte auch einen Tauff Actum. Die Anababtisten kommen fleiβig mit herzu und hőren was bey der Kinder Tauffe erkläret wird." 72/17/March 17, 1743.

explicit instruction in Lutheran beliefs more critical. (Since its founding in 1681, the colony of Pennsylvania offered to all the opportunity to freely exercise their religion, and as a result, Pennsylvania attracted a wide variety of religious groups.) Mühlenberg also held "catechetical examination"—presumably simple instruction in the catechism as well as some evaluation of the state of knowledge. For example, he recorded that on the festival of the Presentation of Our Lord, he preached and held catechetical examination.[9]

MATERIALS USED

A continuing challenge was finding adequate materials to use in instruction. Mühlenberg requested printed catechisms from Germany. Already in December 1742, shortly after arriving in Philadelphia, Mühlenberg wrote to Halle to request one, pleading, "I'd very much like to have a summary of a short but fundamental catechism."[10] And several months later, he repeated his desire for catechesis: "I wait every day with longing for the catechism, which you promised, and expect in advance many blessings from it."[11]

Mühlenberg used Luther's catechisms. In a letter to Johann Helfrich Schaum, he set forth how Schaum should conduct himself in his pastoral call in the Raritan Valley area of New Jersey. The letter includes an order for public worship. Mühlenberg advised, "After the close of the services, call up the youth of your charge, and each time allow them to recite one of the divisions of Luther's Catechism, and also our Glaubens-Lied [hymn setting of the creed]. This instruction of the children should not last more than half an hour."[12] But many versions of Luther's catechism were available, as during and since Luther's time, people had added material to the *Small Catechism*. Other catechisms—some from Reformed and other groups—were available in colonial Pennsylvania as

9 To G. A. Francke and [F. M. Ziegenhagen]: "Mitwochs den 2 Febr. Heute feyerten wir das Fest der Reinigung Mariae. Vormittags predigte hier in der Kirche über das Evangelium, und hielte auch Catechismus Examen." 75/17/March 17, 1743.

10 To G. A. Francke and [F. M. Ziegenhagen]: "mőgte von Hertzen gern einen Abriß von einem kurtzen doch gründlichen Catechismo haben!" 42/14/December 3, 1742.

11 To G. A. Francke and [F. M. Ziegenhagen]: "Den Catechismum welchen Ew. Hochw. versprochen, erwarte alle Tage mit schmertzen und verspreche mir schon zum voraus vielen Seegen daraus." 89/19/June 6, 1743.

12 To J. H. Schaum. 282/64/March 2, 1747.

well. For these reasons Mühlenberg recognized early on the need for a uniform version of the catechism for use in Lutheran congregations:

> A catechism is as necessary for us as dear bread, for in school the children should be grounded in catechetical truths and for this selected phrases are needed. If we have no hope of receiving one from Ziegenhagen,[13] then we must use another proper catechism. When one uses his own meditations, another the Wurtemberg catechism, the third the Giessen catechism and the fourth the Holstein catechism, then confusion ensues.[14]

Sermons were one of the tools he and others used to teach the catechism. Mühlenberg mentioned that he required the catechists,[15] who apparently preached every second Sunday, to memorize and preach on Johann Jakob Rambach's catechetical sermons.[16] Rambach's sermons, based on Luther's catechisms, were a popular pietist product in the eighteenth century. Mühlenberg's approval of these sermons as a means of teaching the catechism was also evidenced by a letter to a pastor, in which he stated, "I wish that you would once

13 Friedrich Michael Ziegenhagen was a German Lutheran clergyman, educated in Halle and Jena. Appointed in 1722 as the German Lutheran court preacher for the Hanoverian king in London, he served there the rest of his life. Mühlenberg visited him in London on his journey to America.

14 To G. A. Francke and [F. M. Ziegenhagen], 196/44–45/November 17, 1745.

15 On Mühlenberg's thinking concerning the question of whether catechists could preach, see Leonard R. Riforgiato, *Missionary of Moderation: Henry Melchior Muhlenberg and the Lutheran Church in English America* (East Brunswick, NJ: Associated University Presses, 1980), 160–61.

16 To G. A. Francke and [F. M. Ziegenhagen]: "Die Umstände, wolten auch nicht anderst erlauben als daβ wir die Catecheten musten mit predigen laβen, wir ordneten deswegen, daβ sie des sel. Rambachs Catechismus Predigten müβen memoriren und in den gemeinen ablegen, da wir den umwechseln, als einen Sontag prediget der Prediger und den nächstren Sontag der Catechet . . . wir sind in voller Arbeit mit predigen und Kinder informiren." 193/43/November 1, 1745. Johann Jakob Rambach was a student of August Hermann Francke and later served on the theological faculty at Halle; see Rambach, *Betrachtungen über den Catechismum Lutheri und über Freylinghausens Ordnung des Heyls* (Frankfurt am Main, 1736).

preach through the blessed Doctor Rambach's catechetical sermons. Your way of preaching would become milder and gentler."[17]

MODES OF INSTRUCTION; LANGUAGE ISSUES

Modes of instruction varied. As mentioned, catechetical sermons aided in teaching the catechism. Mühlenberg's letters mention recitation, exercises, and examinations, with the last of these perhaps including informal quizzes as well as more formal tests of knowledge. Catechizing during and after worship has also been discussed previously.

A letter of call from the Hackensack, New Jersey, congregation to Mühlenberg in 1751 indicates something of the frequency and nature of these duties: "I [plan] to keep divine service in the fore- and afternoon on every first Sunday in every current Month of the year and once at least a Catechetical Exercise in the Week after the appointed monthly Sunday when Health, Wind and Weather will permit it."[18] It is clear that catechization was a priority not only for Mühlenberg but also for the congregations he served. Christian ministry was not only about preaching and presiding but also about instructing.

Mühlenberg recognized the need to teach the catechism in a simple manner. A 1748 letter records that he had assigned the catechist Weygand to instruct the confirmands in New Hannover. He noted that Weygand was untiring in his efforts, "but he preaches too much in the catechizing and cannot chew down the questions into small enough pieces."[19] This comment indicates that Mühlenberg knew something about effective ways to teach the catechism so that learning was easier.

Mühlenberg dealt with a diversity of languages in colonial America and wrote of catechesis taking place not only in German but also in English and Dutch. Writing in 1743, he noted, "A widow brought me her daughter. . . . I had to teach

---

17 To [J. C. Stover]: "Ich wünschete daβ Sie des Sel. D. Rambachs Catechismus Predigten mőgten einmahl durch predigen . . . so würde Ihre Art zu predigen milder und sanffter werden." 266/59/January 20, 1747.

18 426/97/August 19, 1751.

19 To G. A. Francke and [F. M. Ziegenhagen]: "In New-Hannover habe ihn mit an die Information der Confirmatorium gesetzet. Er beweiβet sich unermüdet, nur prediget er noch zu viel im Catechisiren und kan den Kindern die Fragen noch nicht klein genug käuen." 321/72/November 16, 1748.

her doctrine in the English language."[20] A 1745 letter speaks of confirming youth who had been instructed in Dutch but who could understand Mühlenberg's High German: "In November two congregations in Raritan asked me to come. . . . I traveled there, gathered the youth, instructed 24 young people and confirmed them. . . . The young people had themselves practiced well in the main parts of the catechism, and even though they had learned these in the Dutch language, they could also understand High German and give good answers."[21]

Results and Concluding Observations

Mühlenberg viewed the effects of his work in different ways. In some cases, he was happy with the results of his instruction. He reported optimistically on his efforts in February 1743: "From the 7th to the 12th of February I instructed our youth twice a day. The children are learning by God's grace and blessing so that I with God's help will confirm a small group on Maundy Thursday. The children please me the most with their simplicity and honesty."[22] In a 1751 letter, however, he expressed his sorrow that the young people, once confirmed, were scattered and could easily forget what they had learned.[23]

Mühlenberg's correspondence indicates that catechesis was a priority not only for him but also for the congregations he served. Mühlenberg not only preached, presided, and sought to gather people into congregations. Operating in the religiously diverse context of colonial Pennsylvania, he realized that the Lutheran understanding of the Christian faith would only continue if it was explicitly taught and passed on to the next generation. For this task, he used a variety of opportunities and strategies. Amid his diligent and careful catechetical work, he also experienced the uncertainty of ultimately not knowing what its results would be.

---

20 To G. A. Francke and [F. M. Ziegenhagen]: "Eine Witwe brachte mir ihre Tochter. . . . Ich muβ ihr die Glaubens Lehre in der Englischen Sprache beybringen." 17/71/ March 17, 1743.

21 To G. A. Francke and [F. M. Ziegenhagen], 208/45/December 12, 1745.

22 To G. A. Francke and [F. M. Ziegenhagen], 76/17/March 17, 1743.

23 To J. M. Boltzius. "Das ist mein grőstes Leiden mit, daβ die jungen Leute so zerstreuet werden, wenn sie confirmiret worden und nicht unter Aufsicht bleiben, sondern unter allerhand Volck kommen, und leicht wieder vergeβen, was sie gelernet." 462/107/November 23, 1751.

Faith and Love in Luther's *Small Catechism*

Martin J. Lohrmann

Experiencing Luther's *Small Catechism*

How to teach and use Martin Luther's *Small Catechism* remains a living question for Lutheran communities today. For almost five hundred years, it has held a foundational role in Lutheran church life, serving as a basis for Christian education, theological reflection, and spiritual devotion. Even so, connecting the catechism with the gospel freedom and grace held dear by Lutherans has not always been clear to many of the pastors and parishioners who use this little book. In this essay, I suggest that a focus on the pairing of "faith and love" can serve as a useful lens for understanding and using the *Small Catechism* well.

Far too often, the *Small Catechism* has been read and experienced in legalistic or moralistic ways, which ironically works against the lifegiving gospel message that formed the very heart of Luther's Reformation theology. If religious legalism revolves around what people have to do and what they need to believe in order to be loved by God, then the structure of the catechism itself might reinforce this kind of legalistic experience. Its content begins with what to do (in the form of commandments), continues with what to believe (as presented in the Apostles' Creed), moves into ritualized patterns of spiritual life like how to pray and use the sacraments correctly, and concludes with more things to do in its orders for daily prayer and the Table of Duties. Although I may have overstated the potentially legalistic elements of the *Small Catechism*, it might not be surprising that people have found these elements to proclaim something other than good news.

Timothy Wengert's influential work on this central text of the Lutheran tradition has paid attention to precisely this disjuncture between the Lutheran emphasis on grace and many people's less-than-gracious experiences of Luther's *Small Catechism*. Sharing his own negative catechetical experiences in the opening pages of his book *Martin Luther's Catechisms: Forming the Faith*, Wengert wrote,

> Do we know what Martin Luther's Small Catechism is? . . . As a parish pastor, I acted as if the only, or at least the most important use for the catechism was with the "hormonally challenged"—that is, with eighth graders in confirmation. That's the way it had been used on me, when I was taught the catechism in seventh and eighth grade by Pastor Paul Faust—imagine having Faust as a teacher for confirmation instruction! Some of us who are old enough remember those days: "Wengert! The second commandment!" "Thou shalt not take the name . . ." "What does this mean?" "We are to fear and love . . ." The trick was to say it in one breath.[1]

Through his teaching and scholarship, Wengert has sought and found edifying approaches to the *Small Catechism*, especially by describing ways in which the structure of the text promotes gospel grace rather than obscures it.[2] First, Wengert has emphasized that the pattern of starting with commands and moving to statements of who God is (Creed) and how we relate to God (Lord's Prayer and sacraments) structurally enacts the "law and gospel" experience of recognizing sin and turning to a merciful God for reconciliation and peace. Second, the *Small Catechism* presents a concise summary of the church's primary means of grace: God's word—as summarized in the commandments, Creed, and Lord's Prayer—and the sacraments of baptism and the Lord's Supper. Through faith, Christians personally come to know the Lord of Life, a relationship nurtured through the catechetical encounter with word and sacrament. Third, Wengert has pointed out how well the pieces of the catechism teach the basics of Christian faith. Here, one finds biblical texts, clear theological reasoning, guidance for worship, and practical resources. Fourth, Wengert has highlighted how the catechism associates an active spiritual life not with removal from daily

1 Timothy J. Wengert, *Martin Luther's Catechisms: Forming the Faith* (Minneapolis: Fortress, 2009), 1.

2 Wengert, 20–22.

experience but rather as immersion into it, an approach to Christian living that honors the gifts and contributions of all the baptized. Each of these structural observations helps undo potentially legalistic readings of the catechism to highlight gospel-centered moments of grace: (1) the freedom and forgiveness that comes with the move from law to gospel, (2) the personal encounter with God in word and sacrament, (3) lifelong growth in Christian wisdom through instruction and meditation, and (4) the sanctification of daily life through faith.

This essay builds on those four ways to engage the catechism by suggesting one more: namely, Luther's pairing of faith and love. Wengert himself raised the possibility of reading the catechism this way but found reasons not to pursue it further, including the ineffective—and legalistic!—use of "faith and love" in catechisms written by Reformers other than Luther.[3] My own continuing work with the catechism and Luther's theology, however, has given me reason to add "faith and love" as a useful category through which to read and use the *Small Catechism*. In summary, I believe that this pairing brings together many of the elements named above in ways that Luther himself intended: "faith and love" work in partnership to connect belief with action while avoiding an emphasis on human striving that would obscure the righteousness of Christ and gospel freedom.

Faith and Love in Luther's Theology

Like other aspects of Luther's theology, this pairing of "faith and love" appears occasionally throughout his career but rarely received its own detailed treatment, either in Luther's own works or in later studies.[4] This uneven attention to a theological concept is typical of Luther as a theologian who preferred to share primary experiences with God's word rather than secondary reflections about it: Luther lectured on biblical texts directly instead of ruminating on how to

3 Wengert, 8–9.

4 Although not a major theme in Luther research, significant studies of Luther's doctrine of faith and love have appeared in the following sources: Gerhard Ebeling, *Luther: An Introduction to His Thought*, trans. R. A. Wilson (Philadelphia: Fortress, 1970); George Forell, *Faith Active in Love: An Investigation of the Principles Underlying Luther's Social Ethics* (New York: American, 1954); Sun-young Kim, *Luther on Faith and Love: Christ and the Law in the 1535 Galatians Commentary* (Minneapolis: Fortress, 2014); Tuomo Mannermaa, *Christ Present in Faith*, trans. Kirsi I. Stjerna (Minneapolis: Fortress, 2005).

read the Bible; he gave communities a *Small Catechism* for daily use instead of thinking abstractly about what might be in such a resource and what it might do. Despite his reluctance to discuss methodology, though, there are good reasons to lift up Luther's "doctrine of faith and love" as a beneficial framework for reading the *Small Catechism*.

Especially relevant to the personal relationship with God that Luther sought to share through the catechism, we see that "faith and love" was a category that Luther employed for preaching. An early instance of this pairing appears in the *Postils* that Luther began publishing in 1522 and updated throughout his career. His introduction to this preaching resource, "A Brief Instruction on What to Look For and Expect in the Gospels," noted a biblical distinction between the faith of the heart and the good works that spring from faith. His explicit teaching goal was to show preachers how to preach clearly about both faith in God and good works of love:

> Faith redeems you from sin, death, and hell and enables you to overcome all things. O no one can speak enough about this. It is a pity that this kind of preaching has been silenced in the world, and yet boast is made daily of the gospel.
>
> Now when you have Christ as the foundation and chief blessing of your salvation, then the other part follows: that you take him as your example, giving yourself in service to your neighbor just as you see that Christ has given himself for you. See, there faith and love move forward, God's commandment is fulfilled, and a person is happy and fearless to do and to suffer all things. Therefore make note of this, that Christ as a gift nourishes your faith and makes you a Christian. But Christ as an example exercises your works. These do not make you a Christian. Actually they come forth from you because you have already been made a Christian. As widely as a gift differs from an example, so widely does faith differ from works, for faith possesses nothing of its own, only the deeds and life of Christ. Works have something of your own in them, yet they should not belong to you but to your neighbor.[5]

Faith justifies and love follows. Both belong intrinsically to the Christian life, even as Luther explicitly reminded his audience that love does not justify.

5 LW 35:120.

Luther put this "faith and love" model of homiletical clarity into practice in many places in the *Postils.* For instance, in the commentary on Matthew 21:1–9 (Jesus's entry into Jerusalem), Luther organized his material exactly this way, referring readers back to the faith and love that he had discussed in his "Brief Introduction":

> In the preface, I said that there are two things to be noted and considered in the Gospel readings: first, the work of Christ presented to us as a gift and kindness, to which our faith is to cling and in which it is to be exercised; second, the same work offered as an example and model for us to imitate and follow. Thus all the Gospel lessons first teach faith and then works. We will therefore divide this Gospel into three parts: first, faith; second, good works; and third, something of the history and secret meaning [biblical context and allegorical interpretation for application].[6]

Given the *Small Catechism*'s inclusion of the Ten Commandments, the Table of Duties, and repeated injunctions to love and serve our neighbors, this distinction between faith and love provides a helpful way to understand how Luther could emphasize the ethical, action-oriented side of Christian life without confusing it with justification by faith alone. Far from ignoring good works or turning human love into a source of salvation, Luther used the distinction between faith and love both to preach the evangelical freedom that comes through faith alone and to keep a strong emphasis on the fruits of faith expressed as love of neighbor. In this way, Luther gave preachers and parishioners clarity about how faith in Christ transforms hearts and daily lives through God's grace.

This "doctrine of faith and love" informed Luther's influential response to the so-called Wittenberg Unrest of March 1522. To stem the local confusion about gospel preaching and public policy then roiling Wittenberg, Luther began an eight-day preaching series by reminding his fellow citizens about this relationship between faith—which includes the experience of God's word as law and gospel (his first and second points below)—and love:

> In the first place, we must know that we are the children of wrath, and all our works, intentions, and thoughts are nothing at all. Here we need a clear, strong text to bear out this point. Such is the saying of St. Paul

6 LW 75:28.

in Eph. 2[:3]. Note this well; and though there are many such in the Bible, I do not wish to overwhelm you with many texts. "We are all the children of wrath." . . .

Secondly, that God has sent us his only-begotten Son that we may believe in him and that whoever trusts in him shall be free from sin and a child of God, as John declares in his first chapter, "To all who believed in his name, he gave power to become children of God" [John 1:12]. Here we should all be well versed in the Bible and ready to confront the devil with many passages. With respect to these two points I do not feel that there has been anything wrong or lacking. They have been rightly preached to you, and I should be sorry if it were otherwise. . . .

Thirdly, we must also have love and through love we must do to one another as God has done to us through faith. For without love faith is nothing, as St. Paul says (1 Cor 2 [13:1]): If I had the tongues of angels and could speak of the highest things in faith, and have not love, I am nothing. And here, dear friends, have you not grievously failed? I see no signs of love among you, and I observe very well that you have not been grateful to God for his rich gifts and treasures. . . .

I notice that you have a great deal to say of the doctrine of faith and love which is preached to you, and this is no wonder; an ass can almost intone the lessons, and why should you not be able to repeat the doctrines and formulas? Dear friends, the kingdom of God,—and we are that kingdom—does not consist in talk or words [1 Cor 4:20], but in activity, in deeds, in works and exercises. God does not want hearers and repeaters of words [Jas 1:22], but followers and doers, and this occurs in faith through love. For a faith without love is not enough—rather it is not faith at all, but a counterfeit of faith, just as a face seen in a mirror is not a real face, but merely the reflection of a face [1 Cor 13:12].[7]

As the sermons continued, Luther repeatedly returned to his starting point: reforms of faith need to be done in love or else they are not proceeding from faith in Christ at all. It was important for him to be able both to preach salvation through Christ alone and to talk about people's behavior without turning

7 LW 51:70–71.

ethics into the gospel, or vice versa. Applied to the *Small Catechism*, this pattern shows that any faith that removes itself from the love of God and neighbor taught in the Ten Commandments is not saving faith. Rather, recognizing the absence of love in oneself then sends a person back to the beginning: the gospel of justification by faith alone, which—as the First Commandment tells us—looks to God alone as the source of all life and goodness.

Showing that this was not only a category of the Reformer's early career, Luther highlighted the "doctrine of faith and love" in his published Galatians lectures of 1535. In this seminal work, Luther described faith and love as constituting simultaneously the shortest and the longest theology. Commenting on Paul's words about freedom and service in Galatians 5, Luther wrote,

> It is as though [Paul] were saying: "There is no need to burden you with circumcision and the ceremonies of Moses. But above all persevere in the doctrine of faith, which you have received from me. Afterwards, if you want to do good works, I will show you in one word the highest and greatest works, and the way to keep all the laws: Be devoted to one another through love. You will not lack for people to help, for the world is full of people who need the help of others." This is the perfect doctrine of both faith and love. It is also the shortest and the longest kind of theology—the shortest so far as words and sentences are concerned; but in practice and in fact it is wider, longer, deeper, and higher than the whole world.[8]

Indeed, faith and love as "the shortest and the longest kind of theology" wonderfully describes the profound experiences of law and gospel, grace and mercy, belief and action, Scripture and service that Luther managed to pour into his little instructional handbook.

Faith, Love, and the Ten Commandments

In addition to clarifying the relationship between justifying faith and good works of love, a second major advantage to lifting up "faith and love" as a dialectic for reading the *Small Catechism* comes in how it clarifies the role of the Ten Commandments. Despite his consistent and sometimes virulent rejection

8 LW 27:59.

of Judaism as a true faith, Luther loved the Old Testament and the Ten Commandments as God's word, full of both instruction and promise. As he wrote in the longer preface to the *Large Catechism*, "This much is certain: those who know the Ten Commandments perfectly know the entire Scriptures and in all affairs and circumstances are able to counsel, help, comfort, judge, and make decisions in both spiritual and temporal matters. They are qualified to be judge over all doctrines, walks of life [Stände], spirits, legal matters, and everything else in the world. Moreover, what is the whole Psalter but meditation and exercises based on the First Commandment?"[9] Instead of viewing the Ten Commandments in a purely negative light, as divine speech that can only announce law without gospel, Luther valued the Decalogue's witness to faith and love for use in the heart, home, church, and society. The Reformer expanded upon this view that the Ten Commandments advocate not only works but saving faith when he concluded his discussion of them in the *Large Catechism*:

> This is exactly the meaning and the right interpretation of the first and chief commandment, from which all the others proceed. This word, "You shall have no other gods," means simply, "You shall fear, love, and trust me as your one true God." For where your heart has such an attitude toward God, you have fulfilled this commandment and all the others. On the other hand, whoever fears and loves anything else in heaven or on earth will keep neither this one nor any other. Thus the whole Scriptures have proclaimed and presented this commandment everywhere, emphasizing these two things, fear of God and trust in God.[10]

Luther's faith-based (rather than works-based) reading of the Ten Commandments is evident in how he begins his explanations to the commandments by saying, "We are to fear and love God, so that . . ." As seen above in his 1522 sermons in Wittenberg, fear of God and love of God belong to a holistic experience of God's word as law and gospel—that is, as recognition of sin and the promise of grace given freely. Instead of separating the Ten Commandments from faith, Luther embedded them in the trust of the heart that saves apart from works. This follows the logic of the First Commandment itself,

9 BC 382.17–18.

10 BC 429.324–430.325.

which forbids self-justification by sending people to trust in God alone for life, goodness, and salvation.

Luther also showed a dynamic use of the commandments in *A Simple Way to Pray* (1535), as he shared four ways that the commandments informed his prayer life: they served as sources of instruction, thanksgiving, confession, and petition.[11] Although the commandments do not themselves bestow the righteousness that frees from sin, they preach faith by pointing to God alone as the highest good. They also serve as catalysts for prayerful reflection on the blessings and challenges a person encounters in daily life, and as a basis for considering one's ongoing relationships with God and others. Luther's "doctrine of faith and love" lets the commandments take their important place in the lives of believers without turning them into sources of salvation.

Faith and Love across the Catechism

As the *Large Catechism* concludes its discussion of the commandments by commending them to all people (even as it adds an accusatory word against the Jews),[12] Luther foreshadowed his approach to the Apostles' Creed. Here, he did not separate an accusing Lord of the Decalogue from the gracious Triune God of the Creed. Instead, he acknowledged that in our fallen condition, people cannot follow the Decalogue on their own but rather need to be turned to their saving physician, the Lord alone. This physician does not remove the Decalogue but rather conforms believers to it through faith:

> Thus far we have heard the first part of Christian teaching, and in it we have seen all that God wishes us to do and not to do. The Creed properly follows, which sets forth all that we must expect and receive from God: in short, it teaches us to know God perfectly. It is given in order to help us do what the Ten Commandments require of us. For, as we said above, they are set so high that all human ability is far too puny and weak to keep them. Therefore it is just as necessary to learn this part as it is the other so that we may know where and how to obtain the power to do this. If we were able by our own strength to keep the Ten Commandments as they ought to be kept, we would need nothing

11 LW 43:200.

12 BC 430.326–33, with words against the Jews in BC 431.331.

> else, neither the Creed nor the Lord's Prayer. But before we explain the usefulness and necessity of the Creed, it is enough, as a first step, for very simple people to learn and grasp the Creed itself.[13]

The human inability to obey the commandments does not impugn the commandments. Neither does the Creed supplant or undo the Decalogue. To borrow Saint Paul's repeated response to precisely this one-sided view of the law, "By no means!"[14] Instead, the Creed proclaims a God who loves and saves not by human merit or striving but on the basis of God's own righteousness and mercy given freely. The faithful heart that looks to this gracious God for all good, therefore, comes to love the commandments not as a source of self-justification but as a revelation of God's love for creation. As Luther had pointed out already in the *Ninety-Five Theses*, faithful hearts do not despise God's discipline or run from the Decalogue but embrace it: "Christians who are truly contrite seek and love to pay penalties for their sins."[15]

In this way, the doctrine of faith and love adds clarity to the "law and gospel" move from the commandments to the Creed, which might otherwise assign the commandments a purely negative function. Yes, the commandments show sin and drive fallen people to the grace of a loving God. At the same time, a life of faith can do no other than honor God and love neighbors in the ways set forth in the Decalogue. A person is not justified by the commandments but finds in them a guide or companion on the journey of daily life with the God proclaimed and confessed in the Apostles' Creed.

While the "law and gospel" pattern to the catechism is intentional and useful, it should not be interpreted in such a way that the commandments are solely identified with "law" and the Creed and Lord's Prayer as "gospel." The Creed itself announces the death and resurrection of Christ for sinners and the forgiveness of sins through the work of the Holy Spirit. These articles of faith use the law to acknowledge sin even as they proclaim God's work to save. Luther's explanations for each article of the Creed similarly employ a theological

13 BC 431.1–4.

14 Rom 3:31, 6:15, 7:7, 7:13, 9:14, 11:1.

15 LW 31:29, amended for gender inclusiveness. Similarly, see theses 94 and 95: "94. Christians should be exhorted to be diligent in following Christ, their head, through penalties, death, and hell; 95. And thus be confident of entering into heaven through many tribulations rather than through the false security of peace [Acts 14:22]." LW 31:33.

use of the law to highlight human inabilities to believe in the God of the Creed, as in the *Large Catechism*'s explanation to the first article: "If we believe it, this article should humble and terrify all of us. For we sin daily with eyes, ears, hands, body and soul, money and property, and with all that we have, especially those who even fight against the Word of God."[16] In this case, the first article's teaching about a loving and gracious creator also includes a Lutheran second use of the law by naming our inability to love and trust this God completely. In this way, the Decalogue does not merely serve as "law" to the Creed's "gospel." Instead, they each promote a dynamic relationship of trust with a loving and liberating Lord.

The relationship between faith and love is also at work in Luther's explanations of the Lord's Prayer. Describing what it means to hallow God's name, Luther wrote that God's name is hallowed "whenever the word of God is taught clearly and purely"—that is, in such a way that faith is awakened in us—and that "we, as God's children, also live holy lives according to it"—that is, that we love our neighbors as ourselves.[17] Explicitly connecting this petition in the *Large Catechism* with the Second Commandment,[18] Luther described what it means to hallow God's name precisely in terms of faith and love. "The plainest answer that can be given is: when both our teaching and our life are godly and Christian."[19]

Luther used the same faith and love pattern to explain the petition "your kingdom come." As taught in the *Small Catechism*, God's kingdom graciously comes "whenever our heavenly Father gives us his Holy Spirit, so that through his grace we believe his Holy Word and live godly lives here in time and hereafter in eternity."[20] Maintaining the distinction between God's grace and human works, Luther nevertheless connected God's coming kingdom with our reception of it through faith and with our ensuing works of mercy and love.

The doctrine of faith and love also appears in Luther's teaching of what baptism is and what it does. Baptism "signifies that the old person in us with all sins and evil desires is to be drowned and die through daily sorrow for sin and through repentance, and on the other hand that daily a new person is to come

16 BC 433.22.
17 BC 357.8.
18 BC 446.45.
19 BC 445.39.
20 BC 357.11.

forth and rise up to live before God in righteousness and purity forever."[21] Faith receives the promises of baptism. Love lives out these promises "in righteousness and purity," not as impossible standards required so that God will love us, but as effects of what it means to be loved by God and live as people washed and clothed in God's grace.

Luther's guide for morning prayer can also be interpreted in light of faith and love. It starts with making the sign of the cross and praying simple words that entrust hearts to God in faith: "God the Father, Son, and Holy Spirit watch over me. Amen."[22] Luther then suggested that people spend time with the Creed and the Lord's Prayer, not to make God happy or show how pious they might be but to center their lives in God's grace and love. This brief order of prayer continues by giving thanks to God and asking for strength for the day to come: "I give thanks to you, my heavenly Father, through Jesus Christ, your dear Son, that you have graciously protected me this night from all harm and danger, and I ask you that you would protect me today from sin and all evil, so that my life and actions may please you completely. For into your hands I commend myself: my body, my soul, and all that is mine. Let your holy angel be with me, so that the wicked foe may have no power over me. Amen." After praying in faith and asking that the day be filled with God-pleasing actions, Luther would have Christians give thanks for the joyful service that lies ahead of them: "You are to go to your work joyfully."[23] In such a way, faith in God flows seamlessly into love for neighbors.

CONCLUSION

With this study of how Luther put his "doctrine of faith and love" into action in the *Small Catechism*, I hope I have been able to build on the work of Timothy Wengert, one of the preeminent teachers and scholars of Luther's catechisms of our time. Wengert's ability to view the *Small Catechism*'s structure and content not as archaic liabilities but as lively assets for sharing the gospel has been a very welcome contribution to the scholarly field and to personal understandings of this central text of the Lutheran tradition. Beyond my thesis about "faith and love" as a helpful lens for reading the *Small Catechism*, I

21 BC 360.12.

22 BC 363.2.

23 BC 363.2–3.

hope this essay has testified to the enduring richness of Luther's little book as a wellspring for theological thinking and the daily practice of Christian faith. In that spirit, I conclude with words from Luther—which Dr. Wengert also quoted in his writing—about the depths and riches of God's wisdom that are always to be found in the catechism:

> Many regard the catechism as a simple, trifling teaching, which they can absorb and master at one reading and then toss the book into a corner as if they are ashamed to read it again. . . . But this I say for myself: I am also a doctor and a preacher, just as learned and experienced as all of them who are so high and mighty. Nevertheless, each morning, and whenever else I have time, I do as a child who is being taught the catechism and I read and recite word for word the Lord's Prayer, the Ten Commandments, the Creed, the Psalms, etc. I must still read and study the catechism daily, and yet I cannot master it as I wish, but must remain a child and pupil of the catechism—and I also do so gladly.[24]

24 BC 380.5, 7–8. Also cited in Wengert, *Martin Luther's Catechisms*, 22–23.

Courage to Believe

Kirsi Stjerna

Timothy Wengert has been a valued teacher of Lutheran church leaders in North America for several decades. His internationally recognized scholarship on Reformation history has both advanced academic research and enriched local faith communities, sharing treasures of the past for the sake of Christian witness today.

This essay honors Dr. Wengert's abiding concern that faith be alive in real-life, present-day human hearts by presenting a different kind of historical-theological study. It will examine key issues of contemporary faith with two goals: first, to examine Lutheran directions for sharing the gospel amid complex current social situations; second, to leave something of a historical record about this time surrounding Dr. Wengert's seventieth birthday for future scholars who might be interested in these days of global pandemic and civic unrest.

Even though scholars are rightly cautious about making firm assessments of current events, they ironically often love nothing more than digging through the firsthand perspectives and primary sources of others. This is the kind of dynamic that can make a year-old newspaper feel hopelessly out-of-date, while a century-old newspaper can be historically fascinating and socially illuminating. With that sense of self-awareness, this essay takes the risk of making missteps about the interpretation of current events for the sake of contributing a kind of time capsule to this volume and its wider focus on Lutheran theology and proclamation.

An Extraordinary Contemporary Situation

The situation for writing this essay is most unusual: the world is in the grips of a global pandemic. A novel coronavirus, with the COVID-19 disease it causes, spread all over the world in the early months of 2020 via airplanes, church gatherings, birthday parties, funerals, political rallies, sporting events, and workplaces of various sorts. While transmission can be limited by observing practices like washing hands, wearing masks, and social distancing, this virus has nevertheless been powerful enough to change life "as we knew it" throughout the world.

Trust is at stake. Around the world, people are wondering what news information can be trusted, what social media posts are trustworthy, and what public health guidelines can reliably lead communities through these challenges. Should we hope for solutions from political leaders, pharmaceutical labs, or the presumed goodwill and common sense of the individuals in our communities? Perennial questions of whose interests and perspectives matter the most when considering issues of public life have grown increasingly sharp in these days. As long-standing socio-economic problems have risen with new immediacy and urgency during the pandemic, many are acknowledging with new clarity that the "normal times," which the virus interrupted, was never good or fair for a great number of our fellow citizens.

The virus has exposed many ugly truths about the prevalence of power mongering, greed, economic disparity, racism, and other forms of discrimination, even as it has impacted human lives without respect for persons: from global leaders to the world's poor, people of all ages, genders, backgrounds, and fitness levels have contracted the disease, and many have died. Even so, the virus has spread most devastatingly among vulnerable populations, such as elderly people in assisted-living homes, those in incarceration, and workers in crowded factories. These realities have further exposed social iniquities in highly visible ways.

As if the pandemic were not enough of a challenge to presumed notions of "normalcy" around the world, the situation in the United States in 2020 has also included public instances of police using excessive force. Among other deaths that came to national attention, George Floyd, an African American man, was killed by suffocation by a white police officer in front of onlookers in Minneapolis. Recorded on video, the nine-minute-long killing of Mr. Floyd called Americans from all corners of the nation to the streets to protest ongoing manifestations of racism in this country, clearly showing that the safety and dignity of Black and brown bodies are directly at stake. While Mr. Floyd's death brought clear attention to the specific racism of institutional bias in law enforcement, it also coincided with the increasing visibility of white supremacist movements and other violent expressions of hate in words and actions.

Much of our future health as people and communities will depend on how people live out their ultimate concerns in daily life. Individuals will make decisions about a range of behaviors: how to endure a shelter-in-place situation, when to wear a mask, whether to participate in public demonstrations, and, if so, how to do so safely, peacefully, and effectively. Communities will decide which policies to pursue and enforce for the well-being of their people. These decisions are not unrelated to religious grounding. Indeed, the actions that individuals, communities, and governments take regarding public health and social justice are deeply connected to religious values and practices.

THE ROLE OF RELIGION AND ULTIMATE CONCERNS

Contemplating a new possibility for religion in our current time brings to mind the teachings of Paul Tillich, a theologian who was instrumental in rescuing the Lutheran expression of faith from the shadows and damage of World War II. Building on Martin Luther's core insights, Tillich addressed the sad ruins of Europe after bombings and destruction, death camps, and the revelation of extensive crimes committed against humanity under the eyes of ordinary citizens. In such atrocities, the Christian West was collectively implicated in the murder of millions of Jews, Roma, gays, political prisoners, and disabled persons. The church and its people were judged guilty. With pain, Tillich wrote from and to this context in which Christian faith—including its Lutheran expressions—seemed grotesque and maybe even fatally irrelevant and flawed.

As a theologian to whom faith mattered personally and who dared to speak in the moment (including politically), Tillich returned to the essentials of faith and religion. He explored common threads of religious thought, existential questions, doubts, and sources of hope that great thinkers had wrestled with over the centuries. He went back to Jesus, Greco-Roman philosophers, Luther, Schleiermacher, Hegel, and others as his faith sought understanding and his reason explored what it means to believe. Through this intellectual and spiritual journey, he came to express a compelling vision for the constructive, existential power of religion in the lives of individuals and communities—in a markedly purged form—for the new day. He dared to propose the courage to believe that God "is" beyond human doubts and failures.[1]

1 Paul Tillich, *The Courage to Be*, 4th ed. (New Haven, CT: Yale University Press, 2000), 175: "The courage to be is rooted in the God who appears when God has disappeared in the anxiety of doubt."

Tillich's arguments resonated with the insights of Martin Luther over four hundred years earlier, a vision that had arisen from fundamental views about the power of faith. Luther proclaimed a living religion that deals with the realities of life, does not deny suffering, and keeps gospel freedom as its focus. If Tillich and Luther's words sound current for today, then they do so by challenging and inviting Lutheran theologians to rise to the occasion of this moment: to keep religion relevant, to give people reasons to care about God and their neighbors, and to foster the courage to believe in the face of fear, doubt, and failure. Similarly, Tillich and Luther pointed to religion's centrality in dealing with the concerns of utmost importance. Theology that gives people the courage to believe can help people endure the personal moments of despair, temptation, and struggle that Luther called *Anfechtung*.[2] Such a theology also deepens rather than displaces personal engagement with social injustices and communal challenges.

According to Tillich, the deepest fear of all human beings is the fear of not being—that is, the abyss of the abyss. The global pandemic and movements for social justice have made such questions and concerns almost impossible to ignore. These fears of not being and not existing are real, even if they frequently go unvoiced. Religion[3] addresses those moments when one's ultimate concerns and values are tested. In situations that can bring individuals and communities to the brink of despair, the question becomes on what basis, on what foundation, and in whose company does one still dare to believe? In those moments of disorientation, when one's religion might appear empty and distant from a lived reality, one can lose faith. At the same time, especially when staring at the abyss of losing one's religion, one can take another course and re-engage religion as a positive force. In light of Tillich's theology, religion's task is to respond to these fears and guide people away from the abyss. In times of crisis and *Anfechtung*, the fundamental fear of not being is a unifying factor for many who

---

2 See Denis Janz's treatment of Luther's theological discoveries vis-à-vis the "negativities of human existence" and how faith can conquer them in "To Hell (and Back) with Luther: The Dialectic of Anfechtung and Faith," in *Encounters with Luther, ed. Kirsi Stjerna and Brooks Schramm (Louisville: Westminster John Knox, 2016)*, 27f.

3 I am using here mostly the singular *religion*, without elevating any single religion over other religions. Reflections on religion here are general, whereas when speaking of *church* as a Christian expression of religion, I am mostly interested in the Lutheran tradition.

are knocking on the doors of the virtual church or curious about what a church might have to say to them.

Indeed, this has remained constant: people yearn for a supportive faith community and for a religious language that helps make sense of life as it unfolds. This is true regardless of specific religious affiliation. It is also true of the persistent emphasis on faith, grace, and Christian freedom found across the Lutheran tradition. While significant disagreements between religious traditions have not disappeared (and in many cases should remain for the sake of the distinctive gifts and perspectives that diverse communities bring), many of the differences and debates that religious constituencies may have had before the global pandemic might seem less important now. Instead of debates about doctrinal difference, there is an urgency and vital need to experience unity in these challenging moments, to search together for sources of hope in a time of global despair, and to articulate a vision for a firm foundation on which to face the future. A fruitful and energizing task for Lutheran theologians today is to join the tender deliberation about how religious faith can be a positive part of human thriving.

Luther amid Crisis

A Lutheran is tempted to ask, Living today in our situation, what would Martin Luther do? Some answers can be found by examining his actual footsteps: he did leave a record that can resonate with the present moment.

As a reformer of church and society, Luther held fundamental concerns about the functioning of religion in terms of its key parts: the ideas, experiences, and practices informed by faith. In Luther's observation, the dominant church of his time needed purging. People wanted a religion that did something for them, but many things were amiss. It seemed the clergy lived in a world of their own, with many church leaders negligent (if not plain ignorant and ill-prepared) when it came to caring for the needs of the people. Some confessors acted abusively and failed to offer proper pastoral care for suffering souls. Bishops could be absent, wealthy, or interested in lording it over the church rather than shepherding the flock.

The perilous social situations of Luther's time included poverty, illness, miscarriages of justice, armed violence, war, and rebellion. Social divides were real. Luther emerged as a teacher and critic of the status quo in the broken world that he knew, aware that church and religion played major roles in all levels of personal and social life. Luther's reforms, therefore, focused on whether religion was doing what it was supposed to do to support people with the love of God.

Luther had much to say about many of his contemporary realities as he worked to reorient the clergy's and theologians' attention to what was broken and what the church could and should do.[4] He is not one who watched current events from a detached distance. One can easily see from works like the *Ninety-Five Theses*, *The Babylonian Captivity of the Church*, or *The Freedom of a Christian* that his main theological concerns revolved around serving people in tangible and direct ways with a Christian gospel that cared for them in body and soul. He embraced religion as a major force in human life and in society. He identified the dangers of religious leadership to either abuse its power or not use it at all. That is, Luther was highly critical of the church neglecting its proper participation in human affairs, such as caring for the basic needs of human beings who struggle with their daily lives, with their mortality, and with the challenges of human relations.[5]

What fueled Luther's vision and compassion? The Bible and his vocation. As is well established, Luther's primary concern as a biblical theologian was the proper interpretation of God's word. He lived out this deep personal concern and calling both as an academic professor who worked in the classroom and as a preacher called to share the word with the wider community. As a professor and a preacher, Luther dwelled in God's word and discerned its meaning in terms of both credible scholarship and its application as a liberating force of compassion in human life. That compassionate concern, of course, opened a massive amount of conflict about what the church was doing and teaching, what it was standing on, what it authentically offered people, and what would need to happen for the church to have its proper place in peoples' lives. Not unlike Tillich, Luther was in the "rescuing religion" business. He did so with his Bible and scholarship, with his compassion and courage.

---

4 See ample examples of this in TAL 5.

5 See, for example, Carter Lindberg, "Luther on Government Responsibility for the Poor," in *Encounters with Luther*, 220–31. See also two volumes dedicated to unfurling Luther's story and theological impact in light of social issues and reforms: Carter Lindberg and Paul Wee, eds. *Forgotten Luther*, vol. 1 (Minneapolis: Augsburg Fortress, 2016); Ryan Cummings, *Forgotten Luther*, vol. 2 (Minneapolis: Augsburg Fortress, 2019).

Luther's work was interrupted many times with episodes of violence, pain, and suffering, including outbreaks of the plague. These terrifying equalizers infected rich and poor, men and women, elders and children. In earlier times, as many as one-third of Europe's population had died from such outbreaks. Addressing such public health crises, Luther's words have proved their lasting value, continuing to show how a living faith provides a solid point of compassionate involvement and servant leadership. Addressing the ways that people were acting during the health crisis, Luther admonished those who took the situation lightly, selfishly assuming God's protection and thereby "tempting God" rather than doing their part. He wrote,

> It is even more shameful for a person to pay no heed to their own body and to fail to protect it against the plague the best they are able, and then to infect and poison others who might have remained alive if they had taken care of their body as they should have. . . . Indeed, such people behave as though a house were burning in the city and nobody were trying to put the fire out. Instead they let the flames run rampant so that the whole city is consumed, saying that if God so willed, God could save the city without water to quench the fire.
>
> No, my dear friends, that is not good. Use medicine; take potions which can help you; fumigate house, yard, and street; shun persons and places wherever your neighbor does not need your presence or has recovered, and act like a person who wants to help put out the burning city.[6]

These words exemplify a Lutheran orientation in times of crisis: proceed with both faith and reason—neither confusing nor separating the two—always in the spirit of compassion.

In the Lutheran tradition, religion's role in human life is best expressed in the language of the theology of the cross. Theology of the cross sees reality and calls it what it is through the lens of Christ's compassion. Faith starts with the promise of God's unfailing presence and care for human experience, with all its ugliness and beauty, no matter how lost things might seem. Religious practices give embodied expression and patterns to a Christian love that comes from outside oneself and exists to be shared. Preaching speaks of the

6 LW 43:131–32.

belovedness of each person and points to paths toward compassionate engagement in the midst of human reality, which is—despite strong evidence to the contrary—ultimately sacred and godly. Grounded in such a courageous faith, gospel-centered communities nurture respect for life, truth, freedom, and human thriving.[7]

LUTHERAN OFFERINGS

If this essay is to be something of a time capsule, then it might be helpful to contrast some other contemporary approaches that have arisen in American religious life with the Lutheran courage to believe in God and to love their neighbors. During the pandemic, for instance, some have made the news by demanding that churches stay open at full or near-full capacity. They view this as part of their constitutional rights to gather and to practice their religion, even when it has not been deemed safe to do so because of the virus. Some have even called such religious gatherings "essential" and thus urged the speedy opening of churches—against the advice of medical experts and in spite of the evidence of widespread infections originating from specifically these kinds of interactions. Many people have ignored the expert advice for social distancing, emboldened by their faith in God, in whose hands they believe their lives rest. This is precisely the attitude that Luther denounced as "tempting God" and revealing unfaithful, ignorant, and selfish behavior.[8]

---

7 On the basis of Martin Luther's *Heidelberg Disputation* (1518), Vitor Westhelle has powerfully and poetically unfolded the freeing power of Luther's theology of the cross vis-à-vis actual human experience of suffering. See Vitor Westhelle, "Usus Crucis: The Use and Abuse of the Cross and the Practice of Resurrection," in *Encounters with Luther: New Directions for Critical Studies*, ed. Kirsi Stjerna and Brooks Schramm (Louisville, KY: Westminster John Knox, 2016), 85–95. See also Anna Madsen, "Suffering and the Theology of the Cross from a Feminist Perspective," in *Encounters with Luther*, 241–49.

8 See LW 43:131–32, where Luther describes such people as being

> much too rash and reckless, they tempt God and disregard everything that might counteract death and the plague. They disdain the use of medicines; they do not avoid places and persons infected by the plague, but instead they lightheartedly make sport of it and so demonstrate their audacity. They say that the plague is God's punishment, and that if God wants to protect

When the pandemic required citizens to self-isolate and stay away from gatherings and from the public, many churches, including Lutheran congregations, faced a serious challenge. Was the church "closed"? Did ministry stop? What had been the point of church and religious gatherings in the first place?

An enormous splash of creativity occurred, as within days and weeks, religious leaders bravely found ways to care for their communities and maintain basic functions of ministries. They did this through the internet, phone calls, or other "distant" ways. They also embraced various forms of "giving," whether of time, resources, or prayers.

Some church communities have indeed been profoundly damaged by the pandemic through either the deaths of members or the practical inability to continue their ministries. At the same time, amid these pains, some religious communities have found life-giving new paths beyond the walls of any building they may have had before. With church buildings closed for months, congregations have found creative ways to come together as church to offer care in the spirit of Christian faith. In a time when "normalcy" has been undone, many new people have found their way to church communities, either returning to one that already had a place in their lives or engaging one for the first time, eager to hear and experience a community of faith's standing on issues that matter and thereby finding for themselves a firm foundation and a hope-filled vision. In turbulent times, religious communities and faith languages can offer a different perspective in life, one that bolsters a person in faith against the otherwise tempting feelings of devastating loneliness and despair caused by grief.

To provide an example from personal experience, near the beginning of the pandemic in the United States, Finnish Lutherans on the West Coast began gathering for church each week using online technology. Soon, attendance was higher in these online gatherings than when worship had been offered in a variety of physical locations. Many individuals shared that they felt it was now easier to "go to church" and that the technology created a surprisingly welcoming space, including space for relatively anonymous, low-pressure participation.

---

them, then God can do so without medicines or our carefulness. This is not trusting God but tempting God. God has created medicines and provided us with reason to guard and take good care of the body so that we can live in good health. If one makes no use of reason or medicine when they could do so without detriment to their neighbor, such a person injures their own body and must beware lest they become a suicide in God's eyes.

In another example, an English-speaking congregation in Santa Barbara, California, offered worship online every week, along with Sunday morning adult education. Nearly 100 percent of the congregation actively participated. Elderly members were provided printed copies of the worship materials and given pastoral calls (literally, phone calls). New members also joined from different geographic locations. Attendance of this new variety remained high, and the community experienced a strengthening of their faith and fellowship. A special cause of joy was when church members in their nineties (an age bracket not known for familiarity with online technology) eventually became comfortable with using these new resources and joined not only worship but other weekly meetings.

CONCLUSION

Could one say that the most significant offering of Lutheran faith today can be found in the theologically rooted willingness and openness to promote change when the gospel principles of justice, mercy, and freedom are compromised or at risk? In light of the spiritual freedom Luther experienced, the passion he gave to his craft as a theologian, and his conviction to proclaim and share the gospel in words and actions that changed real people's lives, might one say that the authentic Lutheran offering could be best unfolded with the twin concepts of freedom and service?[9] Considering the varied human needs and aspirations, and considering the multifaceted suffering of people around the world in this time and across the centuries, the word *freedom* expresses the ultimate concerns that a religion worth its salt is expected to address: safety, dignity, compassion, and other fundamental matters of life and death.

This essay has applied contemporary questions to ongoing scholarly studies of Luther's views of faith and freedom.[10] The practical changes Luther proposed to the religious world of his time were rooted in his deeper understanding of what faith is and what it does. Religion—the language and experience of belief—offers a ground of being that provides personal, existential

9 For more along these themes, see Kirsi Stjerna, *Lutheran Theology: A Grammar of Faith* (London: Bloomsbury / T&T Clark, 2021).

10 For examples of different ways in which Luther can be re-examined and re-engaged, see Else Marie Wiberg Pedersen, *The Alternative Luther: Lutheran Theology from the Subaltern* (Minneapolis: Lexington/Fortress, 2019).

foundations that allow people to know themselves and their fellow human beings authentically and compassionately, with the courage to be free and to believe that freedom is possible for everyone. The Lutheran conviction that this foundation rests on and revolves around the cross of Christ continues to speak love and grace to a hurting world.

In the spirit of Martin Luther and in recognition of Timothy Wengert's years of faithful teaching, this can be said with confidence: religion matters. Faith matters a great deal, especially, though not exclusively, in times of distress. Time spent revisiting and reshaping the theological language of reality and hope is not wasted. Quite the contrary! With the cross of Christ at the ground of their being, Lutherans know that maintaining a status quo is not the goal of a living religion or the criterion for its relevance. As it adapts to the global pandemic of 2020–2021 and participates in the godly work of overcoming racism and other super-spreader forms of injustice, the church will look different. Outward forms may change, but the church's mission remains the same: to share Christ's self-giving love with a world in need. In this creative, ongoing task of gospel witness, Lutherans are following in the steps of Reformation ancestors who, in their time, also knew what it meant to seek, find, and live out the courage to believe.

A Lutheran Visits La Sagrada Família

Further Reflections on the Marks of the Church

Gordon Lathrop

In a passage of a book that Timothy Wengert and I wrote together in 2004, Professor Wengert made a seemingly passing comment that has impressed itself upon my memory.[1] He stated that, in 1981, he and his family had found the clear presence of the marks of the church at a celebration of the Easter Vigil in a small Roman Catholic community in Tübingen, although they found those marks much more ambiguous—even absent—on the following Easter Sunday morning in the great Lutheran Church, the Stiftskirche, at the heart of that university town. The marks—the characteristics, the tokens, the symbols, the necessary signs—of assembled Christians, marks that enable one to know that here indeed is Christ's church, were for Wengert as for Luther at least these: "baptism and the bread and the gospel." It was those very things the Wengert family found strongly present in that Roman Catholic celebration of the Vigil and painfully absent in the Lutheran assembly the next morning, where the sermon was mostly angry commentary on an event of police action against some university students and where the Eucharist was missing.

This comment was not so much a fruit of Professor Wengert's ecumenism—though we have certainly also known his seriousness about such

1 Gordon Lathrop and Timothy J. Wengert, *Christian Assembly: Marks of the Church in a Pluralistic Age* (Minneapolis: Fortress, 2004), 27. This essay is written in celebration of Timothy Wengert's seventieth birthday and in gratitude for his friendship and for the years we shared teaching together at the Lutheran Theological Seminary at Philadelphia.

engagement[2]—as it was evidence of his commitment to the idea that *church* is a verb, an event that *happens*, and that there are indeed concrete signs that indicate that church is taking place. As he wrote,

> Where was "church" that Easter? Where we heard proclaimed Christ crucified and risen again for us, not where the only word was political commentary on police brutality. Church is not a noun; it is a verb, an event, or, to use the language of the sixties, a happening. The point of the church's marks is not to provide a definition for theologians, ecumenists, and other suspicious people, but to point out "the sign . . . by which we may congregate." The point of the church's marks is always to gather people for the hearing, washing, and eating of God's word.[3]

Far from being a polemicist, Professor Wengert has been very willing to exercise a profound Lutheran ecclesiology by seeing a gathering of *church* wherever those marks evidence its presence, including in Roman Catholic communities.[4]

Luther, Melanchthon, and succeeding generations of Lutherans have found diverse ways to list the "signs of life" that mark and gather the church. The *Augsburg Confession* speaks of the gospel being "purely preached" and the sacraments "administered according to the gospel."[5] A nineteenth-century Danish church bell in northern Wisconsin spoke of "bath and table, prayer and word," and "every seeking soul."[6] Or, in my own favorite formulation, Luther in 1539 asked what signs there are whereby "a poor confused person" might be able to "tell where such a Christian holy people are to be found in this world" and answered with seven marks: the preached word, baptism, the holy supper, the use of absolution, the calling and consecrating of ministers, public thanksgiving and prayer, and "the holy possession of the cross"—that

---

2 See, for example, Timothy J. Wengert and Susan K. Wood, *A Shared Spiritual Journey: Lutherans and Catholics Traveling toward Unity* (Mahwah, NJ: Paulist, 2016).

3 Wengert, *Christian Assembly*, 27.

4 See further in Wengert, *Christian Assembly*, 93. See also Timothy J. Wengert, *A Formula for Parish Practice: Using the Formula of Concord in Congregations* (Grand Rapids, MI: Eerdmans, 2006), 207.

5 Article 7, BC 42.

6 Among other places, see Gordon Lathrop, *Central Things: Worship in Word and Sacrament* (Minneapolis: Augsburg Fortress, 2005), 20–22; Wengert, *Christian Assembly*, 46–52.

is, the presence of suffering as in some sense a mark of communal life.[7] At least some of these marks were what the Wengert family found in that Roman Catholic community on Easter Eve.

I thought of Tim's comment and of our common work on the marks in the midst of a recent experience of my own in Barcelona. I was there in September 2019 as a tourist—or, perhaps, as a pilgrim, given my hope to see the stunning apse paintings of the Romanesque churches of Tahull, preserved in the Museu Nacional d'Art de Catalunya. Besides that museum and other treasures of Barcelona, I did know, of course, about the great, unfinished church, regarded as the "second cathedral" of Barcelona, taken over and thoroughly designed by Antoni Gaudí: La Sagrada Família. But I did not particularly want to see it.

For one thing, I have never had much piety toward the "holy family." The stories of Joseph and Mary and the imagination of life at Nazareth are late New Testament accounts, only present in two Gospels, described quite differently in each of those, and then wildly elaborated in later second- or third-century writings that do not seem to me to catch the genuine heart of the gospel. For another thing, I was aware that Gaudí himself was a conservative—indeed, nearly reactionary—Roman Catholic, and that in his planning together with the "Spiritual Association of the Devotees of St. Joseph," the building was meant to be an "expiatory temple," an act of penance addressed to God for the sins of "modernism," as those sins had been excoriated by Pope Pius IX in 1864.[8] As a person who is far from condemning many of the opinions and movements that Pius IX condemned ("liberalism," "socialism," and "religious freedom," for example) and as a Lutheran Christian who does not believe that God expects "expiation" from us, such a penitential building could not be very interesting to me. On the contrary, perhaps it would be quite offensive.

What is more, while I found that other building projects of Gaudí were marked by a fascinating style—a kind of intensification of "art nouveau" combined with what seemed to me to be an irrepressible whimsy—I could not imagine that this style would be helpful to a church building. Not least, Gaudí was

7 Wengert, *Christian Assembly*, 39–40; for this passage in Luther's "On the Councils and the Church," see TAL 3:422–31.

8 On the beginnings of La Sagrada Família in a reactionary movement, with its sense of being a "new counter-Reformation," see Robert Hughes, *Barcelona* (New York: Knopf, 1992), 526.

famous for making stone look like vegetation—trees or leaves or flowers[9]—and I have long thought such projects to be pretense: a church building, above all, should be honest in its use of materials. And then there was this: the whole undertaking seemed to me to have become simply the ongoing creation of a huge tourist destination, drawing people from all over the world and thus making money for Barcelona and Catalunya.[10] For all of these reasons, La Sagrada Família would seem to me to have little to do with what ought to mark a church building. I would go, but I wouldn't like it.

I was wrong. I loved it. Indeed, it now seems to me one of the most remarkable church buildings in the world.

I need to say clearly that I only saw the building. I did not see "church," since I was not a participant in a liturgical event there, in word and sacrament communally enacted in that space. But the building! I judge this building to be a built symbol of the signs of life that mark the church. That does not mean that church automatically happens there, but it does show that word and sacrament according to the gospel and in assembly have deeply formed what has been built. It does suggest that buildings matter and "doing church" can be and has been resisted and even perverted by some buildings, whereas other buildings—*this* building—can profoundly help.

Let me say more.

For one thing, the exterior of La Sagrada Família is covered with the Bible in images. No, not simply the Bible, but the gospel with which the Bible is full. The three great facades of the church building, above its three principal portals—two of which have been completed—are devoted to the narratives of the incarnation and birth of Jesus, of his death and resurrection, and of his promised coming in judgment and in glory. It is right to say that Gaudí wanted to make a Bible in stone.[11] In many ways, those facades are overwhelming, crammed with images. They are like the *retablos mayores*, the great

9 So, in 1977, Joan Miró wrote, "I think of Gaudí, who turned a stone into a field of stars, with a chrysanthemum in the middle": in a painting on exhibit at the Fundació Joan Miró, Montjuïc, Barcelona. See also the discussion of the "haptic" nature of Gaudí's constructions in Hughes, 470–71.

10 On La Sagrada Família, tourism, and money, see Hughes, 525–26, 537.

11 Gijs van Hensbergen, *The Sagrada Família* (New York: Bloomsbury, 2017), 82. One might argue, however, that the Old Testament is relatively and unfortunately absent, except in the images and texts of some prophets.

crowded collections of statuary and painting that rise behind and above many altars in Spanish churches.[12] But in this case, these images are not inside the building. They are on the outside! When I saw them, they reminded me of what Luther said about images: "Yes, would to God that I could persuade the rich and the mighty that they would permit the whole Bible to be painted on houses, on the inside and outside, so that all can see it. That would be a Christian work."[13] And while there are a few images in the facades that are not actually biblical—Joachim and Anna and an attempt to represent the immaculate conception in the Nativity facade; Veronica in the Passion facade—they are indeed few. The overwhelming sense is of a strange kind of great house covered with images of the biblical events meant for human salvation. At the apex of the Nativity facade, pulling its complexity into a coherent unity, is a Tree of Life, carrying symbols of the Trinity. At the apex of the strikingly different and more severe Passion facade are images of the crucifixion, the empty tomb, and the ascension. Surrounding both facades—as well as the yet unfinished Glory facade—are, in each case, four towers, each named for one of the Twelve, so that, in the end, Jesus's missionary Twelve stand around the biblical message presented in the imagery of the exterior, and that message culminates in the death and resurrection of Jesus and in the availability of the Tree of Life as a way to see and participate in the holy Trinity.[14]

For these facades all crown doorways, entrances into the church building. It is as if Luther's biblical images on the outside of the houses in the town invite us to come into the church. The biblical stories of God's saving mercy bring us to the doors. That is at least an indication of or an arrow pointing toward the first of the marks of the church: the word of God preached.

But the portals are themselves interesting. Under both the Nativity facade and the Passion facade there are three doors, named for Faith, Hope, and Love, with Love in the center. We come into the church through these gifts that Paul

12 Van Hensbergen, 87. On the crowded ornamentation of the Nativity facade, see also Gijs van Hensbergen, *Gaudí: A Biography* (New York: Harper Collins, 2001), 251–56.

13 *Against the Heavenly Prophets in the Matter of Images and Sacraments*, TAL 2:67; in German, WA 18:83.

14 To see the plan of the church as well as many photographs, consult Josep Maria Carandell and Pere Vivas, *The Basilica of the Sagrada Família* (Sant Lluís, Menorca: Triangle, n.d.).

outlines in First Corinthians 13. The doors under the Nativity facade are then surrounded by stone foliage, as if we are coming into that Tree of Life that surmounts the whole. The central door under the Passion facade, however, is covered with carved words from the Passion accounts of the Gospels, as if in coming into the church we are coming into the Bible through its central story. Then the floor of the Passion entranceway has figures—people great and small, branches of trees as if strewn on the floor, a donkey—so that coming into the church joins us to the Passion Sunday procession. The five doors of the Glory facade are not yet finished, but the central one has been installed, and it is covered with the words of the Lord's Prayer in many languages, with "give us this day our daily bread" highlighted. To come into the church is to enter the Lord's Prayer and to come to that bread—in the Eucharist, in care for the poor, and in the promise of the final feast.

But perhaps the greatest surprise attending any visit to La Sagrada Família arises from simply coming inside. If the exterior of the church is complex, covered with carved images and great towers, the interior is nearly empty, a soaring space filled instead with an amazing play of light and organized to represent and enable the flow, or *ordo*, of the liturgy. On one of the bronze doors under the Passion facade a carved quotation from Dante's *Paradiso*, canto 28, reads, "My longing is to gain its end in this amazing and angelic temple that has, as boundaries, only love and light."[15] Suddenly that quotation seems apt. While the exterior has many complex "boundaries," the interior opens onto light and the flow of God's love as it comes to expression in the liturgy. Here, there is simply space for the enacting of the marks: space for movement, space for the assembly to come in and to gather, space for the gospel to be preached, space for that bread to be held out and eaten—and at the rear, flanking what will be the main entrance, there are two circular spaces that will serve as a baptistry and as a place for what Lutherans call "confession and forgiveness." These are built symbols of the marks.

When one looks more closely, there are also interior images and words. Preeminently, at the crossing (for the building is a cruciform basilica), there are four pillars that bear the names of each of the four evangelists and the classic images of the "living creatures" that have been seen as representing them: the fourfold gospel is what this gathering is about. Above these

15 See Carandell and Vivas, 177.

columns, rising from the roof into the sky, are four towers standing for the evangelists and surrounding what will be the central and tallest tower standing for Jesus Christ, thus the living creatures around the Lamb. Then there are great, largely abstract stained glass windows, shedding warm, red and orange colors on the Passion side of the building and cool, blue and green colors on the Nativity side, as if the colors themselves bathe the room with the message that is carved on the exterior. In the apse, there are a few side chapels, including especially a Marian space at the farthest end, and there is a crypt. But none of this detracts from the astonishing space for an assembly in the gospel enacting word and sacrament.

Then there are the columns. Including the pillars of the Gospels, four kinds of columns surround the aisles of the room and support the roof, reaching into and creating this vast and open space. And these columns, too, become a kind of image. At the top of each column, vaults spread out like the arms and leaves of a tree.[16] The assembly has gathered in a kind of open forest. Indeed, when one thinks of that foliage through which one enters from the Nativity side—or, even more, when one sees that outside, on the roof above these interior trees, central pinnacles are topped with images of wheat and grapes, and then twelve side pinnacles are topped with twelve different kinds of fruit, spring and summer fruits on the Nativity side, fall and winter fruits on the Passion side (cf. Rev 22:2)—one might best agree that the whole building is an image of the Tree of God.[17] When I walked in that "forest," under those trees or in that Tree, I thought of Mark 4: as the mustard bush becomes the bird-sheltering tree, so the cross becomes the Tree of Life.[18] And for an assembly to gather in this house, around those gathering marks, is for all the birds to find shelter in the Tree. The building is a Cross become the Tree. More, if the exterior of the building presents biblical stories to invite people to come in, it also presents to the world the fruits and leaves of the Tree of Life, with the sense that what happens in the assembly in the building is deeply intended for the nourishment and the healing of all nations.

16 See van Hensbergen, *Sagrada Família*, 124, and see the photo in Carandell and Vivas, 220.

17 Van Hensbergen, 114. See also Hughes, *Barcelona*, 470.

18 See Gordon Lathrop, *Saving Images: The Presence of the Bible in Christian Liturgy* (Minneapolis: Fortress, 2017), 177.

Again, I do not know how *church* as verb happens in this great building. And I need to say that I am a little sorry that entrance to this "Tree" is now so controlled by timed and purchased tickets. I know that there is still a need to raise funds to finish the construction and a need to monitor the crowds. But if the building is indeed completed by 2024, as is hoped, it would be wonderful were the doors then to be opened, with no fees charged but with the possibility of visitors giving offerings, both to the building and to the poor of Barcelona. After all, Gaudí did imagine that he was working on building "the cathedral of the poor,"[19] and that very idea has at least some connection to the seventh of the marks of the church that Luther listed.

Yet already this built house for the church does support the marks. Its exterior images and its interior light and trees proved me quite wrong in not wanting to see it and rightly reminded me of what Tim Wengert had written about another Roman Catholic community. Now I find myself wishing that all of our houses for the church would give such support to the marks—would use images again, for example, and would use light and space to enable the assembly's liturgy—in so creative a way.

When Dietrich Bonhoeffer was a Lutheran pastor to the German community in Barcelona in the 1920s, he could easily have seen the early construction of Gaudí's great "temple," though there is no evidence I know of that he did. But in a 1928 Barcelona sermon on First Corinthians 12:26–27, on the church as the Body of Christ, he did make a comment useful to a Lutheran visiting La Sagrada Família who wants to do so with a genuine Lutheran ecclesiology, an ecclesiology like Wengert's, in mind. Bonhoeffer said that the word *church* often stirs in Catholics "all the depths of . . . religious sensibility, from dread and awe of the Last Judgment to the sweetness of God's presence," whereas to Protestants ("für den Evangelischen," in Bonhoeffer's German), the word often sounds endlessly banal, unnecessary, a matter of indifference and boredom.[20] La Sagrada Família certainly evidences that dread and awe and that sweetness; it is in Bonhoeffer's sense a "Catholic" building. But when it is seen to be a house recalling, supporting, and evoking those marks of the church

19 Van Hensbergen, *Gaudí*, 244–70.

20 See Eberhard Bethge, *Dietrich Bonhoeffer* (New York: Harper & Row, 1977), 42. The German reads, "Für den Evangelischen den Klang von etwas unendlich Banalem, etwas. . . . Gleichgültigem . . . mit dem sich so oft Gefühle der Langeweile verbinden" (91–92).

whereby we gather, and doing so with such imaginative vigor and beauty, it will be recognized as an ecumenical treasure. And that treasure will have the power to awaken Protestants from their indifference and send them home to rethink their own spaces. In any case, the marks of the church fully enacted are not boring; they are quite capable of radically altering how we see the world itself.

Writings of Timothy J. Wengert

Books: Authored or Coauthored

Philip Melanchthon's "Annotationes in Johannem" of 1523 in Relation to Its Predecessors and Contemporaries. Geneva: Librairie Droz, 1987.

Basics in Lutheran Doctrine. Study book and teacher's guide for the New Journeys series of catechetical instruction. Minneapolis: Augsburg Fortress, 1990.

Law and Gospel: Philip Melanchthon's Debate with John Agricola of Eisleben over "Poenitentia." Grand Rapids, MI: Baker, 1997.

Human Freedom, Christian Righteousness: Philip Melanchthon's Exegetical Dispute with Erasmus of Rotterdam. New York: Oxford University Press, 1998.

With Gordon Lathrop. *Christian Assembly: Marks of the Church in a Pluralistic Age*. Minneapolis: Fortress, 2004.

A Formula for Parish Practice: Using the Formula of Concord in Congregations. Grand Rapids, MI: Eerdmans, 2006.

Priesthood, Pastors, Bishops: Public Ministry for the Reformation and Today. Minneapolis: Fortress, 2008.

Martin Luther's Catechisms: Forming the Faith. Minneapolis: Fortress, 2009.

Philip Melanchthon, Speaker of the Reformation: Wittenberg's Other Reformer. Aldershot, UK: Ashgate, 2010.

Defending Faith: Lutheran Responses to Andreas Osiander's Doctrine of Justification, 1551–1559. Tübingen: Mohr Siebeck, 2012.

Reading the Bible with Martin Luther. Grand Rapids, MI: Baker, 2013.

With Susan K. Wood. *A Shared Spiritual Journey: Lutherans and Catholics Traveling toward Unity*. Mahwah, NJ: Paulist, 2016.

With R. Guy Erwin et al. *By Heart: Conversations with Martin Luther's Small Catechism*. Minneapolis: Augsburg Fortress, 2017.

Word of Life: Introducing Lutheran Hermeneutics. Minneapolis: Fortress, 2019.

The Augsburg Confession: Renewing Lutheran Faith and Practice. Minneapolis: Fortress, 2020.

Books: Edited

With Charles W. Brockwell. *Telling the Churches' Stories: Ecumenical Perspectives on Writing Christian History*. Grand Rapids, MI: Eerdmans, 1995.

With M. Patrick Graham. *Philip Melanchthon (1497–1560) and the Commentary*. Sheffield, UK: Sheffield Academic Press, 1997.

Introduction and annotations to *Martin Luther's Sermons from Holy Week and Easter, 1529*, translated by Irving Sandberg. St. Louis: Concordia, 1999.

With Scott H. Hendrix. *Philip Melanchthon Then and Now (1497–1997)*. Columbia, SC: Lutheran Theological Southern Seminary, 1999.

With Robert Kolb. *The Book of Concord*. Minneapolis: Fortress, 2000.

Harvesting Martin Luther's Reflections on Theology, Ethics, and the Church. Grand Rapids, MI: Eerdmans, 2003.

Centripetal Worship: The Evangelical Heart of Lutheran Worship. Minneapolis: Augsburg Fortress, 2007.

The Pastoral Luther: Essays in Luther's Practical Theology. Grand Rapids, MI: Eerdmans, 2009.

With Wolfgang Splitter. *Correspondence of Heinrich Melchior Mühlenberg*. Vol. 3, *1753–1756*. Rockland, ME: Picton, 2009.

With Wolfgang Splitter. *Correspondence of Heinrich Melchior Mühlenberg*. Vol. 4, *1757–1762*. Rockland, ME: Picton, 2010.

Co-contributor with Irene Dingel, Robert Kolb, and Nicole Kuropka. *Philip Melanchthon: Theologian in Classroom, Confession, and Controversy*. Göttingen: Vandenhoeck & Ruprecht, 2012.

Martin Luther's 95 Theses with Introduction, Commentary, and Study Guide. Minneapolis: Fortress, 2015.

The Roots of Reform. Vol. 1 of *The Annotated Luther*, edited by Timothy J. Wengert. Minneapolis: Fortress, 2015.

General editor. *Dictionary of Martin Luther and the Lutheran Traditions*. Grand Rapids, MI: Baker, 2017.

With Mary Jane Haemig, Chris Halverson, and Robb Harrell. *Minister's Prayer Book*. Revised Edition. Minneapolis: Fortress, 2020.

Articles and Contributions

"Recently Discovered Notes on Two Sermons from 1520 by Martin Luther." *Sixteenth Century Journal* 14 (1983): 189–200.

Contributor to *D. Martin Luthers Werke: Kritische Gesamtausgabe*, 59:223–234. Weimar: H. Böhlaus Nachfolger, 1983.

"Dating Huldrych Zwingli's Lectures on the Gospel of John." *Zwingliana* 17 (1986): 6–10.

"Caspar Cruciger (1504–1548): The Case of the Disappearing Reformer." *Sixteenth Century Journal* 20 (1989): 417–441.

"Hidden Treasure: G. H. Gerberding and the ELCA." *Lutheran Partners* 5, no. 5 (September/October 1989): 26–29.

"The Day Melanchthon Got Mad: A Study in Lutheran Ecclesiology." *Lutheran Quarterly*, n.s., 6 (1991): 419–433.

"Open Letter to a Soldier." *Lutheran Forum* 25, no. 2 (Easter/Pentecost 1991): 10–12.

"What Does This Mean? Luther's Catechisms in the Parish." *Parish Practice Notebook*, no. 34 (Spring 1991): 1–4.

"Caspar Cruciger Sr.'s 1546 'Enarratio' on John's Gospel: An Experiment in Ecclesiological Exegesis." *Church History* 61 (1992): 60–74.

"Scandalized! Preaching the Cross." *Academy Accents* 7, no. 4 (1992): 1–2.

With Charles W. Brockwell Jr. "Christian History in Ecumenical Perspective: Principles of Historiography." *Fides et Historia* 24 (1992): 40–53.

"Wittenberg's Earliest Catechism." *Lutheran Quarterly*, n.s., 7 (1993): 247–260.

"Martin Luther's Movement toward an Apostolic Self-Awareness as Reflected in His Early Letters." *Luther-Jahrbuch* 61 (1994): 54–69.

"Twin Treasures of the Church." *Lutheran Partners* 10, no. 3 (May/June 1994): 28–33.

"'Fear and Love' in the Ten Commandments." *Concordia Journal* 21 (1995): 14–27.

"The Origins of the Lutheran Chorale Service of Holy Communion." *Parish Practice Notebook* 46 (Summer 1995): 4–5.

"Philip Melanchthon." In *The Concise Encyclopedia of Preaching*, edited by Richard Lischer and William Willimon, 328–329. Louisville: John Knox, 1995.

"'With Friends like This . . .': The Biography of Philip Melanchthon by Joachim Camerarius." In *The Rhetorics of Life-Writing in Early Modern Europe: Forms of Biography from Cassandra Fedele to Louis XIV*, edited by Thomas F. Mayer and D. R. Woolf, 115–131. Ann Arbor: University of Michigan, 1995.

With Robert Kolb. "Translating *The Book of Concord* for the 21st Century." *Lutheran Partners*, 11, no. 1 (January/February 1995): 10–16. Later published in *Concordia Journal* 21 (1995): 305–311.

"Adiaphora." In *The Oxford Encyclopedia of the Reformation*, edited by Hans J. Hillerbrand, 51–53. Oxford: Oxford University Press, 1996.

"Antinomianism." In *The Oxford Encyclopedia of the Reformation*, edited by Hans J. Hillerbrand, 1:4–7. Oxford: Oxford University Press, 1996.

"Getting the Most out of the Small Catechism." *Lutheran Partners* 12, no. 4 (July/August 1996): 16–20.

"Martin Luther's Memory in the History of Christianity." *The Periodical* 41, no. 2 (October 1996): 3–4.

"Philip Melanchthon's 1522 Annotations on Romans and the Lutheran Origins of Rhetorical Criticism." In *Biblical Interpretation in the Era of the Reformation*, edited by Richard A. Muller and John L. Thompson, 118–140. Grand Rapids, MI: Eerdmans, 1996.

"The Biblical Commentaries of Philip Melanchthon." In *Philip Melanchthon (1497–1560) and the Commentary*, edited by M. Patrick Graham and Timothy J. Wengert, 106–148. Sheffield, UK: Sheffield Academic Press, 1997.

"Forming the Faith Today through Luther's Catechisms." *Lutheran Quarterly*, n.s., 11 (1997): 379–395.

"Georg Major (1502–1574): Defender of the Wittenberg's Faith and Melanchthonian Exegete." In *Melanchthon in seinen Schülern*, Wolfenbütteler Forschungen 73, edited by Heinz Scheible, 129–156. Wiesbaden: Harrassowitz Verlag, 1997.

"In Celebration of the 500th Anniversary of the Birth of Philip Melanchthon: 1497–1997." *The Periodical* 42, no. 1 (April 1997): 3–5.

"Luther's Catechisms and the Lord's Supper." *Word and World* 17 (1997): 54–60.

"Philip Melanchthon (1497–1560) and His Recently Discovered Prayer for the Church." *Lutheran Quarterly*, n.s., 11 (1997): 131–141.

"The Scope and Contents of Philip Melanchthon's *Opera omnia*, Wittenberg, 1562–1564." *Archive for Reformation History* 88 (1997): 57–76.

"The Unity of Word and Sacrament." *Parish Practice Notebook* 50 (Spring 1997): 1–3.

"Luther on Children: Baptism and the Fourth Commandment." *dialog* 37 (1998): 185–189.

"Philip Melanchthon's Gift to Caspar von Niedbruck." *Lutheran Quarterly*, n.s., 12 (1998): 485–489.

Articles on Philip Melanchthon, Joachim Camerarius, and Caspar Peucer for the *Encyclopedia of the Renaissance*. New York: Scribner's, 1999.

"Beyond Stereotypes: The Real Philip Melanchthon." In *Philip Melanchthon Then and Now (1497–1997)*, edited by Scott H. Hendrix and Timothy J. Wengert, 9–31. Columbia, SC: Lutheran Theological Southern Seminary, 1999.

"Luther and Melanchthon—Melanchthon and Luther." *Luther-Jahrbuch* 66 (1999): 55–88.

"'Qui vigilantissimis oculis veterum omnium commentarios excusserit': Philip Melanchthon's Patristic Exegesis." In *Die Patristik in der Bibelexegese des 16. Jahrhunderts*, edited by David C. Steinmetz, 115–134. Wiesbaden: Harrassowitz, 1999.

"'We Will Feast Together in Heaven Forever': The Epistolary Friendship of John Calvin and Philip Melanchthon." In *Melanchthon in Europe: His Work and Influence beyond Wittenberg*, edited by Karin Maag, 19–44. Grand Rapids, MI: Baker, 1999.

"Gesetz und Buße: Philipp Melanchthons erster Streit mit Johannes Agricola." In *Der Theolog Melanchthon*, edited by Günter Frank, 375–392. Stuttgart: Jan Thorbecke, 2000.

"Philip Melanchthon." In *The Dictionary of Historical Theology*, edited by Trevor A. Hart, 363–364. Grand Rapids, MI: Eerdmans, 2000.

"Philip Melanchthon on Human and Divine Freedom." *dialog* 39 (2000): 262–266.

"Reflections on Confessing the Faith in the New English Translation of *The Book of Concord*." *Lutheran Quarterly* 14 (2000): 1–20.

"Bearing Christ as Melanchthon's Contribution to *The Book of Concord*." *Lutheran Quarterly* 15 (2001): 396–416.

"The Lutheran Confessions: A Handbook for Sharing the Faith." *Lutheran Partners* 17, no. 1 (2001): 24–29.

"Luther and Melanchthon on Consecrated Communion Wine (Eisleben 1542–43)." *Lutheran Quarterly* 15 (2001): 24–42.

"Philip Melanchthon's Last Word to Cardinal Lorenzo Campeggio, Papal Legate at the 1530 Diet of Augsburg." In *Dona Melanchthoniana: Festgabe für Heinz Scheible zum 70. Geburtstag*, edited by Johanna Loehr, 457–483. Stuttgart: Frommann-Holzboog, 2001.

"Certificate of Ordination (1545) for George von Anhalt, Coadjutor Bishop of Merseburg." *Lutheran Quarterly* 16 (2002): 229–233.

"'Peace, Peace . . . Cross, Cross': Reflections on How Martin Luther Relates the Theology of the Cross to Suffering." *Theology Today* 59 (2002): 190–205.

"The Rhetorical Key to the Lutheran Confessions for Faith and Life in Today's Church." *Seminary Ridge Review* 4 (2002): 45–61.

With J. Paul Rajashekar. "Martin Luther, Philip Melanchthon, and the Publication of the Qur'an." *Lutheran Quarterly* 16 (2002): 221–228.

"Philip Melanchthon and a Christian *Politics*." *Lutheran Quarterly* 17 (2003): 29–62.

"Philipp Melanchthon, biblischer Theologe der Neuzeit." In *Melanchthon und die Neuzeit*, edited by Günter Frank and Ulrich Köpf, 23–42. Stuttgart: Frommann-Holzboog, 2003.

"The Tale of a 1580 Book of Concord, Annotated from the Principality of Ansbach to the Commonwealth of Pennsylvania." *Lutheran Quarterly* 17 (2003): 386–419.

"Episcopacy in Lutheran Ecumenical Statements." *Lutheran Quarterly* 18 (2004): 207–231.

"Luther on Prayer in the Large Catechism." *Lutheran Quarterly* 18 (2004): 249–274.

"Martin Luther and the Ten Commandments in the Large Catechism." *Currents in Theology and Mission* 31 (2004): 104–114.

"Philip Melanchthon's Contribution to Luther's Debate with Erasmus over the Bondage of the Will." In *By Faith Alone: Essays on Justification in Honor of Gerhard O. Forde*, edited by Joseph A. Burgess and Marc Kolden, 110–124. Grand Rapids, MI: Eerdmans, 2004.

"Famous Last Words: The Final Epistolary Exchange between Erasmus of Rotterdam and Philip Melanchthon in 1536." *Erasmus of Rotterdam Society Yearbook* 25 (2005): 18–38.

"Georg Major as Exegete of First Timothy." In *Georg Major (1502–1574): Ein Theologe der Wittenberger Reformation*, edited by Irene Dingel and Günther Wartenberg, 69–92. Leipzig: Evangelische Verlagsanstalt, 2005.

"Philip Melanchthon on Time and History in the Reformation." *Consensus* 30, no. 2 (2005): 9–33.

"The Formula of Concord and the Comfort of Election." *Lutheran Quarterly* 20 (2006): 44–62.

"Philip Melanchthon and the Jews: A Reappraisal." In *Jews, Judaism, and the Reformation in Sixteenth-Century Germany*, edited by Dean Phillip Bell and Stephen G. Burnett, 105–135. Leiden: Brill, 2006.

With Robert Kolb. "The Future of Lutheran Confessional Studies: Reflections in Historical Context." *dialog* 45 (2006): 118–126.

"Martin Luther on Spousal Abuse." *Lutheran Quarterly* 21 (2007): 337–339.

"'Not by Nature *Philoneikos*': Philip Melanchthon's Initial Reactions to the Augsburg Interim." In *Politik und Bekenntnis: Die Reaktionen auf das Interim von 1548*, edited by Irene Dingel and Günther Wartenberg, 33–49. Leipzig: Evangelische Verlagsanstalt, 2007.

"Per mutuum colloquium et consolationem fratrum: Monastische Züge in Luthers ökumenischer Theologie." In *Luther und das monastische Erbe*, edited by Christoph Bultmann et al., 243–268. Tübingen: Mohr Siebeck, 2007.

"The Priesthood of All Believers and Other Pious Myths." In *Saying and Doing the Gospel Today*, Institute of Liturgical Studies Occasional Papers 12, edited by Rhoda Schuler, 92–115. Valparaiso, IN: Institute of Liturgical Studies, 2007.

"An Introduction to Centripital Worship" and "Martin Luther's Witness to the Center of Worship." In *Centripetal Worship: The Evangelical Heart of Lutheran Worship*.

With Philip D. W. Krey. "A June 1546 Exorcism in Wittenberg as a Pastoral Act." *Archive for Reformation History* 98 (2007): 71–83.

"Georg Major: An 'Eyewitness' to the Posting of Martin Luther's Ninety-Five Theses." In *Luthers Thesenanschlag—Faktum oder Fiktion*, edited by Joachim Ott and Martin Treu. Leipzig: Evangelische Verlagsanstalt, 2008.

"Higher Education and Vocation: The University of Wittenberg (1517–1533) between Renaissance and Reform." In *The Lutheran Doctrine of Vocation*, Pieper Lectures 11, edited by John A. Maxfield, 1–21. St. Louis: Concordia Historical Institute, 2008.

"Martin Luther's Practical Theology." *Lutheran Quarterly* 22 (2008).

"Philip Melanchthon and Augustine of Hippo." *Lutheran Quarterly* 22 (2008): 249–267.

"Biblical Interpretation in the Works of Philip Melanchthon." In *A History of Biblical Interpretation*, vol. 2, *The Medieval through the Reformation Periods*, edited by Alan J. Hauser and Duane F. Watson, 319–340. Grand Rapids, MI: Eerdmans, 2009.

"*The Book of Concord* and Human Sexuality, Seen through the Institution of Marriage." *dialog* 48, no. 1 (Spring 2009): 9–18.

"Martin Luther (1483–1546), *The Freedom of a Christian*." In *Christian Spirituality: The Classics*, edited by Arthur Holder, 184–196. London: Routledge, 2009.

"The Rhetorical Paul: Philip Melanchthon's Interpretation of the Pauline Epistles." In *A Companion to Paul in the Reformation*, edited by R. Ward Holder, 129–164. Leiden: Brill, 2009.

"Commentary as Polemic: Philip Melanchthon's 1556 *Enarratio ad Romanos* against Andreas Osiander." In *Hermeneutica Sacra: Studies of the Interpretation of Holy Scripture in the Sixteenth and Seventeenth Centuries*, edited by Torbjörn Johansson, Robert Kolb, and Johann Anselm Steiger, 147–163. Berlin: De Gruyter, 2010.

"Martin Luther." In *The Cambridge Dictionary of Christian Theology*, edited by Ian A. McFarland et al., 290–291. Cambridge: Cambridge University Press, 2011.

"A Note on 'Sola Scriptura' in Martin Luther's Writings." *Luther-Bulletin* 20 (2011): 21–31.

"Martin Luther." In *The Decalogue through the Centuries: From the Hebrew Scriptures to Benedict XVI*, edited by Jeffrey P. Greenman and Timothy Larsen, 97–118. Louisville: Westminster John Knox, 2012.

"Philip Melanchthon and Martin Luther as Partners in Evangelical Conversation." In *Lutheranism Legacy and Future: Essays in Honor of Eric W. Gritsch on the 50th Anniversary of His Ordination*, edited by Holger Roggelin and Scott Gustafson, 59–79. West Conshohocken, PA: Infinity, 2012.

"Philip Melanchthon and the Origins of the 'Three Causes' (1533–1535): An Examination of the Roots of the Controversy over the Freedom of the Will." In *Philip Melanchthon: Theologian in Classroom, Confession, and Controversy*, by Irene Dingel et al., 183–208. Göttingen: Vandenhoeck & Ruprecht, 2012.

"Philip Melanchthon on 'Christianity.'" In *Reformation as Christianization: Essays on Scott Hendrix's Christianization Thesis*, edited by Anna Marie Johnson and John A. Maxfield, 79–100. Tübingen: Mohr Siebeck, 2012.

"Philip Melanchthon's 1557 Lecture on Colossians 3:1–2: Christology as Context for the Controversy over the Lord's Supper." In *Philip Melanchthon: Theologian in Classroom, Confession, and Controversy*, by Irene Dingel et al., 209–235. Göttingen: Vandenhoeck & Ruprecht, 2012.

"Philip Melanchthon and John Calvin against Andreas Osiander: Coming to Terms with Forensic Justification." In *Calvin and Luther: The Continuing Relationship*, edited by R. Ward Holder, 63–87. Göttingen: Vandenhoeck & Ruprecht, 2013.

"Philip Melanchthon and Wittenberg's Reform of the Theological Curriculum." In *Church and School in Early Modern Protestantism: Studies in Honor of Richard A. Muller on the Maturation of a Theological Tradition*, edited by Jordan J. Ballor et al., 17–33. Leiden: Brill, 2013.

"Rejoicing with the Angels: Martin Luther on the Incarnation." *Cross Accent* 21, no. 1 (March 2013): 6–19.

"Face-to-Face Meetings between Philip Melanchthon and Johannes Brenz: Differentiated Consensus in the Reformation." In *Collaboration, Conflict, and Continuity in the Reformation: Essays in Honour of James M. Estes on His Eightieth Birthday*, edited by Konrad Eisenbichler, 83–106. Toronto: Centre for Reformation and Renaissance Studies, 2014.

"Glaubensbekenntnis." In *Das Luther-Lexikon*, edited by Volker Leppin and Gury Schneider-Ludorff, 261–263. Regensburg: Bückle & Böhm, 2014.

"Gospel: Christianity." In *Encyclopedia of the Bible and Its Reception*, 9:677–680. Berlin: De Gruyter, 2014.

"Luther's *Freedom of a Christian* for Today's Church." *Lutheran Quarterly* 28 (2014): 1–21.

"The Reformation and Education." In *Renewing Church and University*, edited by M. Patrick Graham, 7–18. Atlanta: Pitts Theology Library, 2014.

"The Wittenberg Circle." In *The Oxford Handbook of Martin Luther's Theology*, edited by Robert Kolb et al., 491–501. Oxford: Oxford University Press, 2014.

"Building on the One Foundation with Straw: Martin Luther and the Epistle of James." *Word and World* 35 (2015): 251–261.

"Luther's Liturgical Reforms and the Origins of *Evangelical Lutheran Worship*." *Cross-Accent* 23, no. 3 (Fall/Winter 2015): 27–41.

"Martin Luther's Preaching an Indulgence in January 1517." *Lutheran Quarterly* 29 (2015): 62–75.

"Matthew's Gospel for the Reformation: 'The Messiah . . . Sent and Manifested.'" In *To All the Nations: Lutheran Hermeneutics and the Gospel of Matthew*, edited by Kenneth Mtata and Craig Koester, 45–58. Geneva: Lutheran World Federation, 2015.

"Philip Melanchthon: Speaking for the Reformation." *Expository Times* 126 (2015): 313–325.

With Volker Leppin. "Sources for and against the Posting of the Ninety-Five Theses." *Lutheran Quarterly* 29 (2015): 373–398.

"The First Biography of Martin Luther, Compiled by Johannes Policarius." In *Memoria—theologische Synthese—Authoritätenkonflikt: Die Rezeption Luthers und Melanchthons in der Schülergeneration*, edited by Irene Dingel. Tübingen: Mohr Siebeck, 2016.

"Martin Luther, Philip Melanchthon, and Their Wittenberg Colleagues." *Oxford Research Encyclopedia of Religion*, July 2016. https://doi.org/10.1093/acrefore/9780199340378.013.271.

"Philipp Melanchthon (1497–1560)." In *Together by Grace: Introducing the Lutherans*, edited by Kathryn A. Kleinhans, 58–61. Minneapolis: Fortress, 2016.

"Biblische Übersetzungen und Kommentare." In *Philipp Melanchthon: Der Reformator zwischen Glauben und Wissen: Ein Handbuch*, edited by Günter Frank, 233–250. Berlin: De Gruyter, 2017.

"How People Are to Be Taught to Confess." In *By Heart: Conversations with Martin Luther's Small Catechism*, 143–147. Minneapolis: Fortress, 2017.

"Martin Luther's *September Testament*: The Untold Story." *The Report: A Journal of German-American History* 47 (2017): 51–61.

"The 95 Theses as Luther's Template for Reading Scripture." *Lutheran Quarterly* 31 (2017): 249–266.

"'Mehr Licht'—Die letzte Exegese Philipp Melanchthons." In *Melanchthon: Der Reformator zwischen Eigenständigkeit und Erkenntnisgemeinschaft*, edited by Rainer Rausch and Tobias Jammerthal, 33–63. Leipzig: Evangelische Verlagsanstalt, 2018.

"The Ninety-Five Theses as a Literary and Theological Event." *Luther-Jahrbuch* 85 (2018): 37–60.

"Martin Luther's Proclamation of Justification by Faith Alone." In *Justification by Grace in East Asia: A Lutheran-Anglican Dialogue on the Occasion of the 500th Anniversary of the Reformation*, 9–18. Hong Kong: Lutheran Theological Seminary, 2019.

"Matthias Flacius's Attacks on Andreas Osiander from 1552." In *Matthias Flacius Illyricus: Biographical Contexts, Theological Impact, Historical Reception*, edited by Irene Dingel, Johannes Hund, and Luka Ilic, 207–226, 319–323. Göttingen: Vandenhoeck & Ruprecht, 2019.

"Philip Melanchthon and the Earliest Report on the Leipzig Debates." In *Luther at Leipzig: Martin Luther, the Leipzig Debate, and the Sixteenth-Century Reformations*, edited by Mickey L. Mattox et al., 171–193. Leiden: Brill, 2019.

"Philip Melanchthon on Bible Translation and Commentaries." *Lutheran Quarterly* 33 (2019): 26–45.

"Martin Luther and Philip Melanchthon on the Care and Feeding of [Future] Pastors." *dialog* 59, no. 2 (June 2020): 130–137.

Works in Progress

Encounters with Philip Melanchthon: An Intellectual Biography.

With Derek Cooper. *Translation of Melanchthon's Commentary on Proverbs.*

Book Reviews

In *Currents in Theology and Mission*, *dialog*, *Theology Today*, *Theological Studies*, *Interpretation*, *Journal of Religion*, *Church History*, *Lutheran Quarterly*, *Renaissance Quarterly*, *Theologische Literaturzeitung*, *Journal of Ecclesiastical History*, *Catholic Historical Review*, and *Sixteenth Century Journal*.

Audio and Video Presentations

"Luther's Catechisms and the Parish." An audio tape presentation. *RESOURCE* 18, no. 7. Minneapolis: Augsburg Fortress, 1991.

"Using Luther's Catechisms in the Congregation." A twelve-session video course for *SELECT*, Continuing Education for Clergy or Laity Meeting in Small Groups, sponsored by the Evangelical Lutheran Church in America. 1991.

"The Augsburg Confession." A five-session video course for *SELECT*, Continuing Education for Clergy or Laity Meeting in Small Groups, sponsored by the Evangelical Lutheran Church in America. 1996.

"The Augsburg Confession and Small Catechism." A video course for *SELECT*, Continuing Education for Clergy or Laity Meeting in Small Groups, sponsored by the Evangelical Lutheran Church in America. 2008.

Translations

From the German: Heinz Scheible. "Luther and Melanchthon." *Lutheran Quarterly* 4 (1990): 317–339.

From the German: Lothar Graf zu Dohna. "Staupitz and Luther: Continuity and Breakthrough at the Beginning of the Reformation." In *Via Augustini: Augustine in the Later Middle Ages, Renaissance and Reformation*, edited by Heiko A. Oberman and Frank A. James III, 116–129. Leiden: E. J. Brill, 1991.

From the German with introduction: *A Contemporary Translation of Luther's Small Catechism*. Minneapolis: Augsburg Fortress, 1994.

From the Latin with annotations (see above): "Recently Discovered Notes on Two Sermons from 1520 by Martin Luther." *Sixteenth Century Journal* 14 (1983): 189–200.

From the German: Helmar Junghans. "Luther on the Reform of Worship." *Lutheran Quarterly* 13 (1999): 315–333.

From the German: John Agricola. *Booklet for Laity and Children*. In *Sources and Contexts of the Book of Concord*, edited by Robert Kolb and James Arne Nestingen, 1–12. Minneapolis: Fortress, 2001.

From the German: John Agricola. *130 Common Questions for the Girl's School in Eisleben*. In *Sources and Contexts of the Book of Concord*, edited by Robert Kolb and James Arne Nestingen, 13–82. Minneapolis: Fortress, 2001.

From the German: *Freedom of a Christian*. Vol. 1 of *The Annotated Luther*, edited by Timothy J. Wengert. Minneapolis: Fortress, 2015.

From the German: *The Ninety-Five Theses*. Vol. 1 of *The Annotated Luther*, edited by Timothy J. Wengert. Minneapolis: Fortress, 2015.

From the German: *Sermon on Indulgences and Grace*. Vol. 1 of *The Annotated Luther*, edited by Timothy J. Wengert. Minneapolis: Fortress, 2015.

From the German: *Treatise on Good Works*. Vol. 1 of *The Annotated Luther*, edited by Timothy J. Wengert. Minneapolis: Fortress, 2015.

From the German: *The Small Catechism*. Vol. 5 of *The Annotated Luther*, edited by Hans Hillerbrand. Minneapolis: Fortress Press, 2017.

Index of Names

This index does not include references to Martin Luther and Philip Melanchthon, who appear extensively throughout the book.

Index of Places

Lutheran Quarterly Books

Living by Faith: Justification and Sanctification, by Oswald Bayer (2003).

Harvesting Martin Luther's Reflections on Theology, Ethics and the Church, essays from *Lutheran Quarterly*, edited by Timothy J. Wengert, with foreword by David C. Steinmetz (2004).

A More Radical Gospel: Essays on Eschatology, Authority, Atonement, and Ecumenism, by Gerhard O. Forde, edited by Mark Mattes and Steven Paulson (2004).

The Role of Justification in Contemporary Theology, by Mark C. Mattes (2004).

The Captivation of the Will: Luther vs. Erasmus on Freedom and Bondage, by Gerhard O. Forde (2005).

Bound Choice, Election, and Wittenberg Theological Method: From Martin Luther to the Formula of Concord, by Robert Kolb (2005).

A Formula for Parish Practice: Using the Formula of Concord in Congregations, by Timothy J. Wengert (2006).

Luther's Liturgical Music: Principles and Implications, by Robin A. Leaver (2006).

The Preached God: Proclamation in Word and Sacrament, by Gerhard O. Forde, edited by Mark C. Mattes and Steven D. Paulson (2007).

Theology the Lutheran Way, by Oswald Bayer (2007).

A Time for Confessing, by Robert W. Bertram (2008).

The Pastoral Luther: Essays on Martin Luther's Practical Theology, edited by Timothy J. Wengert (2009).

Preaching from Home: The Stories of Seven Lutheran Women Hymn Writers, by Gracia Grindal (2011).

The Early Luther: Stages in a Reformation Reorientation, by Berndt Hamm (2013).

The Life, Works, and Witness of Tsehay Tolessa and Gudina Tumsa, the Ethiopian Bonhoeffer, edited by Samuel Yonas Deressa and Sarah Hinlicky (2017).

The Wittenberg Concord: Creating Space for Dialogue, by Gordon A. Jensen (2018).

Luther's Outlaw God: Volume 1: Hiddenness, Evil, and Predestination, by Steven D. Paulson (2018).

The Essential Forde: Distinguishing Law and Gospel, by Gerhard O. Forde, edited by Nicholas Hopman, Mark C. Mattes, and Steven D. Paulson (2019).

Luther's Outlaw God: Volume 2: Hidden in the Cross, by Steven D. Paulson (2019).

The Augsburg Confession: Renewing Lutheran Faith and Practice, by Timothy J. Wengert (2020).

Luther's Outlaw God: Volume 3: Sacraments and God's Attack on the Promise, by Steven D. Paulson (2020).

Stories from Global Lutheranism: A Historical Timeline, by Martin J. Lohrmann (2021).